RED

My Autobiography

GARY NEVILLE

BANTAM PRESS

LONDON · TORONTO · SYDNEY · AUCKLAND · JOHANNESBURG

TRANSWORLD PUBLISHERS
61–63 Uxbridge Road, London W5 5SA
A Random House Group Company
www.transworldbooks.co.uk

First published in Great Britain
in 2011 by Bantam Press
an imprint of Transworld Publishers

A CIP catalogue record for this book
is available from the British Library.

ISBNs 9780593065594 (cased)
9780593065600 (tpb)

Addresses for Random House Group Ltd companies outside the UK
can be found at: www.randomhouse.co.uk
The Random House Group Ltd Reg. No. 954009

The Random House Group Limited supports the Forest Stewardship Council (FSC®),
the leading international forest-certification organization. Our books carrying the FSC
label are printed on FSC®-certified paper. FSC is the only forest-certification scheme
endorsed by the leading environmental organizations, including Greenpeace. Our
paper-procurement policy can be found at www.randomhouse.co.uk/environment.

Typeset in 11.5/16.5pt Times New Roman by
Falcon Oast Graphic Art Ltd.
Printed and bound by
CPI Group (UK) Ltd, Croydon, CR0 4YY

2 4 6 8 10 9 7 5 3 1

MIX
Paper from
responsible sources
FSC   FSC® C016897

To my girls: Emma, Molly, Sophie – all my love. xxxxxxxx

Mum and Dad – none of this would have happened without you. You have given me everything you could and more than I could ever have asked. All my love. x

Tracey and Philip – the best sister and brother. All my love. x

Nan/Bill/Nan/Grandad – thank you. I love you all so much. x

Manchester United: the Boss, the Staff, the Players, the Fans. Thank you for all you have done for me. To be around people who demand the best from you, that you can trust, that look after you, that fight with you and love their own, has been inspiring and the experience of a lifetime. I will miss being with you every day. I love you all!

Gary

Contents

Prologue

The lights went out. Suddenly the Old Trafford dressing room was plunged into darkness. A television flickered into life. And there was my career being played out in front of me.

Leading out the team, lifting trophies, celebrating with Wazza, Scholesy, Becks, even scoring a few goals (they had to do some digging through the archives for those) – and finally a handshake from the boss with the words 'Thank you, son', up on the screen.

I'd had no idea the film was coming but I couldn't have devised a better way to finish than being gathered in that dressing room with the boss, the present-day United lads and all the old gang including Becks, Phil and Butty, all back for my testimonial.

You play football because you love the game, but in many ways it's the dressing room which gives you the most cherished memories. That's where you share the banter, you come together with your mates, you crack jokes, and celebrate titles. It's the private chamber where you learn what it is to be a team.

I was determined not to become emotional on my testimonial night. I've never been comfortable with too much fuss. I'd just wanted to get it over with. But as the film played, I could feel myself welling up. I'd lived my dream.

They say some sportsmen find retirement hard to take. For them it's like falling off a cliff. They become depressed and struggle to find purpose in their life. But retirement held no fears for me. In that moment, as I watched that film, I just felt incredibly lucky.

I played for United all my life – not just a one-club man but at the greatest club on the planet. Something grabs you when you are a child and gives you a passion. Mine was always United.

There's a banner I always looked out for at games – it must have been there for fifteen years – which reads 'United, Kids, Wife'. In that order. I was thinking of making that the title of this book, and my wife wouldn't have been surprised. The club has shaped my life. It's been the one constant, along with my family.

I played all those years with my brother, sharing so many happy times. I was part of the greatest youth team there may ever be, making true, loyal, lifelong friends of Becks, Butty, Scholesy and Giggsy. I'd seen all our teenage hopes and dreams miraculously come true with the Treble.

Since boyhood I'd been taught by the greatest manager of them all. I'd seen him restore United from a club with a famous past into English football's most revered and celebrated sporting institution, not just winning trophies but playing brilliant attacking football. I'd shared a dressing room with Robson, Cantona, Keane, Ronaldo and other living legends.

I played through the most successful period in the club's history. At the end of it all, the club won a record nineteenth title. Who could have believed that was possible when I made my debut in 1992 and the club was on only seven championships? Passing Liverpool was a special moment in history.

It was an amazing ride to get there, with plenty of fantastic moments but some hard times too when the boss, the club, the players were doubted. There were bust-ups and moments of despair. There were times when our characters were tested.

Through it all, the many, many highs and the occasional lows, I've felt privileged to be wearing the shirt. You can't have a bad day playing for United. That's what I've always told the young players coming through. You may feel like you're having a crap time but when you look down and see that United badge on your chest it's always a great day. And I wore that shirt for the best part of twenty years.

1

Boy from the K-Stand

'Gary Neville is a Red, he hates Scousers.'

Right from the start, I loved United and I loved an argument. So it was always going to be a volatile mix when I went to a school full of Liverpool fans.

I grew up in Bury, just up the road from Manchester. But looking at all the Liverpool FC football shirts, my school might as well have been yards from Anfield.

This was the eighties. Liverpool were the glamorous, successful team of the moment so pretty much all the kids at school supported them, like kids do. There we were, less than ten miles from Old Trafford, but it could have been the heart of Merseyside. I wasn't the only United fan in the playground, but it felt that way to me.

I don't know how you react to being outnumbered, but it brought out the fighter in me. My dad's side of the family have a stubborn, argumentative streak, and school is where I first discovered that I'm a Neville to my core. If I have an abiding memory of my school days, it is squabbling with all those Liverpool fans. I must have spent more time bickering with them than focused on my studies. We'd argue about who had the best players, the best ground, the best kit. It's an argument that's never stopped. I don't suppose it ever will.

In those days Liverpool were my tormentors. At school I'd have their success shoved down my throat day after day. That's how the feuding started.

They were winning everything at the time, but the more crowing I heard about Liverpool's triumphs, the more I'd defend my club. I'd stubbornly argue for United all day long. Anyone who thinks I've been a one-eyed defender of United in recent years should have heard me in the playground at Chantlers Primary.

United were the most magical thing in my life. As a kid, I lived for watching games. Going to Old Trafford was the highlight of my week. The club was in the blood, thanks to my dad.

He's been a devoted Red all his life. He went to the 1958 FA Cup final as a nine-year-old, when United lost bravely to Bolton Wanderers just a few months after the tragedy of the Munich air crash. He saw the glory years under Sir Matt Busby, with Best, Law and Charlton. He followed loyally through the lean years of the seventies; he was watching when United were relegated in 1974. Win or lose, following United was his passion. Once he'd started earning his own money, he hardly missed a match.

From my earliest days, I was desperate to join him. I nagged him to take me. I begged, I pleaded. Finally, he agreed, on one condition: I could join him and his mates at the game as long as I wasn't a pain or a distraction.

I can't remember my first journey down from our house in Bury to Old Trafford. My dad reckons I was four years old, which would put it in 1979. I don't recall that first game but I can still feel the excitement, the anticipation, the goosebumps of those early trips.

As soon as we crossed Barton Bridge, over the Manchester Ship Canal, my heart would skip quicker. It was a sign that we were close to the ground. Soon I'd see those towering stands and we'd be parked up. Always early, we'd get to the stadium by noon and have something to eat in Marina's Grill. It's still there at the top of Sir Matt Busby Way, just up the road from the stadium. Pie and chips, the same every time, and then we'd be at the front of the queue at one o'clock to go into the old K-Stand.

My dad would meet his mates, but that was fine with me. I was happy in my own company. He'd have a pint at the bottom and I'd go up and sit in my seat, taking in the sights inside the stadium. I never got bored of it, sitting on my own in that spot. Old Trafford would be empty but I'd look around, mesmerised by the place. I'd take in the noise, the sights, the smells. They have stayed with me all my life.

When the players came out to warm up I would be transfixed. I can still see Arnold Muhren practising those swerving shots. The earliest memory of my life is big, battling Joe Jordan jumping for a header. I was at Old Trafford the day Bryan Robson signed for United out on the pitch, an English record at £1.5 million. I was only six but the image is fixed in my head. To think that I would share a pitch with my hero thirteen years later, in his last league match.

Robson was my idol, though I was never one for posters on the bedroom wall. I've never asked for an autograph in my life and I've never really understood why kids do. I owned a United shirt but I never wore it to Old Trafford. The thrill for me was not in the personalities. Even if I'd had a camera-phone in those days I'd never have wanted to grab a cheesy picture with a player. My love was for the game. Nothing could beat the atmosphere of a Saturday afternoon watching United.

Right from the start I loved wholehearted players, which is why Robson was instantly my favourite. He epitomised every-thing I thought a United player should be. He flogged himself to the end of every game and gave blood, sweat and tears. He was a true leader. When he burst into the box, it was like his life depended on it. You could see it in his face and his running style. Everything was a fight and a battle. He made a massive impression on me.

Later I would love Mark Hughes, too, and Norman Whiteside. They were the three players I looked up to the most. They had plenty of talent, but what I really loved was how they gave their all. I've always admired grafters.

I loved the players who seemed to care about United as much as I did, but devotion to the cause wasn't going to win us titles. We had some good players, like Arthur Albiston and Mick Duxbury, but nothing like the depth of Liverpool, how-ever much I tried to pretend otherwise. United won a couple of FA Cups during my school years – against Brighton in 1983, and Everton in 1985 – but Liverpool were winning championships and European Cups. They were dominant.

Looking back now, I have to respect what Liverpool achieved. I wasn't blind to the qualities of their team even if I hated to admit it. You'd have to be stupid not to acknowledge the brilliance of Kenny Dalglish. Which fan wouldn't covet Graeme Souness, Peter Beardsley and John Aldridge? I had a secret admiration for Steve Nicol. John Barnes was vastly talented, and I hated him for it.

Now I am able to appreciate Liverpool as another true working city of the north. I can recognise the loyalty of their supporters and admire how Liverpool, like Manchester, has punched above its weight when it comes to music and football. But back then, I loathed Liverpool and I loathed their success.

United were my team and I'd stand up for them in the face of logic. At school, I'd brag about how we had Robson, the England captain and the best player in the country. I'd shout about Old Trafford being bigger than Anfield. And the reply would come back like a slap in the face: 'Yeah, but Liverpool won the league and you finished thirty-one points behind.'

I'd cling to the great heritage of Busby, Best, Law and Charlton that I'd learnt from my dad and tell myself that United would be back on top soon enough. But even I was struggling to believe it when we finished thirteenth in the league behind Coventry City and QPR.

We were spending fortunes and winning nothing. We'd buy Garry Birtles or Peter Davenport and there would be a big fanfare but we'd soon be let down again. We'd threaten to challenge but it would peter out into nothing. But still I wouldn't be shouted down.

I must have sounded like City fans have done all these years, bleating away with a massive chip on their shoulder. City fans would blather on about the derby being such a massive game, and how they were the true fans of

Manchester, but United–City was never the crunch match for me. That was always Liverpool, and it always will be thanks to this childhood rivalry.

Being a football supporter has never just been about the team you love. It's also about the teams you love to hate. English football is brilliant for being so tribal and there'll always be an edge between United and Liverpool.

As a kid, I had to suffer at their hands again and again. But that's why every victory later in life tasted so sweet. That's why I charged up and down the pitch celebrating every win over Liverpool. It's why I kissed the United badge in front of them, like any true fan.

My passion would eventually cost me £5,000, when the FA fined me for celebrating a winning goal at Old Trafford. I thought it was a ridiculous punishment. As I said at the time, do they want to turn us all into robots? How many times do we hear that players are too distant from the fans and don't care about the clubs they represent? And then they punish someone for being real. Pathetic.

I was giving some stick back to Liverpool fans, just as I've taken plenty. I've never complained about all the abuse I've had from Liverpool supporters – and there's been enough, stretching right back to those school days.

For years I've had to listen to the songs. I've had Liverpool fans try to turn my car over on Salford Keys on the way back from a match. They tried to force open the doors, and when they couldn't get in, they started to rock me over. Luckily the traffic started moving so I could make my escape before they rocked me off my wheels.

One night, on the eve of another Liverpool game at Old Trafford, the police told me I had to move out of my house because they had intelligence that a gang of lads from Merseyside were on the way to give me a sleepless night. I had to pack my bags and move to a hotel.

I've always known this stick is the price for nailing my colours to the mast like I've done ever since I was a kid. But what's football about if it's not about taking sides, my club against yours, whether that's on the pitch, on the terraces, in the bar or in the school playground?

United till I die. And to hell with the rest.

2

Brotherly Love

How does an ordinary family from an ordinary street produce three England internationals?

There was nothing to distinguish the Nevilles from anyone else in Bury. We grew up, like most families in the town, in a little two-up, two-down. I was the eldest, born on 18 February 1975. Tracey and Phil, the twins, followed two years later.

We are a normal working-class family. There are no famous sporting ancestors. Yet, somehow, we won a combined 218 caps for our country – at football and netball – between us. Tracey went twice to the Commonwealth Games and World Championships, representing England seventy-four times before she suffered injury problems. Phil has played fifty-nine times for England and could still do a good job for his country now. I won eighty-five caps and went to five major tournaments.

Perhaps other families – the Murray brothers, the Williams

sisters, the world-famous Charltons – have their own explanation for how they all came to succeed at sport. Speaking for the Nevilles, I can only point to Mum and Dad. It was our parents who gave us a love of sport and the tools to succeed at it.

People often ask who my heroes are, and I normally say Bryan Robson. But it is my mum and dad really. They have been great parents, now wonderful grandparents, in just about every way. They deserve all our medals and caps.

Thanks to them, sport was at the heart of family life. Mum and Dad were never professional athletes but they were mad keen amateurs. My mum played rounders, netball and hockey to a decent county level. She'd take us kids along to netball and we'd play with a ball in the corridor of the gym. We'd go to her rounders matches and play in the field. My dad played cricket and we'd be kicking a football or bowling at each other in the outfield.

All the while we were picking up the habits and joys of sport. To us kids it was just fun but, looking back, I guess we were also laying the foundations of our future careers. We always seemed to have a ball in our hands or at our feet.

My parents also passed down the qualities of hard work and a determination to give your very best every day. When we were growing up, my dad was a lorry driver for a luggage company based in Oldham. He would leave our house while it was still dark, sometimes at four a.m., for his run down to Northamptonshire just so that he could be back by early afternoon to play sport himself or, more often than not, to give us a lift to football or cricket. It didn't matter if he had all day to do a job, we'd still hear him creeping out of the house before light to get his day's work finished as early as possible. That attitude would rub off and serve us kids well down the years: get up, get on with things; make the most of your day, don't waste time. I've been up early all my life. I don't do lie-ins. Attack the day!

Mum and Dad also taught us to value loyalty. As kids, we'd have our squabbles, but we quickly understood that nothing mattered more than family. We loved each other even if we didn't say so. That bond is unbreakable, and it would prove invaluable for Phil and me as we grew up not just as teammates at Manchester United but at times as rivals for the same jersey.

I can honestly say, for both of us, that we never forgot that family came first. If I had to give up my place in the team to anybody, I'd always prefer it to go to Phil more than anyone in the world. I don't know if that's unusual. You hear a lot about sibling rivalry but, because of the way our parents brought us up, there's never been a place for jealousy or selfishness in the Neville family.

We shared a bedroom right up to the days when I was a United regular at nineteen, and I know I must have driven him mad as a bossy older brother. But we weren't just brothers, we were best mates.

We have different natures. The Nevilles are incredibly tight-knit. My dad is an extremely sociable bloke and he likes nothing better than a drink and a chat. But we rarely entertained at home. The family house was like our castle. He just didn't want people inside. I've picked up the same trait. I can be begrudging of intruders. I like my space and limit those who get close. We're such a tight family that it can be hard for others to break inside.

I've also got the Neville stubborn streak. To understand the

Neville stubbornness you only have to know the story of how my dad got the name Neville Neville.

Just after he was born, a midwife came in and picked up a clipboard on the end of the hospital bed. 'Neville?' she said. 'Oh, that's a nice name for your new boy.'

My great-aunt was there and she jumped in. 'Oh no, it's not Neville. That's his surname. Neville Neville? We can't be having that.'

My nan was not a woman to be messed with. She wasn't going to be told which name she could or couldn't pick for her own son. 'And why not Neville Neville? I'll call him what I want.'

So it was out of sheer bloody-mindedness that my dad came to have his name. And plenty of people would say I inherited that streak of pig-headedness from my nan.

My mum's side are more placid, and that's Phil. He's always been the most easy-going of the three of us, and I'm certainly the most intense. Tracey sits in between. There was a slightly closer relationship between the two of them in the early years. Being twins, they were in the same class at school. But we all became equally close. You just can't fall out with Philip. He won't row with anyone and he's been like that since he was a kid.

We had our little scraps on the floor but my dad would have battered us if it had gone any further. Discipline was important. We never took liberties with my parents. If they said we had to be back by nine, we'd be back. I remember at the age of thirteen coming in a quarter of an hour late one evening and my dad leathered me up the stairs. I didn't do it again. A lesson always stayed taught in our house.

Mostly it was sport that brought me and Phil together.

Whenever there was a minute spare, we played football and cricket. We would play all day and all evening. Two years isn't a big age gap so we did everything together.

We used to head down the road to this huge field in Bury, the Barracks. We'd put a jumper down on the ground, I'd whack the ball high into the air, and the competition was to see who could get the ball on to the jumper, trapped under their foot. It was one against one, just the two of us locked in battle. Imagine it, two Nevilles going at each other for hours at a time. You wouldn't have sold many tickets. Or seen many goals, even if we'd played until midnight.

There were times, many times, when we went to the field together and walked back separately, one ten yards in front of the other, after taking lumps out of each other. But it was never more than healthy competition. Even though I was older by a couple of years, we were well matched. Phil was quick to mature physically, playing above his age group all the way through school. I never did that.

It became obvious early on that my little brother was naturally gifted. He found sport easy – at least that's how it seemed to me. He was two-footed right from those early games at the Barracks. Playing cricket, he was a left-handed batsman who threw with his right. That summed him up: brilliant off both sides. Phil had this grace which marked him out as a natural.

At football, I had a chance of making it as a player; Phil was a certainty. I struggled to make the county team; he played for England schoolboys at every level, going down to Wembley in his smart blazer, the cream of the crop. Teams wanted me; they begged to have Phil.

It was the same in cricket. I was pretty good, an aggressive right-hand batsman who could give the ball a whack. At thirteen I made it into the Greenmount first team in the Bolton League, competing with grown men. It was a high standard with professionals, including some frighteningly fast bowlers from the West Indies. I learnt a lot about courage from facing down the quickies.

I scored enough runs to be selected for Lancashire Under 14s and then the North of England schoolboys team. I was picked to bat at number three, with a lad called Michael Vaughan at four. I might have made it into the England junior team. The Bunbury Festival was effectively the trials for the national squad, but I broke a finger slip-fielding.

I was decent, maybe good enough to have made it as a pro, but Phil was a cut above. He was selected for Lancashire Under 13s, 14s and 15s and was easily the stand-out player in a team that included Andrew Flintoff. At fifteen, Phil was playing for Lancashire seconds. That's the men's team. If it hadn't been for football he could have gone on to play cricket dozens of times for England at every level, there's absolutely no doubt about that.

For both of us sports-mad kids, it helped to have this competition. I had a younger brother keeping me on my toes and he had a bigger brother to topple. We were great for each other, pushing each other on, though I remember one cricket game when I decided to put him in his place. He'd annoyed me, so when we batted together I kept taking singles off the last ball of every over, hogging the strike. I don't think he faced a ball for about half an hour. Then, as he got more and more frustrated, I ran him out. It was one of those rare occasions when Phil blew his top. He was fuming as we drove home, me and my dad laughing our heads off about it.

Most of the time Phil sailed on, calm, skilful, in control. He was a class act with gifts that set him apart from me. Like millions of young boys, I dreamt of being a footballer. In my imagination, I was the next Bryan Robson. But I wasn't even the best sportsman in my own family.

3

Starting Out

It all began on the pitches of Littleton Road in Salford. I was one among around two hundred kids having a trial for the great Manchester United. I was a midfield player, the next Bryan Robson in my dreams, but I wondered how the scouts could detect talent in this sea of schoolboy footballers. There were so many of us. How could I hope to stand out?

This was 1986, a year that will go down in history because that's when Alex Ferguson came down to Old Trafford to start his revolution. It was the year I joined United too, on the very bottom rung of the ladder, aged eleven, though that's less celebrated.

Our head teacher had put in a few of us for the trial and, despite my doubts, I must have done OK because a letter arrived a few weeks later asking me to join United's Centre of Excellence. It was like a golden ticket inviting me inside the chocolate factory.

On Mondays and Thursdays after school my dad would drive me to the Cliff, the training ground nestling between houses in Salford where Best and Charlton honed their skills. These days United train at a massive out-of-town base at Carrington with security gates barring the entrance to a huge complex of pitches and state-of-the-art facilities. The Cliff had one outdoor field and an old sports hall, but it was a hallowed place for a young United fanatic.

It was at the Cliff that I said hello for the first time to Nicky Butt and Paul Scholes, who joined a couple of years after me. Though, looking back, I suspect it was less of a hello and more of a grunt. Butty and Scholesy weren't the types for niceties.

My first impression of Butty, even at thirteen, was that he was hard as nails. He wasn't the biggest but he didn't care less who he came up against, he'd just rattle right through them. I was central midfield at the time and I hated facing him. He was intimidating, a schoolboy Roy Keane.

Scholesy's talent was less obvious to the eye. He was small for his age. You certainly didn't think that you were seeing a guy who would become one of the best in the world. He was asthmatic and struggled to get up and down the pitch.

It's amazing to think that I was still playing with Scholesy twenty-five years later. I can't say we clicked straight away, but we became great mates. He's never been someone to waste words, but in later years we'd always go to the same café in the middle of Manchester on the morning of a match for a natter. It became our way of relaxing.

Scholesy's attitude to the game has always been brilliantly straightforward. He thinks football's a simple game complicated by idiots. Others can talk all day about formations and tactics. 'Give me a ball,' he'd say, 'and let's just get on the pitch.'

Training with Butty and Scholesy, I realised how high the bar was set – and in my mind I fell a long way short. I was probably the best player at my local club Bury Juniors, but they'd come through a far tougher school. They'd both been scouted playing for Boundary Park, the best youth team in the area. Compared to them I was timid. Eventually I joined them at Boundary, turning my back on my pals, so I could try to keep up with them.

I needed to give myself every chance to improve. Ben Thornley had joined us at the Centre of Excellence and you couldn't tell whether he was left- or right-footed. Each year seemed to bring a new crop of talent.

I was a decent town player, but I honestly didn't know whether I would make it through the first big cull of our young lives at fourteen, when we would find out if the club wanted us to sign schoolboy forms for the next two years. I didn't know what to expect when my dad said he was off to see Brian Kidd, the head of the youth system.

My game was coming on and I couldn't be faulted for effort. I'd turned up for every session, loyally driven down by my dad. But was I really going to make the grade with all these better players around me? Butty and Scholesy were certain to be picked. I had no confidence that I'd hear good news from my dad.

There are a few moments you look back on – those cross-roads moments – and wonder how life might have played out differently. I wasn't nailed on to be a professional footballer. I knew that. United were out there grabbing every kid they could find with talent. A whole different path might have

opened up that day, one that didn't involve United, or football. I knew the club couldn't keep us all on.

I can still see the look on Dad's face when he came to pick me up at school to tell me about his meeting with Kiddo, the smile he couldn't suppress. I'd made it over the first big hurdle. And as I sat in the Steven Street chippy eating my chips and gravy, the news just kept getting better. I'd not only been offered two years of schoolboy forms to the age of sixteen but a two-year apprenticeship to follow. Four years at United, an invitation to become a YTS on £29.50 a week.

I couldn't believe it. United wanted me. I'm not the type to become too emotional, but I did shed a little tear.

What I couldn't know or appreciate at the time was that, desperate to turn around the fortunes of United, the boss had decided to overhaul the youth structure. He was staking the club's future on bringing through players. He was following the great tradition of Sir Matt Busby who'd built the club on home-grown talent.

Who knows what might have been if the manager hadn't possessed that bravery and vision? He'd taken over a massive, underachieving football club. The pressure for instant results must have been intense. But he was willing to put in the time, the resources and the energy to build a lasting youth structure. And then he had the guts to put his talented kids into the team.

Appointing Kiddo to head up the academy was a masterstroke. He was one of United's 1968 European Cup-winning heroes, though the great thing about Kiddo was his ability to make you feel at ease. Right from the start, he was your mate, the guy always looking out for you, his arm round your shoulder. I loved the way he was always happy and buzzing.

Kiddo was the good cop compared to Eric Harrison, a scary Yorkshireman who became a huge presence in our lives as schoolboy trainees. But what was really amazing, reflecting the manager's determination to make this youth policy work, was how much the first-team coaches were also involved. The standard of coaching we'd receive on Monday and Thursday nights was out of this world for fourteen-year-old kids.

The manager's assistant, Archie Knox, would pay us visits, and occasionally the manager himself. He'd have been at work since the early hours but still he'd walk across the Cliff car park and come and cast an eye over us in the evening as we played in the freezing-cold indoor hall. He was already showing the attention to detail that would drive us on throughout our professional lives.

We'd be practising and Archie would come in. You felt like standing to attention as soon as he walked through the door. He'd put on these passing sessions and speak to us in a Scottish accent so thick most of us couldn't understand a word he was saying. Until we screwed up – then you'd hear every word loud and clear.

The intensity was incredible. Pass, pass, pass. Get it wrong and you'd be called out to do it again. It was tough, physically and mentally. There was to be no larking about. Do it right or do it again. Drive your passes. First touch. Control the ball. Pass. Move. We were learning the courage and skill necessary to take the ball under pressure and move it on quickly and precisely. Everything had to be done at speed. I can still hear Archie barking at me not to 'tippy-tap'.

It was a hard school, and just to make it that bit tougher, in the school holidays there would be an influx of talented kids from out of town competing for places. David Beckham arrived one summer, aged fourteen. We were training when the boss himself walked over, his arm around the shoulder of this skinny kid with gel in his hair. He was wearing a brand-new United tracksuit and his best trainers. Apparently he'd won a Bobby Charlton soccer schools competition, but we were just thinking, 'Who's this flash git?' A Cockney, too.

He was so slim he looked like he'd be blown over in a gale. At first glance you wondered what could be so special, but when we started training he could deliver a ball better than anyone I'd seen. His technique was straight out of a text-book; the body angle, the grace, the spin on the ball. He looked stylish. He played midfield too, my position, so here was another rival.

Robbie Savage, a flash kid from Wales with terrible dress sense, and Keith Gillespie, from Northern Ireland, were two more who would turn up in the holidays, and suddenly from being in the first XI among the schoolboys I'd find myself on the bench feeling like a spare part. I'd play for the Under 15s and Under 16s in regular games through the winter but be left out when the big matches came around.

The biggest of all was the match against Lilleshall, the FA's academy. They included the best hand-picked lads in the country. All the top coaches and scouts came to watch, including the boss. I was on the sidelines, a substitute, when Ryan Wilson – who'd become better known as Ryan Giggs – scored an unbelievable goal, an overhead kick that was out of this world. I'm sure I cheered – I hope I cheered – but I felt a pang of anxiety that makes me shudder to this day. What a goal. I couldn't even dream of pulling off a skill like that.

I didn't have the flair or natural ability of others, but I

flatter myself that I was a good learner with organisational qualities. Maybe it comes from being an older brother, but I've always been bossy. And I was a hard worker, sticking in the hours, doing everything I was asked, never slacking. But those were the minimum requirements when the time came to leave school at sixteen and, alongside Becks, Scholesy, Butty and the rest of the apprentices, see if I could carve out a full-time career at United.

4

Apprentice

Making love to Clayton Blackmore was one of the worst things about being an apprentice at United. Not the real Clayton Blackmore, obviously. He was sat in the dressing room pissing himself with laughter like the rest of the first-teamers.

No, this was a lifesize picture of our pin-up defender which would be stuck on to the treatment table by a senior player with a vicious sense of humour. As Barry White music played, I, or whichever unlucky apprentice had been chosen, would have to dance around the table and pretend to get off with Wales's right-back. I can't tell you how excruciating that is for a sixteen-year-old in front of an audience of his heroes like Mark Hughes and Bryan Robson.

Young players breaking in at United these days don't know how lucky they are. They might have to endure an initiation rite like being ordered to stand on a chair and sing a song.

They might face some embarrassing questions in front of the squad if they haven't done their chores properly, like pumping up the balls or filling the drinks fridge. But in our day it was brutal.

Refuse to make love to Clayton properly and a second-year apprentice would smash you over the head with a ball wrapped up in a towel. God it hurt. Be late for training and the second-years would line up while you sat on the massage bed and give you a dead arm. You'd ache for days.

Giggsy was one of the chief tormentors. He was only a year older but he'd broken into the first team at seventeen which gave him exalted status. He was leader of the pack among the second-year apprentices. 'Chatting up the mop' was one of his favourites. He'd pretend to be a girl in a nightclub, hiding his face behind a mop. You had to talk to the mop and try to get 'her' home.

'What's your name?'

'Who wants to know?' Giggsy would say from behind his mop in some daft girly voice.

'What's your phone number?'

'Don't I even get a drink?'

Everyone would slaughter you for not doing it well enough. You're trying to do this as a teenager with all these first-team legends telling you how crap you are. Robbie Savage, who has never lacked self-confidence, was a showman who could pull it off. He couldn't wait for his chance to stand up in front of everyone and make a fool of himself – like he carried on doing for the next twenty years. He'd have everyone screaming with laughter. I wish we'd filmed some of his performances.

Being a bit of a show-off, Sav was up there all the time, but the rest of us had to be forced at gunpoint. The older lads might say you had to do it for two minutes, but I'd try to sit down after twenty seconds and hope I got away with it. Scholesy was the same and he never got pushed too badly. The digs lads from out of town, like Becks, would get it worse. Becks never liked being dragged up in front of a crowd but if you were called, you had to get on with it. There was no soft way out.

Perhaps the worst of these punishments was being stripped naked and having the whole United kit – the shorts, the shirt, even the number on your back – rubbed on to you in dubbin with a wire wool brush. I can still feel the sharp bristles ripping my skin. Then it would be into an ice-cold bath and stay there for two minutes. Sometimes, just to finish things off, you'd be thrown into a tumble dryer and the machine set on spin.

This was the introduction to apprenticeship at United, and even if these tests only lasted the first few months, they were the hardest months of my life. At the time I was a quiet, conscientious sixteen-year-old. I preferred to keep my head down. I'd been brought up a United fanatic and the last thing I wanted was to be humiliated in front of players I worshipped.

I dreaded going in the changing room between morning and afternoon sessions in case I got picked on. I worried that they might make me go skateboarding – another little initiation rite involving a training cone on your head, shin-pads on your arms, then standing on a rolled-up towel pretending you were skateboarding down the street. Other players would try to knock you off. And, yes, if you did fall off the towel, it was another flurry of digs.

They used to test our nerves by making us stand on a bench, right arm fully extended, holding a full pint of water. Some players would be shaking so much there'd be half a pint left by the time they were allowed to step down.

I think the coaches must have seen it as part of our education because they would look out of the windows at the Cliff and see an apprentice running round the pitch in the freezing cold in nothing but his boots, yet they'd just turn a blind eye.

It eventually stopped when things got a bit out of hand. We'd had a mock trial, complete with senior players as judge and jury. It was another little ritual if a player stepped out of line. The punishment was called 'the lap' which would involve the guilty party – you were always found guilty – having his head held down over the wooden treatment table and a ball kicked in his face.

Once, Butty and Steven Riley left a first-team game early to grab the bus home and someone dropped them in it. Riser got so annoyed by all the punishment whacks that he started swinging back and it all got a bit rough. Kiddo got wind of it and summoned all the second-years together. They were told to cut it out.

I'm sure they have all sorts of initiations at other clubs. It is all part of the process of turning boys into men and, while I cringe to look back on some of the humiliations we endured, there's no doubt it helped to bond us. We rallied round if one of our mates was getting a hard time, and I can trace that spirit right through our glory years with United. The camaraderie, the friendships and the trust forged as teenagers carried us through many challenges.

*

There's a continuing bond between all of us who played in the youth teams of 1992–94 because we know we were part of something special. As much as the Treble, the success of our generation will be a part of Alex Ferguson's legacy because it is every bit as incredible. In fact I'd say it's even more remarkable than what we did in 1999, and harder to repeat.

None of us will ever claim to have the aura of the Busby Babes, but 'Fergie's Fledglings' have gone down as one of the greatest gatherings of youth talent ever seen, given that the club had Giggs, Beckham, Scholes, Butt and me coming together at the same time, and then my brother a year later. In that group, you are talking about the most decorated player in the history of the English game, the most famous footballer on the planet, the most technically gifted English footballer in decades, the most capped brothers in English history and Butty who matched all our achievements with six championships, three FA Cups, a Champions League win and thirty-nine appearances for England.

And even that's not the whole story. Robbie Savage played thirty-nine times for Wales on top of hundreds of games in the top flight; Keith Gillespie won eighty-six caps for Northern Ireland; Ben Thornley would have been an England player but for injury. And there's more: Chris Casper, Kevin Pilkington, Simon Davies – they all had professional careers and were really good players in their own right. Simon and Casp would go on to become two of the youngest managers in the league.

So what made us special? Well, the talent hardly needs to be spelt out. Giggs, Beckham, Scholes, Butt – that's a rare, special crop brought together by the scouting system the manager had put in place. On top of it we had a relentless will to succeed. 'Practice makes players' the manager would often say, but we didn't need to be told. You have never seen a harder-working group of sixteen-year-olds in your life than the class of 1992 at United.

I don't want to sound like a moaning old pro saying kids don't work hard enough these days – some do. But there's no doubt that we had an unbelievable work ethic. At the time we thought it was normal, but there's no doubt looking back that we were an extraordinary group in our eagerness to practise.

We loved to play and work at the game. It's no coincidence that we've all played into our mid-thirties, and beyond in Giggsy's case. We've wanted to squeeze every last drop out of our careers from first kick to last.

In my case, it was fear of failure that drove me. When I started as an apprentice, my dad said: 'Gary, make sure you don't look back thinking I wish I'd done more.' Maybe everyone's dad says that – but I took it to heart.

If I thought my left foot needed working on, I would go out on my own and kick a ball against a wall non-stop for an hour. One day after weights, I stayed out on the pitch at the Cliff and started passing the ball against a big brick wall. Left foot, right foot, left, right, left, right, hundreds of times. That's where my nickname 'Busy' came from. It stayed with me for years.

You could see everything out of the windows where the players ate lunch so all the older apprentices started banging on the glass, screaming 'Busy, Busy!' They thought I was trying to become the teacher's pet. Eric Harrison heard about it and called me into the office to ask if I was worried about the stick from the older lads.

'No, I'm fine,' I told him.

I was still kicking that ball against the wall six months later, and by then, so were the other first-years.

As part of our warm-up, we ran around the pitches at Littleton Road near the Cliff. One day things felt a bit, sluggish so four of us – me, Becks, Sav and Casp – thought, 'Sod this' and started running off ahead of the pack. The next day we sprinted off again, but this time six or seven of the other first-years followed. Soon it was all of our year. Again the second-years just thought we were being busy but, in every sense, we were leaving them behind. When the youth team was picked, there'd be only three of them to eight of us.

People say that Eric Cantona taught the United players about staying behind for extra training, that he changed the culture of the club on the practice ground. Among the first team that was true, but, as a group, we were doing this religiously every day at sixteen. We were desperate to improve. We were desperate to play for United.

I was willing to ditch everything else in my life apart from football and family. So much for my wild teenage years. If there was a game on a Saturday, I was in bed by 9.15 every Thursday and Friday night. I was a robot.

I cast off all my mates from school, never saw them again. I decided, ruthlessly, that I was going to make friends with my new teammates who shared the same goals as me. As far as I was concerned, the lives of athletes and non-athletes were incompatible. Going out to bars, drinking beer and staying up till all hours – well, it sounded like fun, but I couldn't see how I was going to have that fun and play for United.

Between the ages of sixteen and twenty I dropped women completely (and, I'll be honest, I might have struggled any-way). They were always going to want to go to the cinema or a bar on a Friday night. They were going to be expecting phone calls and pestering me to do this or that. My only priority on a Friday night was resting up in bed.

It was extreme, and I know others were different. Scholesy and Butty would go for a few pints in the week, sometimes even on a Friday. Becks, Casp and Ben always had girlfriends. But I knew my talent wasn't at their level. As far as I was concerned, I couldn't afford even to sniff a pint of lager.

I wasn't going to let anything mess it up – not even my passion for cricket. Which was a shame because I was playing to a decent standard. A talented Aussie lad called Matthew Hayden had joined us at Greenmount and one day we shared an unbroken stand of 236 against Astley Bridge, centuries for both of us. He'd go on to make more than a hundred Test appearances for Australia, but it was my last big innings. The story of our stand got into the local papers and someone at the club must have pointed it out to Eric.

Straight to the point, he came up to me: 'What the bloody hell are you playing at with this cricket nonsense? No more of that.'

So that was the end of my career as a batsman.

Eric liked my dedication. Maybe he saw something of himself in me. He'd call us up individually to his office every couple of months just to chat about how we were getting on. I'd not been there long when he said, 'You've surprised me, you've got a chance.'

That was all I ever wanted to hear.

5

Fergie's Fledglings

We'd been brought together from all over the place, and there could easily have been a split between the out-of-town lads like Becks, Sav, Keith and John O'Kane and those of us from Salford, Bury and Oldham. It had always felt like they'd had preferential treatment in the past. We'd heard how Becks had been taken into the dressing room to meet the players when the team was down in London. How he'd been sent a brand-new United kit in the post.

Becks was a southerner, and you'd think we were very different. But there was far more that brought us together and we quickly became best mates, once I realised that a Cockney could love United. We'd both been brought up United fanatics, we loved the game, and we had a desire to do whatever it took to make the grade at Old Trafford. In Becks I quickly recognised someone who shared my dedication, and had bags of talent to go with it. Our families became close, standing on the touchline together on cold nights watching the youth team. Becks' mum and dad, Ted and Sandra, would drive all over the place to support him, just like my parents. It was the start of a lifelong friendship.

We had a great spirit in the squad. Inevitably there were groups of mates, but no cliques. Among the local lads, I was great pals with Casp and Ben, and the more I got to know the lads in digs, the more I got to like them too. People might think me and Robbie Savage are unlikely pals – even more than me and Becks – and we certainly didn't share tastes in fashion. He'd go around in the worst purple Ralph Lauren shirts and shell suits with highlights in his hair. I took him to Toni and Guy in Manchester once because I was the one with a car. He had his hair cut too short and when he saw his reflection in a shop window, he burst into tears. He'll deny it, but it's true.

We had a good laugh together. We'd pile into my car and go to the snooker club in Salford.

Another place we'd hang out was the bookie's along the road from the Cliff. Keith Gillespie was a gambler even then. Me, Casp and Sav would sit in there for two or three hours just having a laugh, maybe sticking the odd few quid on, but Keith always had a tip and would put money on every race. For us it was social, but he really enjoyed it.

One day we were in there when a bloke walked in and said, 'Whoever owns that black Golf, it's being smashed up by some lads.' That would be my black Golf. I looked outside and, sure enough, there was a gang of lads on bikes, all shaven heads, smashing the windows and trying to rip out the radio.

I went outside. 'Oi, what the fuck you doing?' That's when two of them started walking over. Now I might have a big mouth, but I'm no Ricky Hatton. Me and Keith legged it back into the bookie's until they disappeared.

People might think from this that life at United must have been a privileged existence for a teenager. But Eric took it upon himself to make us feel like nothing was ever going to come easy. He made us do every job you could think of, like sweeping out the bogs and mopping the corridors, even cleaning all the staff's boots, including the manager's.

On other days you'd be sent over to Old Trafford to shadow the groundsman or help the secretaries in the general office. And that was how Ben and I ended up in Sir Matt Busby's office one day. We were walking past, going about our chores, when an old Scottish voice called us in. There was Sir Matt sitting behind his desk, puffing on his cigar.

'Hi boys, you OK? How are you doing?'

I don't think we managed more than a mumbled 'Fine, thanks'.

We knew we were in the presence of greatness, a United god. I remember telling my dad later; he would have killed for the opportunity. If I'd met Sir Matt when I was older and more experienced, I'd have bombarded him with questions. But, to be honest, it was a moment wasted on two young tongue-tied lads.

Doing those jobs around the club was all good for our grounding, but it was on the pitch that we'd be judged, and

Eric tested us in every way there as well. He was brilliant. Standing on the pitch for the first time as apprentices, he'd said to us, 'You're all talented players, that's why you're here at Manchester United. But you've only got one chance and that's by listening to me. Don't listen and you're finished before you've started.'

I didn't just listen, I hung off every word. If Eric had said, 'Stand in a bucket for two hours a day and you'll play for United', I'd have done it.

He could be a tough man. In the first year, he'd rip our heads off during training. He'd scream at me and Casp for losing headers, Becks for hitting 'Hollywood passes', Butty and Scholesy for losing control of midfield. Of course he'd praise you at times, and when he did it meant everything. But even that was a test. Could we handle a compliment or would we get full of ourselves?

Eric took boys and turned them into men. He made us better footballers, and, just as importantly, he made sure we would compete. Every second of every training session under Eric had to be treated like a cup final. At an England gathering a few years later some of the other lads were shocked at how hard me, Butty and Scholesy were going into tackles. 'Come on, lads, it's just training,' they said. But Eric's attitude was that if you weren't full-on in practice, it was no preparation for Saturday.

He'd make us play heading games, the biggest lads against the smallest, with no allowance made. Be aggressive. Assisting him was Nobby Stiles – European Cup winner, World Cup winner and a good man to have on your side in any battle. Nobby sent us out one day with the words 'your best friends out there are your six studs'. Of course Eric and Nobby taught us to use the ball, but if they instilled one thing, it was that wearing the United badge meant you had to win the fight.

They made you understand the prestige of representing United at any level. The history was all around you. We went over to the Milk Cup in Northern Ireland once and stayed at a hotel run by Harry Gregg, the great United goalkeeper and hero of the Munich air crash. We sat there as sixteen-year-olds listening to Harry and Nobby's stories about George Best, Denis Law and Bobby Charlton.

With our relish for practice and Eric and Nobby driving us on, before long we were beating most opponents and playing fantastic football. We always had the beating of the Everton and Liverpool youth teams, though they did have a standout player in Robbie Fowler. His movement around the box was exceptional even then.

There were bad days. The Oldham pair Ian Marshall and Graham Sharpe gave us a torrid time in a reserve team game. 'Think you're players?' Eric told me and Casp afterwards. 'A million fucking miles away.'

We played one game against Chester as first-year apprentices and were winning 5–0 at half-time. Butty had scored a hat-trick. We were feeling very pleased with ourselves when the boss walked in. 'Why are you doing this? Why aren't you doing that?' Five goals up and he still wasn't satisfied.

But there was a buzz about the place, about our team, and in the Youth Cup we were on a roll. United had not won the competition since 1964 and, under the manager with his insatiable demands, these things mattered.

We'd play games at the Cliff and there would be more than a thousand people watching us on a Saturday morning. The crowd would include first-team players, which made us feel ten feet tall. We were building the confidence that we could do anything, beat anyone.

My own self-belief was growing. I'd never seen myself as a centre-half but that's where I ended up in my first year as an apprentice. It was obvious I wasn't going to make it in midfield with the competition. Eric pushed me back, but with a word of warning: 'If you're going to be a defender, you'd better start tackling.' It's funny to admit, but I didn't like putting a foot in then. Laugh if you like, but I regarded myself as a passer.

My first big test at centre-back came in a Youth Cup match against Sunderland. I'd never been as nervous, but we won, and I felt assured. For the first time I felt that I belonged in that company.

Everyone knew we had one prodigy in our ranks: Giggsy. He was such a sensation that he was playing regularly in the first team even as he joined us in those Youth Cup matches. Giggsy's impact for a seventeen-year-old was incredible. He had this unbelievable balance, the ability to make swaying runs at top speed that would leave a defender on his arse. Quite often that would be me on the training pitch. I spent years having to face him down in practice and there probably wasn't a day when he didn't nutmeg me, and then I'd clobber him back. He must have called me a 'clumsy bastard' a million times after I'd taken him down rather than let him skip past.

Showing the versatility that would help turn Giggsy into a United legend, playing over two decades, he mostly played as centre-forward in the youth team. That was the one position we were short in; there was no truly prolific striker. Sav and Colin McKee were never true goalscorers. Striker has always been the hardest position to prove yourself in at a big club like United. Up front and goalkeeper are the two specialist positions where we've always ended up buying players more than bringing through our own. Still, Giggsy wasn't a bad stand-in.

Reaching the final of the Youth Cup in 1992 was a very big deal, and it showed how good we were – and how competitive – that Scholesy wasn't even on the bench as he worked to improve his strength and stamina. A 3–1 win over Crystal Palace in the first leg in London set us up nicely for the return.

In front of 14,681, a team that read Pilkington – Switzer, Neville, Casper, O'Kane – Thornley, Beckham, Butt, Davies – Giggs, McKee (with Savage and Gillespie on the bench) beat Palace 3–2 to make it 6–3 on aggregate. It was Giggsy who lifted the first major silverware of our young lives.

Let no one be in any doubt about how important that moment was. A group of talented sixteen- and seventeen-year-olds had tasted success. And God did we like it.

After all the championships, and even the Champions League, that Youth Cup is still one of my proudest achievements. Not just because we won it, which gave us all a great rush of joy and self-belief, but because it was such a fantastic team to be part of. There was a real togetherness because we were great pals.

It's inevitable that Giggsy, Becks, Butty, Scholesy and me and Phil are the focus, but to concentrate on the six of us actually undersells the phenomenal success of that squad.

Take Sav. He should count as a success for the United youth system, even if he was eventually released. The fact is, he didn't have the most natural ability among us, and he was never going to be a United centre-forward, but given his limitations he made for himself a brilliant career out of football. When he left Old Trafford for Crewe Alexandra as a teenager, he could easily have disappeared out of the game. But he battled back and ended up spending many seasons in the Premiership. And I bet his years at United underpinned that career. He had learnt to extract every ounce of ability from himself – a quality driven into us by Kiddo and Eric.

I only have to look at him on telly and I laugh. And I can see why a lot of other people might think he's a pain in the backside. But he's not to be underestimated. I have huge respect for his career.

Keith also went on to have a fine career, playing Champions League with Newcastle United. Casp was a classy centre-half until he suffered a terrible injury, and then became one of the youngest managers in the league at Bury. He's currently working for the Premier League in the youth department and passing on all those valuable lessons he learnt at United. Ben would have been a top-class winger had he not also been struck down by injury. Kevin Pilkington has hundreds of league appearances to his name.

It's only John O'Kane whose career you can trace and say he should have done better. John was a good lad, a right-back with far more gifts than me. Six foot, great on the ball, quick, and he could use both feet. But he was the one member of the group who couldn't get his head round our basic ethos: if the coach said run five miles, we'd run six.

In a game against Rotor Volgograd in the Uefa Cup in September 1995, Phil was picked at left-back, John on the right. But John came in after his warm-up, turned to the manager and asked to play on the left instead. Here was a young right-footed defender asking the manager of Manchester United fifteen minutes before a European tie at Old Trafford if he could swap positions. The boss did it, but he took John off after twenty-seven minutes and he never started for United again.

I don't want to pick on John, but he didn't come close to fulfilling his potential at his subsequent clubs Everton and Bury. He ended up at Hyde United.

It was unheard of for a whole youth squad to be invited to turn professional, but all of us were given that chance. Only George Switzer and Sav would never play a game in the United first team. Eleven out of thirteen making it into the first XI, however briefly, isn't bad. It's sensational.

To have a group which combined our love of the game, our ability and our dedication to practice – well, any club would kill for it. There was no one like us. We were fitter and stronger, better prepared, and possessed more ability as a group than all of our rivals. We weren't in it for the money, we were in it to become United players.

It shows how rare a group we were that United, despite all the resources it pours into the youth system, has not had a crop like us since. There are dozens of Premiership players who have been through the United academy, like Ryan Shawcross, Phil Bardsley, Kieran Richardson and Chris Eagles, who are all proof that the club still produces very good players. No club in England works harder to bring through its own. But to make it at United in this era is to be among the very best.

We were a rare generation, so much so that I honestly wouldn't speculate when there will be another group like it. Fergie's Fledglings – to be honest, it's not the greatest title in the world, but it makes me shiver to think that I was part of a team that will go down in history.

6

The First Time

We still had plenty to learn, and who better to learn it from than one of the most ferociously competitive teams in the history of English football?

The boss has gone on record many times to say that his favourite United team, if not his best, was the 1992–94 vintage, and I can understand why. They played the game the same way they behaved off the pitch, with power and presence. They reflected the manager's character. This was a team that could win the championship not just through ability but sheer force of personality.

Schmeichel, Bruce, Ince, Robson, Hughes, Cantona – they weren't just great players but fierce competitors and real men. Perhaps it took those qualities to shoulder the responsibility of finally bringing the title to Old Trafford after twenty-six years.

That long wait had been an embarrassment for a club of

United's stature but a new era, finally, was dawning. And as history was being made at Old Trafford, young players like me had front-row seats.

As apprentices, we would travel with the first team helping Norman, the kit man, with the laundry skips. We would watch close-up as this squad of huge characters stormed their way to the title. We witnessed their fire and passion – which led to some explosive clashes in the dressing room.

We went to Anfield one day and it all kicked off in the dressing room between the boss and Peter. It was the first time I'd truly seen what people call 'the hairdryer', though the players never referred to it as that.

'You're slipping!' the boss shouted at Schmeichel.

'So are you,' the big goalie replied, just in earshot.

Everyone looked up, thinking, 'Oh my God, here he comes'. And sure enough, the boss ripped Peter's head off. I'd thought Eric Harrison had a temper, but this was something else. I think Peter was fined for that bit of backchat, but the worst of it was the manager's four-letter ear-bashing.

Then there was the time in 1994 when we got thrashed by Barcelona at the Nou Camp, torn to shreds by Stoichkov and Romario, and at half-time the boss ripped into Incey. At one point Kiddo half stood up ready to intervene, thinking it was about to go off.

I loved to see this competitive spirit come alive in the dressing room, though for us young lads it was intimidating to say the least. We'd had brilliant coaching from Eric and Nobby, we'd had a taste of success, and now we were witnessing what it took to be champions from seeing Schmeichel, Hughes, Ince and Robson with their ferocious determination. This was the final part of our education, the perfect schooling.

I experienced first-hand the exacting standards one day in September 1992 when, totally out of the blue, Kiddo told me I was in the first-team squad for the visit of Torpedo Moscow.

I could hardly believe it. I was still a raw apprentice, seventeen years old. None of our age group had been near the first team, not Butty, Becks or Scholesy. Never mind playing for the first team, we still had to knock on the door before we could even enter their dressing room. Mark Hughes, in particular, was a stickler for manners like that. I wouldn't have dreamed of speaking to a player like Sparky unless he said something first so I was nervous as hell as Kiddo told me where and when to meet.

I kept myself to myself as we were taken on a bus to the Midland Hotel in central Manchester for a pre-game nap. Even the hotel was an eye-opener for me. I hardly ventured into the city centre in those days and I'd never seen anywhere so posh.

When we reached Old Trafford, the manager told me I was going to be among the substitutes. I assumed that I'd just be filling out the numbers for a European game, making sure we had enough on the bench, but with the clock running down Kiddo told me to get ready.

Of the 19,998 fans in the ground, I expect only my dad noticed the kid running up and down the sidelines. Then, as the clock counted down on a drab goalless draw, the signal came for me to strip off. I was going to make my debut. I was going to be running out at Old Trafford to play alongside Hughes, Bruce and Brian McClair. The boy who'd sat in the K-Stand all those years was about to get his big chance, tucked in behind Andrei Kanchelskis.

I shook out my nerves as Lee Martin trotted over to the

bench. It wasn't much of an appearance, or much of a game, but my dream had come true.

It was a moment to cherish and remember – and I haven't forgotten what happened afterwards, either. We won a throw-in down in the right-hand corner and taking it was the only touch I got in those three minutes. I lobbed it into the box – I've always had a decent throw on me – but like everything else that night the move came to nothing.

Afterwards, as we stripped off in a subdued dressing room, the manager started laying into Gary Pallister.

'Pally, have you ever watched the youth team? Have you not seen his long throw?'

'Yes.'

'Then why weren't you in the box then!'

He wasn't happy we'd been held to a 0–0 draw at home – we'd go out on penalties in the second leg two weeks later – and Pally was getting it in the neck for a tiny detail. As I sat there thrilled, eager to see my dad and relive the experience, I'd witnessed yet another stark reminder that the boss wouldn't let standards drop for a minute.

You can never beat the first time. Of all my hundreds of appearances for United, that debut will always have a special place in my memory. We were brought up at Old Trafford always to strive for more, but I remember the night after that tie with Torpedo Moscow thinking, 'If I die tomorrow, I die happy.'

A dream really had come true, but I'd be lying if I said it was the blossoming of my career at United. My promotion was short-lived. It was straight back to the youth team, back to learning my trade. It would be months, many months, before I got another sniff of the first team.

Rather than dreaming about running out at Old Trafford again, I had to knuckle down to the job of defending the Youth Cup and earning a professional contract. With such quality in our ranks we should have retained the trophy in 1992/93, our second year as apprentices. But we ended up losing the final to a Leeds United team with Noel Whelan, Jamie Forrester and Mark Tinkler but few others who made the grade.

We were sitting in the dressing room at Elland Road gutted after defeat in front of thirty thousand fans. 'I couldn't have asked for more from you over two years, you've made me proud,' Eric told us. It was a fond farewell as we headed off to the senior ranks. And we really couldn't have worked harder for Eric. We'd given him everything.

Then the door opened and the manager walked in. 'You lot,' he said, with one of those looks. 'You can have all the ability in the world, but if you haven't got the temperament, you won't play for my team.'

This was how it was at United under the boss – a constant test of your desire, your determination, your concentration. We were very self-motivated as a group, but as we moved up to the senior ranks, we saw competitiveness in a whole new dimension.

Liverpool beat us in a reserve game one day. We hadn't played that badly but the manager was apoplectic. We were hauled in, knackered, for training at 7.30 a.m. the next day and told to buck up our ideas, or else. The message was clear: any defeat was bad, but some were worse than others. No United team would be allowed to come second to Liverpool under any circumstances.

Most of the time we trained with the reserves, though some

days we'd be called in to work with the first team. It was a hard school. Some of the players would look out for you. Brucey generally had a kind word. Incey, despite his reputation for cockiness, would offer helpful advice. Schmeichel was a different animal. I had to give him crossing practice and if I hit even one bad ball he'd shout, 'What's he training with us for? He's fucking shite.'

It was tough, but we were starting to make the transition. We would play in A-team games or for the reserves alongside some of the first-teamers who were coming back from injury, and through doing that we started to feel more comfortable alongside senior pros. We'd play with the likes of Clayton Blackmore and Lee Martin and, no disrespect, we started to realise that they were no better than us. We'd seen them from the stands, watched them play in cup finals, but suddenly it hit us that they weren't gods, they weren't untouchable. Robbo tells the story himself about going to take a free-kick in an A-team game and Becks shooing him away. And Robbo was captain of England.

Because he was my childhood hero, it was Robbo who gave me the biggest boost of my young career, though he won't know it. A mate rang me up one morning and said that Robbo had done an article in the papers talking about the young lads who had come through, the class of '92. I remember reading that newspaper like it was yesterday and seeing what Robbo had said about me: 'I'll be amazed if he doesn't become a top player.' This was my idol saying that I could go all the way. It sounds a small thing, just a line in a paper, but, honestly, I never looked back from there. If Robbo believed that I could make it to the top, that was good enough for me.

Robbo wasn't the only one singing our praises. My dad has still got a scrapbook at home full of cuttings from that time, including an article where the boss says, 'If this lot don't make it we can all pack in.' You think about how cautious the manager generally is about building up young players, how he likes to play down the hype – but in our case he was willing to make a bold prediction.

Outside the club, there were other managers comparing us to the Busby Babes. We were getting amazing write-ups, and I had another reason to believe in myself when I was part of the England squad that won the European Under 18 Championship in the summer of 1993. The tournament only lasted just over a week, with four matches crammed in, but it was fantastic experience. It was the first time I played at right-back, and in a really good team. Five of us – me, Butty, Scholesy, Sol Campbell and Robbie Fowler – would go on to play for England, though that tournament is a good example of how players develop at different speeds. The stars at the time were Julian Joachim, who had bags of power and pace, and Darren Caskey, the captain, who was a bit older and had the most experience.

We beat Turkey in the final at the City Ground in Nottingham in front of more than twenty thousand fans. It was a useful part of the learning experience of facing European sides – I remember a young Clarence Seedorf playing for the Dutch – but the best thing of all was the taste of victory. Trophies, medals, give you confidence. You become ambitious to win more.

Obviously I couldn't have known at the time that this would be the only success of my international career.

*

As a United fan I was overjoyed that we were back on the summit of English football with that title in 1993. The manager had transformed the club after decades of frustration. Winning that first title was a major turning point in the club's history and, honestly, I was as happy about that championship as any I played in.

The night we celebrated at home to Blackburn Rovers was as euphoric as I've seen Old Trafford, before or since. You can never beat the first time. It was a night when you felt the hairs stand up on the back of your neck. We'd had to wait so long. There'd been the agony of just missing out the season before, and we'd endured heart-stopping moments in the run-in, famously the game against Sheffield Wednesday when Brucey's two late headers saved the day. That night at Old Trafford is a memory I'll take to the grave.

The downside of the club's new era of success was that it was going to be even harder for the likes of me, Becks and Butty to break into the team. As a centre-half, my path was blocked by Brucey, a brilliant, brave defender and a respected captain. Alongside him, Pally was one of the best centre-halves United have ever had. Opportunities for an eighteen-year-old central defender were going to be limited. So the coaches decided I was now a full-back.

Jim Ryan, our reserve-team coach, and 'Pop' Robson, his assistant, took me aside one day and pointed out that Paul Parker was getting more injuries. Perhaps he wasn't as assured as he used to be. They told me, bluntly, that right-back was my best chance of making the first team. I disagreed and told them I wanted to stay at centre-half.

I can't say I enjoyed full-back at first. I'd loved the authority that came with being in the centre – organising the defence, pushing people forward and back. I could yell out instructions from the middle. I couldn't see myself as the next Josimar, making overlapping runs. Even before I learnt to attack and cross the ball I'd have to become more mobile, get lower to the ground and snap quicker into tackles. But the coaches had made it clear it was my only chance of moving up through the ranks.

When it came to my education, I couldn't have been luckier than to have Denis Irwin to study. Has there been a more versatile full-back in English football? He was able to switch from left to right wing without skipping a beat, he could attack and defend with equal ability, take free-kicks and penalties – and he stayed modest and hard-working throughout. He must be the best left- and right-back United have ever had.

I wasn't in his class, but I must have been doing something right because in the 1993/94 season I made it on to the pitch for a second time. We younger lads would often find ourselves as unused substitutes in Europe when the manager needed a bigger squad. But for the trip to Istanbul in November 1993 I got on to the pitch for five minutes – though it wasn't my appearance that made this a memorable evening.

We were playing in the Ali Sami Yen Stadium and the Galatasaray fans were up for it. One of their supporters had run on to the pitch in the first leg and Peter had given chase and chucked him to the ground. Now thousands of them were giving us hell.

An hour and a half before the game, the crowd was frenzied. I'd never experienced an atmosphere like it. There were so many flares and so much smoke it looked as though the whole stadium was on fire. By the time the game kicked off the noise was deafening. We couldn't understand a word of what the fans were chanting, but we didn't need a translator when we saw a banner that read 'Manchester United RIP'.

After the 3–3 draw at Old Trafford, the game was heading towards a goalless draw and we were sliding out of the European Cup (I still prefer the old title to 'the Champions League') in only the second round when I came on for Mike Phelan.

It had been a trying, frustrating evening and it was all too much for Eric Cantona, who was sent off right on the final whistle for a gesture to the referee. The crowd grew even more frenzied, and as we walked off a couple of missiles landed at our feet. Suddenly we were being surrounded by a gang of policemen with shields. I'm guessing their job was to protect us, but you wouldn't have known it as we were shoved down the stairs which led from the pitch to the dressing rooms. Eric was steaming, and then he took a whack on the back of the head with a truncheon. He flipped. Suddenly it was a riot, with police batons flying and shields clashing everywhere.

Kiddo and the other coaches were grabbing us, trying to pull us into the dressing room. We bundled through the door into sanctuary but all the shouting carried on outside. Pally, Robbo and Brucey had to drag Eric in and hold him there. The experienced lads were going to the shower two by two so that Eric was never left alone in the dressing room. They ended up walking him to the coach to stop him going back after the police.

There's no doubt that team – the club's first Double winners after they thrashed Chelsea in the 1994 FA Cup final – had a massive influence on me and the rest of the young players coming through. They established the standards for the rest of us to match.

Just to train with the likes of Ince, Hughes and Cantona was a thrill. Eric could make an average pass look brilliant. But even the slightest mishit, or a lost tackle, would earn you a glare. You'd feel two inches tall. A mistake was a crime in that team.

As if it hadn't been competitive enough already, Roy Keane had now taken the squad to another level after joining United and coming in alongside Incey. There was a time, a match at Coventry, when Keano came storming at me after I'd taken an extra touch to steady myself before getting a cross over. Thrusting his head forward – I honestly thought he was going to butt me – he screamed, 'Fucking get the ball over!'

'Can I not take a fucking touch?'

'Who the hell are you talking to? Get the fucking ball over!'

It was like having a snarling pitbull in my face. And I'd thought Schmeichel was a hard taskmaster. One extra touch and Keano was slaughtering me.

We were already fiercely competitive ourselves, but now we were seeing how even the very best players took immense pride in their performance. We were seeing up close what it took to be winners at the highest level.

The ethos had been created by the manager: success was expected, and it was the players' responsibility to go out and seize it. After twenty-six years in the wilderness United had won two titles in a row. From now on, a season without the championship could be measured as a failure. And that's been the case ever since.

It was just my luck, then, that the 1994/95 season would be

one of those years when we fell short – because that was the campaign when I properly became a United first-team player.

After a couple of one-off appearances in the previous two seasons, just before Christmas 1994 the boss gave me a little run of four games at right-back, though you never quite knew what he was thinking. He left me out for a couple of matches when I'd been playing well, never wanting to overexpose a young player. One of them was a trip to Chelsea when there'd been a lot of talk in the build-up about hooligan trouble involving Combat 18. The manager sensed it was a night for the old hands.

I only had myself to blame for another spell out of the team – a rare lapse involving K cider. Strong stuff, that. I'd been travelling with the first team so I was caught totally by surprise when the manager suddenly threw me into an A-team game at Chester on a Monday morning. After a Saturday night out, I was all over the place.

'It's gone to your head, Neville. Well, you won't be travelling with us again any day soon.'

And I didn't travel with the first team for six weeks. That would teach me to take my eye off the ball, even for one night. No more K cider for me.

That Premiership campaign was shaped, unforgettably, by Eric's kung-fu attack on a supporter at Crystal Palace in January. I was out in a bar in Manchester that night when someone said to turn on the telly because Eric had been involved in some bother. I'd seen Eric lose his rag spectacularly in Istanbul, and everyone knew he wore his heart on his sleeve. I couldn't say I blamed him. Eric had a unique personality and didn't give a stuff what anyone else thought of him.

The club, rightly, stuck by him, but Eric was a huge player to miss. It was always going to be hard without our talisman but we were still chasing the league and the FA Cup as we went into March and I enjoyed another run in the side.

We were in a frantic race with Blackburn Rovers for the title. They didn't have United's flair, but they had a goal-scoring phenomenon in Alan Shearer and an experienced manager in Kenny Dalglish. It was obvious from a long way out that the title would be tight, and it went right down to the final game of the season.

Our last fixture was at West Ham United – and all to play for. Blackburn were two points ahead but had their own tricky trip to Liverpool so we had to give ourselves a good chance of overtaking them. That's why I was surprised, like all the lads, when the boss left out Sparky. Sparky had started every game in the previous few months. He was a fixed point in the team, one of our leaders. I'm still not quite sure why the boss didn't play him in a game we needed to win.

We fell behind but had enough opportunities to win several matches. Brian McClair equalised and we had three or four chances to win in the last ten minutes but it just wouldn't fall for us. One goal to win the league – that's all we needed. That's the fine line you are treading sometimes between triumph and disaster.

Afterwards in the dressing room it was the most disappointed I've ever been at a football match. Throughout my career I've been able to handle defeat pretty well. Particularly as you get older, you learn to take the blows. But that was one of the real low points. My first championship race, and it had ended disastrously. As we made the long journey home I felt physically sick.

Perhaps the FA Cup final could provide some comfort. I'd been cleared to play by the FA despite amassing eleven bookings. In my eagerness to become a tackling full-back I'd been launching myself into some shocking challenges. I'll admit I was a bit of a maniac in those early months. There was one tackle, on Jason Dodd at Southampton, that was terrible, deserving a straight red. I can also remember going into a fifty-fifty with Carlton Palmer against Sheffield Wednesday and cutting him in half. The coaches had told me to make my mark and, typically, I'd taken it to heart. I knew I had to take my chance, to make an impression. It's always been said, rightly, that you can't be ordinary at United and expect to survive for long, but maybe I'd got a bit carried away in my eagerness.

I was due to miss the final, but we appealed against the suspension. You know, a young lad, making his way in the game – just over-enthusiasm. I went down to London to plead my case, explain that I hadn't been booked for anything too bad and it wasn't fair to deprive a twenty-year-old of participating in such a big occasion. And they let me play. I did, however, have to pay a £1,000 fine for the privilege of a Wembley appearance. I didn't have the cash – I was earning £210 a week on my first professional contract – so I had to borrow the money off my dad.

It was my first hearing in front of the FA disciplinary panel and I thought they were a fair bunch then. That wouldn't last.

I loved all the build-up to my first big game at Wembley. Call me sad, but I like the tradition of the cup song, even if ours for that year – 'We're Gonna Do It Again' with a rapper called Stryker – is probably best forgotten. I felt in good form and I was really confident we were going to win. Ince, Keane,

Bruce, Pallister, Hughes – these guys were winners. We knew Everton were beatable.

I don't remember much about the game apart from the gaffer going mad at us for the goal when they broke on us to take the lead. Scholesy almost scored, then Sparky went close. But after letting the league slip on the last day, again we just couldn't get the vital goal.

So that was two crushing disappointments in a week. A Double gone in two tight games. I'd made twenty-seven appearances, which should have been something to be pleased about, but this was no time to smile. United were not in the business of trophyless seasons.

They say you learn most from defeats, and that campaign would certainly lead to major changes at the club. But that was for later. Coming straight off defeat in that 1995 FA Cup final, we headed off for a team party. It came as a bit of a shock to see how the senior lads stayed up drinking until breakfast – but there's something to be said for drowning your disappointment. I sank a few myself, but next time I hoped I'd be drinking out of a trophy.

7

Win Nothing With Kids

I'll always remember one newspaper article at the time when the manager was being asked a lot about the gamble to promote his 'Fledglings'. One line stuck in my head. The great thing with young players, the boss said, is that if you confront them with a barbed-wire fence, they'll run straight through it; an older player will walk two hundred yards to find a gate.

That's the sort of hunger he knew he would get from us. We were so eager, so willing. We would have run through a brick wall for him, never mind a barbed-wire fence. This was the Busby philosophy, moulding young players so that you know exactly what you will get from them when they break into the first XI. We were already steeped in the disciplines of the club, the way to play the game, the work ethic, the way to behave.

It doesn't matter how much homework you do, sign a

player for £20 million and you are always taking a gamble on whether he will adapt to a new environment, a new style of playing, the new level of pressure that comes with representing United. With us, the manager knew our games and our characters inside out.

He knew that Butty wasn't scared of anything, and never has been. He's got this fantastic temperament to confront whatever's in front of him. Put him up against the best player in the world, or the hardest, and Butty would roll up his sleeves and get on with the job.

The only time I've ever seen Butty run away from anything was after he'd held a scalding-hot teapot right next to a naked Schmeichel in the dressing room so that when Peter turned round his privates got burnt. Everyone found it funny, apart from the big Dane. As Butty legged it, Peter picked up one of those massive drinks containers and hurled it across the room. 'I'm going to kill you!' he screamed, sounding like Ivan Drago from *Rocky IV*. But Butty was long gone, leaving Peter nursing his burns.

Scholesy, the late developer, was blossoming into the player the coaches always knew he'd become. He had eyes in the back of his head and a pass as accurate as a laser. Half the time he'd use it on the training ground to smack you on the back of the head when you weren't looking. You'd turn round and he'd be about sixty yards away pissing his sides.

It would be another year before Becks scored from the halfway line, but he had started to come through, stronger and better after a loan spell at Preston, and already plenty of people were taking notice of his technical prowess. He could hit a brilliant pass off any part of his foot – spinning, dipping, a low grass-cutter or whipped into the box. And, game after game, you've never seen anyone cover so much ground.

It must still have taken massive courage for the manager to throw us in together, but he's never lacked that quality. Plenty of other clubs talk about bringing through young players. They spout a good game about youth philosophy. Our boss has demonstrated as far back as his days at Aberdeen that he's willing to put his trust in kids. 'Young players will surprise you,' he says. And we certainly did.

My first championship would be unforgettable for a few reasons, but perhaps mostly because Alan Hansen claimed we couldn't win it. Mind you, it wasn't Hansen who put the wind up me after we were thrashed at Aston Villa on the opening day of the season in August 1995, even if it was his remark – 'you'll win nothing with kids' – which has gone down in folklore.

When we came in to train on the Sunday morning after our drubbing, 'Choccy' McClair demonstrated a nice line in dry wit: 'Well, lads, only forty points to avoid relegation.' Everyone laughed, but they were nervous giggles.

We'd been shambolic at Villa Park, playing three at the back. We must have looked a mile from championship contenders with a team that contained Butty, Scholesy, me and Phil in the starting XI, and Becks and John O'Kane off the bench – unknown youngsters to most of the country. On *Match of the Day* that night we were pulled apart a second time. Win nothing with kids . . . on that evidence, it didn't sound a daft thing to say.

Plenty of people wondered what the boss was doing. After the disastrous conclusion to the previous campaign, he'd wielded the axe. Incey was off to Inter Milan. I was sad to see him go. A lot was said about his self-styled reputation as the Guv'nor. He could be brash, but what did you expect? He was from the south. He'd been encouraging us young lads and looked after us on the pitch. He was a fantastic midfielder for United.

Andrei Kanchelskis was next out after some row about his contract. On his day, there was no better right-winger in Europe, though it was fair to wonder if we'd seen the best of him.

The big shock was Sparky. I was in my car when I heard on the radio that he'd left for Chelsea. I was as stunned as any Stretford Ender. With Incey, I half knew he'd reached the point where his relationship with the manager was strained. And Andrei had agitated for a move. But Sparky was a United legend. I guess he must have known that Cole–Cantona was the first-choice partnership, and being left out of that title-decider at West Ham can't have helped. He was too good and too proud to be sitting on the bench.

The fans, and the media, were in uproar. The *Manchester Evening News* conducted a poll asking 'Should Fergie go?' It couldn't have been more ludicrous, looking back, but it showed the pressure we were under.

It was the first of many little crises we'd confront over the years. The world would be going crazy outside, but inside the camp the manager would tell us to keep our heads down and get on with our jobs. And we had plenty to think about that late summer of 1995 with three big games in a week straight on the back of our humbling at Villa.

First up was West Ham, when Becks would face Julian Dicks. We knew Dicks would want to clatter him early, put the kid in his place, so Becks made sure he got stuck in early, showed that he wouldn't be pushed around. He gave Dicks a torrid time as we ran out winners.

Next up was Wimbledon, Vinny Jones and the rest. They might have had an intimidating reputation as the Crazy Gang but we thrashed them 3–1. So recently written off as kids, now we were proving ourselves men. I walked off with the knowledge that we had nothing to be scared of.

We made it three wins in six days with a massive victory at Blackburn, the reigning champions. Becks scored in front of our travelling fans, and as they went crazy we jumped all over Becks like we'd just won the league. The relief was overpowering. The manager had put his trust in us. Perhaps now the rest of the country would give us some slack.

We kept up the momentum: 4–1 away at Chelsea then eight goals against Southampton and Coventry City in back-to-back matches. But standards only needed to drop a fraction and the manager would be straight on to us.

That November, I experienced his anger on full blast for the first time. I'd just come back from international duty when we drew 1–1 away at Nottingham Forest. Not a great result, but I didn't think I'd done too much wrong, until I walked into the dressing room.

'What's happened to you, Neville?' he shouted. 'The only reason I'm picking you is because you're playing for England.'

I went home feeling distraught.

More than Butty or Scholesy, who had thicker skins, I would turn an incident like that over and over in my mind. After your hundredth bollocking you become a bit more immune to it, but at that age I would take it to heart. In fact I would hate it. I wouldn't sleep. It was like the end of the world. Was he just bringing me back down to earth now that I was an established international? Or did he really think I was too big for my boots? I fretted, but that's my personality.

If you told Scholesy he was playing in an FA Cup final, he'd shrug his shoulders and saunter off. Butty would say, 'Why wouldn't I be playing?' Becks would be straight on the phone. I'd immediately start thinking of my opponent and how I was going to combat him.

But we never let our momentum slip, and by the spring of 1996 we were chasing the Double. Newcastle had been the early pace-setters, impressing everyone with their cavalier football under Kevin Keegan and storming twelve points clear. But we'd welcomed Eric back from his ban in October, straight into a massive game against Liverpool, and he'd scored the equalizer from the penalty spot. What a man.

And now Newcastle were in reverse. Crucially, we beat them up at St James's Park in March, despite a personal nightmare. I was at centre-back with Steve Bruce against Faustino Asprilla and Les Ferdinand. We got battered – at least I did. I kicked fresh air one time in the first half as Asprilla tormented me. At half-time the manager was on turbo-charge. 'Asprilla is beating you on the ground, he's beating you in the air. What's going on? Play like that second half and you've cost us the title.'

Out we came for the second half, and this time we had the slope. It's a big old slope at Newcastle, the biggest in the league. In the first half it felt like we were stuck at the bottom of a hill being pounded, but now we were up at the top and, while it might sound odd, I felt taller.

That second half was an occasion when I felt the Manchester United spirit course through the team. It relies on excellence from individuals – from Schmeichel and Bruce, who were immense that evening, and from Eric, who popped up to score the winner – but there is also something collective. It's unspoken but unmistakeable: let's get this match won. It's our time.

We weren't playing well but we seized the moment and the whole world knew then that Newcastle were never going to win the league. They should have been 3–0 up and cruising but they lacked the ability to get the job done. We had it in us to fight, to dig in and survive. Do that and, more often than not, you get your rewards. And of course Eric delivered for us, after a great cross from Phil, just as he did so many times. As wins go, it was huge, season-defining.

Newcastle were the type of team that gave you a chance, and that's what the manager kept saying to us even when they were streets ahead. It might have been very different if we'd been chasing a battle-hardened team like the 1998 Arsenal side or Mourinho's Chelsea. Once Newcastle started slipping, even the young players among us sensed the opportunity. Pavel Srnicek was inconsistent in goal, the full-backs Barton and Beresford were a weakness, and they were soft in the centre. Keep up the pressure and we knew we stood a good chance.

With four games to go we were in the driving seat when we travelled to the Dell to face Southampton. The first half was disastrous – 3–0 down! The Dell could be a tricky place to visit, but this was terrible.

'Get that kit off, you're getting changed,' the manager said in the dressing room at half-time.

I can't say I liked our grey shirts – United colours are red, white and black, and I've never thought we should play in anything else – but it hadn't occurred to me that our strip might be the problem. I just thought we were playing really badly.

I didn't know it at the time, but the manager had been talking to Gail Stephenson, an eye and vision expert at Liverpool University. She would later work with all of us on our peripheral vision. She gave me eye exercises to do before a game and I'd work on them just like stretching my calves or hamstrings. Attention to detail.

She'd warned the boss that grey shirts would be hard to spot against a crowd, and perhaps she had a point, given that we wore that kit five times and lost four of the games and drew the other. So off they came – good riddance – and we did pull one goal back through Giggsy in our blue and white change strip. But it didn't stop everyone having a good laugh at our expense.

Fortunately Newcastle's jitters were worse, as the whole country saw when Keegan lost the plot live on Sky with his 'I'd love it' rant. He was jabbing at the camera with his fingers. Watching at home, I couldn't believe my eyes.

The manager always says, 'Never become emotional.' He wants hardened winners, and I was surrounded by players who knew how to get us over the finishing line. After thrashing Nottingham Forest 5–0 we needed just one more win to clinch the title. I ended up on the bench at Middlesbrough as we won 3–0.

We had done it with kids, though there is no doubting who made the greatest contribution. Eric was immense. As young players we'd looked to him for leadership and he'd been incredible as a match-winner. Winning titles is all about teamwork, but there are a couple from my time – certainly that year, and also 2006/07 with Cristiano Ronaldo – when you are so indebted to one player that you feel like giving him your medal. That was Eric's championship.

He was in his pomp, but we also had a fantastic, well-balanced team. Some of the media were urging the manager to push Becks into central midfield because of his way of spraying around passes, but that would have made him too static. Using him on the right made the most of his energy and stamina. And the relentless accuracy of his crosses was unbelievable. We already had fantastic options in central midfield with Keane, Scholesy and Butty, and with Giggs and Becks on opposite flanks we had a dribbler and a crosser. There were not two harder-working, more productive wingers in the world.

We were already starting to develop the ability to wear out opponents. If we didn't succeed in blitzing them early on, we'd keep moving the ball around midfield, making our opponents run and run without the ball. We'd keep at them, knowing that we had the penetration from Giggsy and the unfailing accuracy of Becks to make a killer blow when their legs had gone in the last fifteen minutes.

We had won the league, and we had the FA Cup final to come. Except, just like for the title-decider, I wouldn't be starting. By now I was a regular for my country but I couldn't even get a place in my club team. And it was my brother keeping me out.

It wasn't the first time it had happened. When Phil made his debut at City the previous year I'd been told I wasn't playing the day before. Tracey was at home, and she'd asked me who was in the team the next day.

'Phil is, I'm not,' I said.

'What, he's playing ahead of you?' Like a sensitive sister, she burst out laughing.

I got over it quickly – what choice do you have? – and Phil was brilliant in that game, as he was at full-back for the next couple of years, when I often played in the middle. It crossed my mind that he'd be the one who'd keep me out long-term, but it only ever acted as a little spur to drive me on. We were only ever supportive to each other.

We'd go round to each other's rooms before games. We were a comfort to each other, a sounding board. We'd offer advice about a particular opponent. It was the same with Scholesy and Becks. When you are making these big leaps up, it's great to have familiar faces around you. We'd travel in the same seats on the bus, all sitting together. We were like each other's security blankets.

Phil was brilliant, and there was no jealousy from me. That has never been our nature. We were too busy keeping up to worry about any petty rivalry. Phil was playing so well that he couldn't be dropped. It was up to me to accept my place on the bench and not to mope as we prepared for the final.

The Liverpool team we faced had talent but their professionalism wasn't close to ours at United. We would let our hair down but only on rare occasions, when the time was right.

They turned up at Wembley wearing shocking white suits, looking like they had done most of their preparations in the tailors. Their lifestyle even featured in our team talk. 'Keep playing the ball around their area because David James will probably be waving at Giorgio Armani up in the directors' box,' the manager said.

Fair or not, that's the image they had, and the manager could claim, 'I told you so' when Jamo half-punched a corner from Becks to the edge of the area. Eric had been quiet by his standards, but he volleyed the ball straight through a crowded box. Now we'd won the Double with kids – as all the banners and T-shirts around Wembley reminded Hansen.

I came on for a few minutes at the end and was on the pitch when we did our lap of honour afterwards. The fans were singing their favourite chant of the moment: 'Cheer up Kevin Keegan, oh what can it mean . . .' Full of joy, I joined in.

I didn't think anything of it until someone from the club pulled me afterwards to say it had been caught on television. I didn't know Kevin Keegan, I'd never spoken to him, but he was an England legend so I sent him a letter of apology.

Perhaps those Liverpool lads have no regrets from their careers. I don't doubt they enjoyed themselves. But at United the time to party is when you've won something. There's no denying that there had been a drinking culture in English football for decades, but the world was wising up, and our boss was one of the managers who would not tolerate boozing players.

We'd go on the odd piss-up, though, and we always had a great Christmas party. December 1995 might be my personal best. A lightweight drinker at twenty, I knew I was in trouble when someone passed me a sixth pint of cider and it slipped straight through my hands and smashed on the floor. Later we staggered on to a Chinese and I ended up falling asleep on the pavement outside the Golden Rice Bowl. I was throwing up so badly that Ben and Casp had to put me in a cab. I could barely talk, but I managed to ask the driver to take me straight to hospital.

He took me to the Royal Infirmary, and I was so terrified of being recognised that I checked in under the first name I could think of – Simon Brown. The lads got years of fun out of that. 'Pass the ball, Simon.' I crashed out on a bed and woke up in the middle of the night to find about fifty missed calls on my phone. I rang Casp to come and pick me up and he found me sitting in reception in a wheelchair barely able to speak. He could hardly push the chair for laughing.

As well as Christmas, we'd celebrate the titles. And did we celebrate. After that first title we went to the Amblehurst Hotel in Sale, a traditional den for the United boys, and got bladdered. There's a great photo of Phil sat outside the bus stop the next morning with his club blazer on, looking like Keith Richards.

I think it was the following year when I surpassed myself by spewing all over the hotel reception. I was necking vodka straight out of the bottle, half a pint of the stuff, and I couldn't stand up. About all I can remember is Keano pissing his sides and taunting me as I threw up everywhere. 'Neville, you're a shambles. I'm ringing Hoddle in the morning to tell him you're a fucking disgrace.'

My mum went berserk when Phil and my dad had to carry me into the house. 'What have you done to my boy?' Only a mum could be sympathetic in those circumstances.

They're the best nights, those celebrations. Absolutely the best. You've been under pressure all season with the expectations of the fans, the manager, everyone connected with the club. You've put yourself under pressure just to keep your place in the team. And then it all comes pouring out of you in a great wave of euphoria.

I honestly don't think you can appreciate the high unless you've been there and done it. Having a kid? Well, most people can do that. It's a very small, privileged group who get to experience the thrill of winning a championship with their best mates, playing for United.

But if I couldn't handle my drink on those special occasions, it was because I rationed myself the rest of the time. Training and preparation were crucial to me – obsessively so. You could set your watch by my pre-match rituals.

Week after week I'd go to bed like clockwork and eat the same meals. I didn't want to take any chances. The day before a game, it was always the same:

8 a.m.: breakfast of cereal and orange juice

Noon: fish, potatoes and vegetables

3.30 p.m.: cereal and a piece of toast

7 p.m.: pasta with soup

9.15 p.m.: lights out.

I'd even take cereal and my own bowl and spoon on the train if we were going down to London. I'd sit there at 3.30 precisely munching my Weetabix as the train rolled through the countryside and the other lads pissed their sides. They could laugh, but these rituals mattered to me.

Most of them started out as good professional habits – healthy diet, plenty of rest – but they quickly bordered on superstitions. It's common enough among sportsmen. You are constantly looking for a little confidence booster, a reassurance that it will turn out all right on the night. Sticking to the same rituals offered me the comfort that I had done everything I could to be perfectly prepared, mentally and physically.

At the end of the final training session before every match I would sprint off to the changing rooms. If you didn't know my habits, you would assume I had a bladder problem. This was my last exercise before the game and I wanted to feel sharp (for the same reason, I'd always jump up first when we posed for team photos before a match). I'd hurtle off, leaving the rest of the lads cracking up.

On match day, another strict routine would start with stretches at 9.30 in the morning and the ten o'clock call to my mum. Every game I ever played, I spoke to my mum five hours before kick-off. 'Go stuff 'em,' she would tell me, every single time, over twenty years.

I'd always be early into Old Trafford, say 11.40 a.m. before a three p.m. kick-off. Well, who wants to be late? It used to drive me mad when players turned up for the team bus seconds before we were due to leave. I swear Louis Saha was never earlier than 11.59 and fifty-nine seconds if we had a noon departure. It would drive me crazy.

After a noon lunch – Ribena, spaghetti with a bit of sauce, and a yoghurt – and the manager's team talk, I always needed my private time. I'd grab a programme and head into the right-hand toilet cubicle. In the dressing room the rest of the lads would be laughing and joking. Someone would be kicking a ball around. But I always needed time on my own to think about the game or my direct opponent. I might be facing a lightning-quick winger with bags of skill, so to get some positive thoughts in my mind I'd say to myself,

'Will he want it as much as me? Will he run as far as me?'

Sometimes, if I was feeling edgy and nervous, I'd think about the meal I'd be eating later. I'd reassure myself that all this hullabaloo would be over in three hours and I'd be enjoying my salt-and-pepper spare ribs and my chicken curry in town with my family. People think you need to fire yourself up before a match, but it's often about calming your-self down.

Play for long enough and you get into some daft habits. I had a quick back massage once when I was seventeen and played well. So that was it, a rub-down for every game after that, even though I've never had a bad back in my life. Walking out, I always insisted on being fifth in line with Becks just behind me. I've no idea why.

Plenty of sportsmen have rituals like this. Mine were based on knowing that I had done everything to give myself an edge. The early nights, the 3.30 p.m. Weetabix, the pre-match stretches – I didn't want to leave anything to chance.

It doesn't work for every player. A dressing room full of Gary Nevilles would be boring. But you cannot stay at the top in professional sport for very long without commitment and sacrifice – and there's no doubt that, as a squad, we had good habits. Times were changing. Gone were the days when foot-ballers could afford to get pissed in the week.

There's nothing worse than not making the most of your abilities. And that's what the boss would remind us day after day after day. In the manager's team talks, no one has been name-checked more times than a billionaire he knows. He's got more money than he can spend, he can retire to the golf course, but, according to the boss, this bloke is still first into work every day. It was a speech we heard often: 'Be proud to say you work hard.'

You might think hard work should be taken for granted, especially with the millions that footballers can earn. But in a macho environment like a dressing room, it's cooler to act like you don't give a damn. And maybe that was the difference between the talented Liverpool squad of those days and us at United – they acted cool, and we won the championship.

8

Terry

Sitting on the team bus, we crawled through a sea of smiling England fans, all of them willing us on to win the European Championship on home soil. The whole country was buzzing. Stuart Pearce turned to me. 'Enjoy it,' he said, 'because it might not get as good as this again.'

Being young, I shrugged it off, thinking, 'There'll be plenty more good times to come'. But he turned out to be right. There weren't nearly enough good times, not when it came to playing for my country. Euro 96 was the pinnacle.

I loved playing under Terry Venables, although it wasn't all plain sailing. Being a United player at that time was to be a target for some terrible stick at Wembley. People either loved us or hated us now that we were winning trophies every year. And in Hughes and Ince, then Keane and Cantona, we had a really hard, aggressive edge.

England, not having to qualify for the tournament, played

a run of friendlies with the old stadium half empty. Less than thirty thousand fans watched us play Bulgaria one night so you could hear every shout. 'Munich bastard!' 'Red bastard!' It was always at its worst down one side, across from the dug- outs and the royal box. There would be groups of West Ham and Chelsea supporters, lads who had come not to cheer England but to get pissed and hammer a few United players on a Wednesday night. I'd be running up and down the touch- line, playing my guts out for my country, then I'd go to pick up the ball for a throw-in and hear a shout of 'Fuck off Neville, you're shit!'

I was delighted when that tired old ground, with its crap facilities and its pockets of bitter fans, got smashed into little pieces. I never mourned the Twin Towers, not for a minute.

Still, I didn't let the minority of idiots spoil the experience of playing for England or for Terry. I loved it right from my debut in the summer of 1995.

I was out in Zurich for an end-of-season youth competition for under 20s involving some of the top European clubs when one of the United coaches came over.

'Gary,' he said, 'you've been called up by England.'

I couldn't believe it. I was out there playing with youth players. But I rang my dad and he confirmed it. So I was on the first plane out of there to meet up with the senior England team.

Gary Pallister was the only other United player in the squad so I travelled down with him to the hotel at Burnham Beeches. It was one of those nervous moments. I didn't say much, which isn't like me. I must have come over as someone quite shy to Terry and the rest of the players, and it didn't help when Pally went home a few days later carrying an injury. I felt isolated, lonely for the first time in a football environment. I was used to being around my pals.

Every time I went down to dinner I was already looking forward to getting back to my room without any fuss or bother. If I wasn't training, I'd lie in my room watching telly or having a nap. The other lads, like Gazza, David Platt and Alan Shearer, weren't unfriendly. I was just a youngster staying out of their way. Stan Collymore was in his first squad, too, but he had Liverpool teammates like Steve McManaman and John Barnes to hang around with. There was a big Liverpool contingent, but they were a different clique to me – a bit louder, a bit more outgoing and confident. If I was going to make an impression it would have to be on the pitch.

At twenty, and after only nineteen Premiership matches, I made my England debut in a three-match series, the Umbro Cup, against Japan at Wembley – admittedly a low-key game, with a crowd of just 21,142 – playing in a defence that featured John Scales and David Unsworth at centre-back and Stuart Pearce on the other side. I acquitted myself pretty well, and though Warren Barton came in for the next game against Sweden, I returned against Brazil – a 3–1 defeat in front of a much bigger crowd and with Ronaldo, Roberto Carlos and Dunga in opposition.

As a defender, I learnt so much from Don Howe, Terry's assistant. He used to take the back four for sessions while Terry and Bryan Robson worked on the attacking side of the game. We'd split into different groups straight after the warm-up for half an hour before coming back together to work as a team.

That was new to me. At United we'd always based training around small-sided games together. We'd go to ball-work quickly. Under Don it was much more about tactical shape and co-ordinating everyone's movements. As a defence, we were drilled with military precision.

Don's attitude was that you had to get the foundations right in any team, and that meant building from the back. You could win a game 4–1 but if the goal conceded was a bad one, he'd be livid.

Terry had a crane installed by the practice pitch so he could film the sessions from on high and then go back over the video to show you your movements. It's common now to have that sort of analysis but at the time it was a novel approach, and very educational for me.

Armed with those tapes, Don hammered us until we were as co-ordinated as synchronised swimmers. They were brilliant sessions, as good as I've seen. I learnt how to antici-pate angled passes behind me, and to close down my winger. At that time, more than in later years, my job was mainly about stopping my opponent. It was a crime if I let him swing a cross in.

One of the first things Don, astute as ever, said to me was this: 'I've watched you, I like you and you defend quite well, but you don't set up a lot of goals. You don't go forward much.' At that time, it was a fair observation.

But my game suited him and Terry so, as Euro 96 loomed, I was firmly established as right-back in a four-man defence. I could also operate as a third centre-back, which was a big advantage because we'd worked on swapping between forma-tions when necessary. Warren Barton wasn't really Don's type and Rob Jones had had terrible injury problems at Liverpool.

So I was a regular, and Phil, precocious as ever, was my understudy, at nineteen.

Before the tournament we went on tour to the Far East – a chance to warm up with a match against China and to bond together as a squad. In the interests of camaraderie, Terry gave us all a night off before we were due to fly home. I was up for a few beers, but David Platt sensed trouble brewing. As one of the senior pros, he approached me, Phil, Nicky Barmby and Jason Wilcox, the young lads, with some friendly words of advice. 'This could be one to miss,' he said. So as Teddy Sheringham, Alan Shearer, Gazza and the boys all went out to explore Hong Kong's nightlife, the three of us sat in our hotel having dinner. We didn't know what a riotous time we were missing.

The first I knew about anything was when I came down for lunch the next day. I walked into the dining room and Gazza was lighting a cigar with something that looked like a Bunsen burner from a chemistry class. I swear it's one of the funniest things I've seen in my life. The flame must have been about three feet long and Gazza, in the dining room of a five-star hotel, was almost setting fire to himself. Phil and I were crying with laughter. If anyone had done that at United you wouldn't have waited for the bollocking from the manager, you would have just packed your bags and gone. I do know the boss wanted to bring Gazza to Old Trafford. It's a real shame it never happened because I think Alex Ferguson would have been great for him.

It was clear from Gazza's state, and the sore heads among the rest of the lads, that they'd had a cracking night out. Part of me was kicking myself for not going, and I wouldn't have missed it in later years. But Platty had looked after us younger lads and I can't imagine how our manager at home would have reacted if we'd been all over the front pages. I wasn't exactly a hardened drinker. A quick appointment in the infamous dentist's chair having vodka poured down my throat would have finished me off for days. But I wished I'd been there to enjoy it.

There was more mayhem to come. When we flew home all the players were upstairs in the bubble of the jumbo jet. Gazza was sat next to Phil and me. He'd been drinking for hours and Terry wanted someone to make sure he didn't get out of control. Terry sent Doc Crane, the England team doctor, to keep an eye on him, but he liked a tipple himself and fell asleep.

Alan Shearer came down to play cards. As he was walking past Gazza he slapped the back of his head. A big clout. Gazza woke up with a start and thought it was McManaman or Fowler because they were sat a couple of rows behind. Gazza's revenge was to go and smash up their TV consoles.

We got off the plane and didn't really think much about the damage that had been left behind, but the next day all hell broke loose. It had kicked off in the Sunday papers, with pictures of everyone getting pissed in the China Jump and a story about the wreckage on the plane.

Back in the team hotel, Terry met the senior players and told them they'd better come up with a way out of this mess. Around the country there was a bit of impatience with our form so there wasn't much credit in the bank with the media or the public. The wolves were out.

We had a full meeting of the squad at Burnham Beeches. The senior players – Platt, Shearer and Pearce – had their say and came out with the line about collective responsibility. We'd all take the rap and give two match fees to pay for the damage and the rest to charity. This was another lesson that stayed with me through my England career: teams stick together. Never chuck your teammate overboard, or show divisions.

Sharing the blame was going to cost me a lot of money. Our match fee was £1,500, which was a fortune to me at the time, and I had a moan to my brother. We hadn't been on the piss-up or caused any of the damage. But looking back, it was the right way to handle it. We had to keep the group together. And the truth was that the players were willing to make allowances for Gazza because they knew what he could do for the team. He was our match-winner, and as popular a player as any in the squad. There was nothing to be gained by us hanging Gazza out to dry.

We went into the tournament with a great team, as well as home advantage. We had David Seaman, Tony Adams, Platt, Ince, Gazza, Shearer, Pearce and Sheringham, all established and in their prime. You could have made a captain out of any of them. It was a joy for the young players like Steve McManaman, Darren Anderton, Nick Barmby and me to look around the dressing room and see all this talent and hardened experience.

In the dressing room before matches, Adams would kick a ball against a wall or the door like he was ready to batter it down. I used to sit next to Pearce and he scared the life out of me the first time he warmed up for a match at Wembley. 'This is our fuckin' turf, this is my fuckin' turf,' he kept snarling.

Even though there were big characters at United, the

dressing room at Old Trafford was generally composed in the minutes leading up to kick-off. Not so with England. There'd be shouting, chest-beating, patriotic roars. I'd sit there and think, 'This lot are wound up.' I wanted to put on *Football Focus* and chill out. It was the opposite from what I knew at United where we had music, the telly on until half an hour before kick-off, lads laughing and joking.

For a young defender, Adams was someone to look up to. Our manager once described him as a United player in the wrong shirt, and I can see what he meant. His intensity, his drive, his courage would have made him a legend at Old Trafford.

Shearer was another who could – make that should – have played for United. I thought he was going to join us that summer of '96. The club were sniffing around him when Becks and I bumped into him at a Bryan Adams concert. We did our best to talk him round but he chose Newcastle, and to this day I think of what might have been had he come to United. For all his achievements in the game, there will always be something missing from his career because he never played consistently at the top European club level. At United he would have done that and become adored every bit as much as he was at Newcastle. He could have been embraced like Charlton and Robson, two other United legends from the north-east. I thought it was madness for him not to want to come to Old Trafford, where he would have won countless medals. But then I'm not a Geordie.

We also had Gazza, who'd been to a World Cup semi-final and who, despite his injuries, was still a world-class talent. He was everything you've heard – mad, hilarious, warm-hearted, and a match-winner.

That squad had power, strength, experience, a proven goalscorer, depth and confidence. And thanks to Terry's abilities, we had players who were better for their country than their clubs. Anderton was one, Barmby another, because they were bright and adaptable. Jamie Redknapp was a bit like that as well, although very unlucky with injury. These were players who weren't in a rush, who could hold the ball, who could use it intelligently. McManaman was another. Just going through the squad makes me wonder what might have been.

We began with a scrappy draw against Switzerland so we needed to raise our game against Scotland in our second group game. Everyone remembers the second goal, that brilliant individual strike by Gazza which he celebrated as if he was back in the dentist's chair. But it was the first goal that gave me one of the most satisfying moments of my England career.

It was a cross, just a cross, but I remember it as one of my best ever, landing right on Shearer's head at the far post. He was never going to miss from there. I ran off up the touchline, pumping my fists, Gazza chasing after me. After all the stick at Wembley, it felt like the whole country was united behind every one of us, even Phil and me, the United lads. The atmosphere was fantastic.

We'd not been great against Scotland, suffering a nightmare twenty minutes and needing Big Dave Seaman to make a big penalty save. But we were gathering momentum, which is what matters in tournaments. We were full of confidence going into our third game, against Holland, and both tactically and technically it was the best international performance I've been involved in, a real tribute to Terry's preparations.

Football is always going to be unpredictable, but under a top coach like Terry you would go out with a picture in your mind of how the game should unfold. And more often than not, and particularly in that match against Holland, it would happen as he had anticipated.

He'd been working for months on the plans. When Big Dave had the ball in his hands, Terry had me and Stuart Pearce push high up the field, pressing Holland right back on their flanks. One of the midfield players would drop so we wouldn't be exposed defensively, but, with one tweak, we had control of the pitch. We were playing a team you would expect to dominate possession, but it was as though England became foreigners for a night. That 4–1 victory is one of only a handful of England games when we looked a higher class than the opposition.

It was a brilliant team performance, but we couldn't match it in a really tough, tight quarter-final against Spain. I was as tired as I've ever been on the pitch. There was such a buzz around the country that I was barely sleeping at night, and I felt it in that game. We went through on penalties, Stuart Pearce providing one of the great England moments with his celebration, but I was booked for a tired tackle on the left-back Sergi which meant I'd miss the semi-final through suspension. I was gutted, and I'd probably have been even more upset if I'd known there'd be no more semi-finals with England in my time.

Terry came up to me in the dressing room after the Spain game. 'Don't worry, you'll be back for the final,' he said. I had every reason to believe him. We were certain we could beat Germany to reach the final. We were on home soil, the team was packed with talent and experience, and the spirit was fantastic under Terry. Everything was in place. Germany weren't great. We had the beating of them.

The fans believed it too. There seemed to be a St George's flag flying from every house. Everywhere we went there were thousands out on the streets.

I felt the hairs rise on the back of my neck as I took my seat for the match and the whole stadium sang 'Football's Coming Home'. I'm not sure I've seen Wembley like that, before or since.

It was heartbreaking to lose, especially the way we did. There would be a lot of self-inflicted disasters with England, but this was a genuine hard-luck story. We'd been the better team, with Gazza just inches away from converting one cross deep into injury-time that would have been an historic Golden Goal. And when we went to penalties, we'd actually scored them. All five had flown in when Gareth Southgate, my replacement, stepped up. You know the rest. We went out to the eventual champions, but by the narrowest of margins.

The sense of disappointment was massive around the whole country, and among the players. If there was a consolation for me it was that the experience of a major tournament at the age of twenty-one was incredible. My performances had been very decent. I'd felt at home, whether it was at right-back, right centre-back or wing-back (I played all three positions in four games). It had been a joy to play because Wembley was right behind us. There were spine-tingling experiences sitting on the team bus on the way to games, with the streets lined with fans from Burnham Beeches right into London.

I'd learnt so much from the older players, but mostly from Terry. People talk about his knowledge of the game, his tactical brain, and rightly so, but the thing that most impressed me was that he was never afraid to have really strong people around him like Don Howe and Bryan Robson. He'd encourage everyone, including the players, to join a discussion but never in a way that made him seem weak or indecisive. Don might come into the dressing room and contradict him. Don might win the argument. Maybe it showed Terry's self-confidence and experience that he was able to be talked round without it seeming as though he was being undermined.

The FA's failure to give Terry a contract to take us on after Euro 96 remains one of the great disappointments of my career. I know there was a massive clash of personalities with Noel White, the chairman of the international committee, but only at the FA could it be the elite coach who packs his bags and the blazer who wins the day.

Terry was at his peak. He'd had experience of being a club manager at the top level, he'd enjoyed success at Barcelona, where he'd expanded his vision of the game and his expertise, and he'd gained a fantastic knowledge of the players. Even if Terry was a bit stubborn in his dealings with the FA, it was a massive cock-up to let him go. It was a decision that undermined England for years.

But that was the trouble with the FA. Too many suits, too many guys with agendas, too many people listening to the press and panicking at the first sign of controversy. So what that some of the media had it in for Terry because of his business dealings? So what if Terry used to invite us for a few drinks at his club, Scribes? So what if he wouldn't bow before the international committee? The bottom line is that he'd not only restored pride in the national team after the Graham

Taylor shambles but also put us within a whisker of winning our first tournament in thirty years. Tactically and technically, we had no reason to be afraid of anyone. We had good players and, thanks to Terry and his staff, we were a very good team.

The great imponderable of my international career is what might have happened had Terry Venables been allowed to lead us after Euro 96. The simple fact is that we haven't been as close to winning a tournament since.

But back then, as a twenty-one-year-old, I didn't know this was going to be as good as it got for me, as Stuart Pearce had predicted when we were sat on that coach together. He said it just after the Spain game when there was national euphoria, with fans dancing in the fountains at Trafalgar Square. I thought I had all the time in the world. I thought I'd soon be back contesting another tournament, perhaps even winning one. Why not?

9

Au Revoir, Cantona

'Together, we will win the European Cup.' It was quite a promise to make, but this wasn't coming from just anyone. The man saying it across the pub table was Eric Cantona.

We were in the Bull's Head in Hale on a team day out. It was December 1996, and our Frenchman had pulled up a seat with me and Becks. The young lads had always been in awe of him and Eric was a quiet man in the changing room. But this time we got chatting properly. Over a drink, Eric told us we were going to become kings of Europe.

It was a big claim given the club's record. Conquering the continent was obviously the challenge for us now that we'd won the title, but the task loomed as high as Everest. More than a decade had passed since any English club had won the European Cup. As a country, we'd endured the post-Heysel exile. The stars of the game were still being drawn to the big clubs in Italy and Spain. At Old Trafford, you had to look

Above: The Chantlers School Under-11 team with me (*front row, second from right*) and Phil (*back row, far left*).

Left and below: On Saturdays we played for the ICE junior team, under the watchful eye of my dad. I'm the captain in this team photo, with Phil standing (*back row, far right*).

Above left and right: We both loved cricket, and Phil certainly could have played at the very highest level. Here we are (*front row, centre and second from right*) representing Lancashire.

Below: The North of England schoolboys team featured a future England captain in Michael Vaughan (*front row, third from left*), but as you can just see from the sling (*back row, second from left*), I broke my finger slip-fielding at what was effectively the national trials.

Above: With Phil at my dad's last game. He scored a six to win the match.

Below: I scored an unbeaten 110 for Greenmount against Astley Bridge in July 1992 in partnership with a young Australian called Matthew Hayden (140 not out), as the *Bury Times* reported, but it was football only for me from then on.

Two ton route to cup final

GREENMOUNT emerged triumphant from a semi-final tie which produced more than 500 runs on Sunday afternoon.

They amassed 278 for 2 against Astley Bridge, thanks largely to two individual hundreds, and were then forced to sweat it out as their visitors made a tremendous effort to snatch a place in the Bolton League's Hamer Cup final.

The home side were 42 for 2 when 17 years old Gary Neville, an apprentice footballer with Manchester United, strolled to the middle to join 21 years old Australian professional Matthew Hayden.

Some 40 overs later the big Queenslander, who has high hopes of a place in the Aussie Test squad, was 140 not out and his less experienced partner (right) was unbeaten on 110. Neville's maiden first team 'ton' after a previous best of 49. It was Hayden's fourth century for the club this summer.

Bridge professional Brendan McArdle (102) and Mark Warren (74) bravely led the reply but when they both fell to Mark Stewart (6 for 74) in the same over, the chase became a lost cause and they were eventually all out for 256.

*Matthew Hayden is organising cricket coaching for all juniors of any age. The sessions, at Greenmount CC, are from 10am to 4pm on August 4, 5 and 6 and then 11, 12 and 13, each week costing £20 per person. For details telephone 020-4

Above: Tracey, Gary and Phil Neville: 218 caps between us.

Above: I signed my registration form for the Manchester United Centre of Excellence in August 1987.

Left: At the age of sixteen, in the summer of 1991, this letter came from Brian Kidd inviting me for pre-season training with United.

SUNDERLAND INFORMATION

![Sunderland AFC crest]

SUNDERLAND ASSOCIATION FOOTBALL CLUB LIMITED

Registered Offices and Ground
Roker Park Ground,
Sunderland, SR6 9SW
Telephone: 091 514 0332
Fax: 091 5145854
Clubcall: 0898 121140
Ticketcall: 0898 121881

Honours:
League Division One
Champions:
1891-92, 92-93, 94-95,
1901-02, 1912-13, 1935-36
League Division Two
Champions:
1975-76
League Division Three
Champions:
1987-88
F.A. Cup Winners
1937, 1973

Manager: DENIS SMITH
Chief Coach: VIV BUSBY
Coaches:
ROGER JONES
MALCOLM CROSBY
JIM MORROW
Physiotherapist
STEVE SMELT
Football in the Community Officer:
MICK FERGUSON
Hon. Club Consultant Surgeon:
R. G. CHECKETTS, M.D., F.R.C.S.
Hon. Club Doctors:
DR. A. J. CRUMMIE
DR. E. SPAGNOLI
General Manager and Secretary:
GEOFF DAVIDSON, F.C.A.
Marketing and Commercial Executive:
ALEC KING
Ground Administrator:
FRED BAILEY

F. A. YOUTH CUP - 2ND ROUND

SUNDERLAND -V- MANCHESTER UNITED

WEDNESDAY 27TH NOVEMBER, 1991 - KICK-OFF - 7.00 P.M.

T E A M S

SUNDERLAND		MANCHESTER UNITED
1. Sean Musgrave		1. Kevin Pilkington
2. Paul Gate		2. Mark Gordon
3. Andrew Scothern 5		3. George Switzer
4. Gareth Cronin 6		4. John O'Kane
5. Paul Harwood 3		5. Gary Neville
6. Dean McGee 7		6. Keith Gillespie
7. Paul Jeffrey 4		7. Nicky Butt
8. Michael Gray		8. Simon Davies
9. Martin Smith 11		9. Colin McKee
10. Craig Russell 9		10. Robert Savage
11. Ian Lawson 10		11. Ben Thornley

Subs:-

12. David Carr

14. TO BE ADVISED

Subs:-

12. TO BE ADVISED *D BECKHAM*

14. TO BE ADVISED *C. CAPPER*

REFEREE :- J.L. WATSON

LINESMEN :- A. HARRISON & R. LOCKHART

Left: My first youth team match came at Sunderland on 27 November 1991.

Below left and right: It was a proud moment to wear the United shirt and club blazer.

Above: The famous Manchester United youth team. I'm in the back row (*second from left*) with Butty (*second from right*); Becks and Scholesy have the balls at their feet in front of us.

Above and above right: We beat Crystal Palace in the final of the FA Youth Cup in 1992, bringing the trophy to Old Trafford for the first time in twenty-eight years: (*Back row, from left*) Ben Thornley, Nicky Butt, Gary Neville, Simon Davies, Chris Casper, Kevin Pilkington, Keith Gillespie; (*front row, from left*) John O'Kane, Robert Savage, George Switzer, Ryan Giggs, David Beckham, Colin McKee.

MANCHESTER UNITED FOOTBALL CLUB plc
Old Trafford, Manchester M16 0RA

President:
Sir Matt Busby, CBE

Directors:
C. M. Edwards, Chairman,
J. M. Edelson, R. Charlton, CBE,
E. M. Watkins, LLM, A. Midani,
R. L. Olive, R. P. Launders

Chief Executive:
Martin Edwards

Manager:
Alex Ferguson, OBE

Secretary:
Kenneth R. Merrett

HONOURS
European Champion Clubs' Cup
Winners: 1968
European Cup Winners' Cup
Winners: 1991
Football League Division One
Champions: 1908 1911 1952 1956
1957 1965 1967
Runners-up: 1947 1948 1949 1951
1959 1964 1968 1980
1988 1992
Football League Division Two
Champions: 1936 1975
Runners-up 1897 1906 1925 1938
FA Challenge Cup
Winners: 1909 1948 1963 1977
1983 1985 1990
Finalists: 1957 1958 1976 1979
Football League Cup
Winners: 1992
Finalists: 1983 1991
European Super Cup
Winners: 1991
FA Charity Shield
Winners: 1908 1911 1952 1956
1957 1983
Joint
Holders: 1965 1967 1977 1990
Finalists: 1948 1963 1985
FA Youth Cup
Winners: 1953 1954 1955 1956
1957 1964 1992
Finalists: 1982 1986

UNITED REVIEW
The official programme of
Manchester United Football Club plc
Edited by Cliff Butler

Designed and printed by
Trafford Press Ltd., Manchester

*The views expressed by contributors
are not necessarily shared by the Club.*

THE MATCH LINE-UP
Wednesday, 16th September 1992 – 8.05 p.m.

MANCHESTER UNITED	TORPEDO MOSCOW
David Beckham	Andrei Afanasyev
Russell Beardsmore	Sergei Borisov
Steve Bruce (Capt.)	Maxim Cheltsov
Ryan Giggs	Igor Chuganov
Mark Hughes	Guennady Grishin
Denis Irwin	Andrei Kolaichev
Andrei Kanchelskis	Andrei Martinov
Brian McClair	Vladimir Pchelnikov
Lee Martin	(Capt.) Alexander Podshivalov
Gary Neville	Nikolai Savichev
Gary Pallister	Sergei Shustikov
Mike Phelan	Sergei Skachenko
Peter Schmeichel	Andrei Talalayev
Danny Wallace	Yury Tishkov
Gary Walsh	Demitry Ulyanov
Neil Webb	Boris Vostrosablin

Tonight's teams will be chosen from the squads listed above.

MATCH OFFICIALS

Referee
Mr. A. Schmidhuber *(Germany)*

Linesmen
Mr. L. Lommer *(Germany)*
Red Trim

Standby Official
Mr. H. Scheurer *(Germany)*

Mr. R. Dornberg *(Germany)*
Yellow Trim

NEXT HOME MATCH
FA PREMIER LEAGUE
SATURDAY 26th SEPTEMBER, 1992 – 3 p.m.
QUEEN'S PARK RANGERS
FOR TICKET DETAILS SEE PAGE 9

Left: A dream come true. My first team debut came against Torpedo Moscow in the Uefa Cup on 16 September 1992.

Below: With Becks and Butty in Red Square for the return leg of that match.

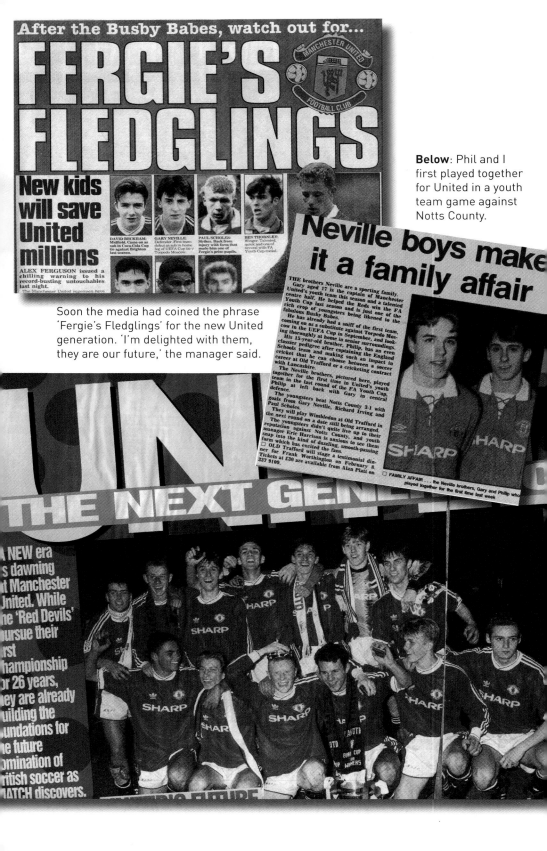

After the Busby Babes, watch out for...

FERGIE'S FLEDGLINGS

New kids will save United millions

ALEX FERGUSON issued a chilling warning to his record-busting untouchables last night.

The Manchester United supermen have

DAVID BECKHAM: Midfield. Came on as sub in Coca-Cola Cup tie against Brighton last season.

GARY NEVILLE: Defender. First team debut as sub in home leg of UEFA Cup tie v Torpedo Moscow.

PAUL SCHOLES: Striker. Back from injury with form that made him one of Fergie's prize pupils.

BEN THORNLEY: Winger. Talented, quick and one of several with FA Youth Cup medal.

Below: Phil and I first played together for United in a youth team game against Notts County.

Soon the media had coined the phrase 'Fergie's Fledglings' for the new United generation. 'I'm delighted with them, they are our future,' the manager said.

Neville boys make it a family affair

THE brothers Neville are a sporting family. Gary aged 17 is the captain of Manchester United's youth team this season and a talented centre half. He helped the Reds win the FA Youth Cup last season and is just one of the rich crop of youngsters being likened to the fabulous Busby Babes.

He has already had a sniff of the first team, coming on as a substitute against Torpedo Moscow in the UEFA Cup in September, and looking thoroughly at home in senior surroundings.

His 15-year-old brother, Philip, has an even classier pedigree after captaining the England Schools team and making such an impact in cricket that he can choose between a soccer career at Old Trafford or a cricketing contract with Lancashire.

The Neville brothers, pictured here, played together for the first time in United's youth team in the last round of the FA Youth Cup, Philip at left back with Gary in central defence.

The youngsters beat Notts County 3-1 with goals from Gary Neville, Richard Irving and Paul Scholes.

They will play Wimbledon at Old Trafford in the next round on a date still being arranged.

The youngsters didn't quite live up to their reputation against Notts County, and youth manager Eric Harrison is anxious to see them snap into the kind of dazzling, smooth-passing form which has excited the fans.

☐ OLD TRAFFORD will stage a testimonial dinner for Frank Worthington on February 8. Tickets at £30 are available from Alan Platt on 337 9109.

☐ FAMILY AFFAIR ... the Neville brothers, Gary and Philip who played together for the first time last week

UNI
THE NEXT GENE

A NEW era is dawning at Manchester United. While the 'Red Devils' pursue their first championship or 26 years, they are already building the foundations for the future domination of British soccer as MATCH discovers.

back as far as flared trousers and George Best in 1968 to remember the last time we'd reached the pinnacle in Europe.

The previous year we'd been knocked out of the Uefa Cup in the first round by Rotor Volgograd. We might be champions of England but this wasn't form to terrify the rest of the world, especially when in the autumn of 1996 we stumbled through the Champions League group stage. We lost the club's 40-year unbeaten record at home, defeated by Fenerbahçe, and went down in both games to Juventus – the European champions, and one of the best teams I ever faced.

Juventus were unbelievably good, so big and powerful as well as packed with talent. Just standing in the tunnel next to them was intimidating. I'd never faced such a formidable team: Ferrara and Montero in defence, Deschamps, Conte and Zidane in midfield, and Del Piero with two big and dangerous strikers in Boksic and Vieri. Big names, big players, in every respect. We lost 1–0 to them in Turin, but it could have been 10–0. It was the biggest battering I've ever had on a football pitch. They took us to school, boys against men. We didn't have a proper chance in the whole match. Manchester United played ninety minutes without a shot, without a sniff of a chance. It's the only time that happened in my 602 games.

Del Piero was a class act, so sharp and elusive and intelligent. There's a lot of thick footballers out there, players with huge talent when the ball's at their feet but no real under-standing of where to move or how best to link with their teammates. That is a criticism you'd never make of Zidane or Del Piero, and Juventus had both of them. These were the guys who made the Champions League such a massive test.

They knew how to play and they were streetwise, too. They could handle themselves, and if anyone did have a go they had tough nuts like Montero to offer protection.

That defeat was as bad as it got, and Giggsy probably had the worst night of all. As the manager was dishing out his half-time criticism, Giggsy bit back. The boss was never going to let that pass, and his response was instant. He hooked Giggsy straight away.

That was a big call for the boss, who was rarely that re-active at half-time, throwing all the plans in the air. You think of Mourinho making early changes all the time, but the boss is generally more patient, more trusting. He'll certainly let you know what you are doing wrong. If we are being dominated by a particular player, he'll come in, look around and say, 'So-and-so is having a nice game isn't he? He's having a lovely time. Did I not mention him in my team talk? You two, get up ten yards. You two, midfield, close him down.' He'll deal with things and dole out whatever criticisms are necessary – 'Gary, you haven't passed to a red shirt yet'; 'Scholesy, watch those tackles' – but he doesn't want to spend the whole of half-time hammering people and he doesn't like to throw a game plan out of the window. But having a go back at the boss, as Giggsy discovered that night – and as I'd find out later – was met with zero tolerance.

So Giggsy watched from the sidelines as the spanking from Juventus continued in the second half. I walked off at the end thinking, 'We're a long way off yet'.

Still, Eric seemed convinced that good times were around the corner as we sat in the Bull's Head. Becks and I left the pub invigorated – and not just because of the beer. For Eric, there wouldn't be many chances left to prove that he could dominate in Europe as he had done so majestically in English football. The rest of us weren't to know it, but Eric had staked everything on winning the Champions League.

None of us got to know Eric well, although there was a vast, unspoken respect for him. In training, if the ball didn't get played to him as he wanted he would look at you like he was going to knock you out. He had massively high standards; he was a perfectionist. But because it was Eric, you didn't feel belittled, it just made you strive to do better. We were desperate to impress him.

Respect for him contained a little dash of fear because we had all seen how he could erupt, even though we knew he'd never take it out on us. There'd been the kung-fu kick, a string of red cards, the punch-up at Galatasaray. We found incidents like that amusing – after the event, anyway – because Eric was so mild-mannered, quiet even, the rest of the time. He wasn't arrogant at all but polite and considered. He always remained real. He drove a modest car, lived in a modest house in Salford. He'd turn up at all the team evenings, the Christmas parties, the nights out with the wives, but he'd be quiet, a bit like Scholesy or Andy Cole – not in a way that excludes you from the team, you're just accepted as being a quieter participant, just like there are louder types.

Eric did things his way and no one interfered, not even the manager sometimes. When we turned up at a civic event at Manchester town hall to celebrate the Double, Eric wandered in wearing a denim jacket instead of a blazer. We looked him up and down and wondered how the boss would react when he arrived. Surely he'd go berserk. The press were there and all sorts of VIPs. But the manager just shook his head and smiled. 'Eh, lads,' he said. 'Some man, that Cantona.'

Eric could get away with it, as Gazza did with England, because he combined his talent with being a committed team-man at heart. He trained as hard as lesser players and strived for improvement. And in that 1996/97 season he was striving, like the rest of us, to win the Champions League.

One problem was that, as a young team, we were still plagued with inconsistency. We thrashed Newcastle United, with the newly signed Alan Shearer, 4–0 in the Charity Shield but then lost 5–0 at St James's Park in October on one of those days when you just want to disappear off the pitch. Everything Newcastle tried came off. I backed a few yards off David Ginola at one point. I should have been tighter, and I managed to get on the wrong side. He turned inside and smashed a shot into the top corner from thirty yards. It was a great bit of skill to buy himself a yard and to finish like that. The minute a player of that quality does you on the turn like that your heart sinks because there's the feeling he's going to pull off something special. I was left praying that Schmeichel would get me out of trouble. This time even Peter couldn't get a hand on it.

It was a great goal, though not the best bit of skill ever done on me. That has to go to Jay Jay Okocha. One moment he was standing in front of me and the next thing I knew he'd disappeared the other side of me, and the ball too. It's probably on YouTube somewhere. I still don't know how he did it.

The Newcastle defeat was a horror, and we let in six at Southampton a week later. Beaten 6–3 at Southampton – it was a bad moment, that, and we had to learn to cope with such set-backs. You'd get them in every season, and that's when the manager came into his own, keeping up morale, maintaining focus and making sure we didn't get distracted by all the noises outside. He had belief in us, and on another day we'd play like world beaters.

In Europe we were proving just as unpredictable. We'd needed victory at Rapid Vienna in the final group match to qualify for the knock-out rounds. Eric's idea of proving ourselves the best team in Europe was looking ambitious, to say the least.

We dared to believe a bit more when we blitzed Porto 4–0 in the first leg of the quarter-finals. We ripped into them on the counter-attack, flying forward at 100mph to score fantastic goals through Giggsy and Andy Cole. We were through to our first Champions League semi-final and felt we had nothing to be scared about facing Borussia Dortmund, even if they were the champions of Germany.

In the first leg in Dortmund, we had the three best chances. Butty hit the post, Eric shot wide from fifteen yards, and Becks had a chance cleared off the line. We deserved better than to lose 1–0 to a deflected shot off Gary Pallister. Still, all to play for, even if Keano was suspended back at our place after a booking in Germany. In his absence, we'd go front foot with Eric behind Andy Cole and Ole Gunnar Solskjaer.

The game had barely started when Lars Ricken put them ahead with their first attack. Now we needed three goals, but we kept at it and created an unbelievable number of chances. The best of them fell to Eric. A cross-shot from Cole was pushed out to him inside the six-yard box. But, as the goal gaped, Jurgen Kohler slid into his path and Eric shot at him. Two 1–0 defeats.

It was to prove the final blow for Eric, even after we went on to win a second championship in a row, celebrated in style at the Hacienda, the nightclub made famous by the Happy Mondays and the Stone Roses. That's my type of music, though hanging around with Giggsy, Becks and Ben Thornley we probably looked more like Take That.

At the weekend we'd drawn 3–3 at Middlesbrough, which included my first goal for United. I'd like to tell a story of great attacking adventure, but truth is I was knackered after a run forward and ended up staying up the field. The ball came across to Eric and, inevitably, he played the perfect pass to slip me in. I remember really concentrating as it came across my body and I just struck it absolutely perfect. It went in, and what a feeling – the greatest goal of my career. Sad, really, that there were only seven of them in 687 games for United and England. That's a crap total by any standards. Sometimes I have thought, 'Christ, is that all I contributed in all those years?'

Anyway, when Liverpool lost and Newcastle could only draw the following day, we'd clinched the championship. 'The goal that won us the title!' I joked to the lads when we danced around the Hacienda with a room full of ecstatic United fans.

We celebrated in style, but Eric's thoughts were elsewhere, as they'd been since our European exit. We'd soon discover that losing to Dortmund, and the way we lost the games, must have had a massive effect on Eric. We hadn't been beaten by a great team, we'd just not taken our chances. Tiny margins. There were several factors, and no one inside the dressing room blamed Eric, except perhaps himself.

But as I knew from that chat in the Bull's Head, he'd set his heart on Europe that season. He'd dominated the English league and he'd wanted to take us to the next level. We'd fallen short, and while there were no recriminations, at the age of thirty he'd decided that he'd given it his best shot. He'd had enough. Time to quit.

A week after our final game, I saw on Teletext that there was going to be a big announcement by the club. I assumed we must be signing someone. Instead Martin Edwards, the chairman, told the world that Eric Cantona had retired. One of United's greatest ever players had decided to walk away while still in his prime.

The news came as a shock to all of us. I'd played with him in a testimonial for David Busst just a few days earlier and he'd got off the team bus and told us, 'Have a good summer, see you later.' But the way he left was typical Eric. There would be no diminishing of his legend, no slide into mediocrity. He'd finish at the top, or as near as he could make it – captain of a club that had won the Premiership. He certainly left us wanting more, which isn't a bad way to go.

I wished he'd stayed because I believe he could have been part of the European Cup-winning team. Failure hadn't been down to him; it was because we were a young, inconsistent side still exploring our potential. His departure means that he fell short of achieving his dream of conquering Europe, but it doesn't lessen his status in my eyes. I played with him for two full seasons and we won a title both times, the first of them almost single-handedly down to him.

He will always have a place in the hearts of the fans because of his charisma and his daring. That temper is part of the legend. People loved him because he did, and said, things they would love to have got away with.

People talk about money and fame affecting footballers, distorting their characters and warping their judgement. And in many cases that might be right. But that wasn't the case with Eric. As with Keano, what you saw was what you got. They'd have been the same fiery individuals whether they were footballers or electricians.

Some players, some people, are capable of counting to ten when they are wound up. Others, like Roy and Eric, are incapable of taking a deep breath. That's not down to the fame or the money. They are firebrands by nature, and I loved having them on my side.

Eric's retirement caused shockwaves in English football but it didn't send the club into meltdown. That's probably the greatest strength of the boss's era. You can be one of the greatest legends United has ever seen – and I was lucky enough to play with a few – but you leave and the club moves on without so much as a glance back. You walk out the door and you'll be lucky if you get a mention. There's never a leaving party, except when a member of staff leaves. There's always someone to fill your boots, and another trophy to be won. It keeps everyone humble, and hungry.

With Eric gone, in the summer of 1997 the boss brought in the experience of Teddy Sheringham. I knew his class on the pitch from my time with England. And you should have heard Scholesy drool about him. He loved playing with Teddy because he recognised another player who had eyes in the back of his head. He'd still be talking about Teddy years after he left – about the awareness, the ability to take a ball in tight areas, the vision. Teddy didn't have the aura of Eric but he was equally good at drawing the best out of his teammates.

Teddy was the significant signing of the summer, but Phil and I were also ready to update our contracts on the back of our success. Wealth has been a happy by-product of my career, but the one thing I always craved was security. So when the club intimated that they would offer us seven-year contracts we couldn't scribble our names quick enough, even though others counselled against it. The negotiations lasted about fifteen minutes.

My dad was on a European trip, and he bumped into Terry Venables. He'd read about the new long-term deals and, in the age of Bosman, of free agency and huge signing-on fees, asked why we'd signed away our futures for as long as seven years. 'Because they wouldn't give us ten,' my dad replied, and he wasn't being sarcastic.

Losing Eric would hinder any team, and then two months into the 1997/98 season we lost our new captain, Keano, to a serious knee injury. We had a terrible time with injuries that season. Another player we lost for a long period was Denis Irwin, after a scandalous tackle by Paul Bosvelt in a Champions League game at Feyenoord. It was a horrible night, with Feyenoord trying to kick lumps out of us, one of those games when you end up going in for every tackle with your own studs up out of self-protection. Julio Cruz, their Argentine striker, spat straight in my face and offered to meet me in the tunnel. When I walked off he wasn't anywhere to be seen.

A young squad was exposed. We had an average age of twenty-three in some matches, and at one stage our oldest outfield player was Andy Cole at twenty-six. We were depleted, but nothing should detract from the Arsenal team that won the championship that year, the best domestic opponents I faced. The best of the bunch, better than Chelsea under Mourinho and Arsenal's Invincibles.

Arsène Wenger had been appointed the previous season. We hadn't known much about him then, but we'd witnessed the coming together of a formidable opponent. That Arsenal team had so many gifts. They were experienced and strong, both mentally and physically. They were tough. They didn't have the touch of arrogance that would come in the Henry years when their attitude was 'you can't touch us, we're French and we're brilliant'.

From back to front, it was hard to detect a weakness. Modern football is a squad game but you know a team is really strong when you can rattle off their first XI without pausing: Seaman, Dixon, Winterburn, Adams, Keown, Vieira, Petit, Parlour, Overmars, Anelka and Bergkamp. If they were fit, they played.

I've rarely come across a physically stronger team – perhaps only Juventus. Arsenal had a top goalkeeper, a fantastic back four, a central midfield pair that could pass, move and never be intimidated, and a hard-working right-midfield player in Parlour who could tuck in complemented by an out-and-out flyer in Overmars on the other flank.

Of all my regular left-wing opponents, Overmars must go down as the toughest I faced.

Ginola was another tricky one, not least because of his physical stature. For a winger he was a big man. But he was never going to run in behind you. He was a lazy winger. He wanted the ball to his feet so he could turn and run. If he did that, if he got his tail up in the first twenty minutes, he could make life a nightmare. That happened one time at White Hart Lane and I was sent off by half-time. But if you nailed him with a few early tackles, if you snapped at him like a terrier, he'd think, 'I'm not having much joy here, I'll go drift inside or see what it's like on the other wing.'

Overmars, and Arsenal, would keep at you. The Dutchman's scorching pace gave any defender a problem. Petit, with that wand of a left foot, would constantly flick the ball over my head for Overmars to run on to. Get tight and he'd beat you in a sprint. Drop off and he had room to build up a head of steam.

And then there was Bergkamp, one of the great number 10s, who would play in the hole and feed the ball through to Anelka, a finisher who had an eye for goal and searing pace.

In terms of fitting the pieces together for 4–4–2, you could not have hand-picked a team with better balance.

Mourinho's Chelsea were an unstoppable force for a couple of seasons. And I know the Arsenal Invincibles of 2003/04 can claim their own unique place in the record books, and they were mesmerising to watch. In Henry they had a forward so elusive that he was almost unplayable at his peak. But, if it's not perverse to say this of a team that went a whole season unbeaten, you always felt you had a chance against that later Arsenal side because you could get about them, bully them. I couldn't say that about Wenger's first champions, and I don't think it's a coincidence that we drew twice against the Invincibles but lost twice to Arsenal in 1997/98. They were the best domestic team we came up against in my time at United.

We were top of the league when they came to Old Trafford in March but it was a sign of our injury problems that I was at centre-half with young John Curtis at right-back. Anelka flicked the ball over the top and Overmars used his speed to spring through and slide the ball through Schmeichel's legs. When big Peter pulled his hamstring going up for a corner it seemed to sum up our problems. Arsenal had won at Old Trafford for the first time in eight seasons.

By the end of the season we weren't far off Arsenal – only a point as it turned out, which wasn't bad considering our injuries – but we couldn't complain when we finished empty-handed. Arsenal were truly impressive.

10

Glenn

It's been said before because it's true: if only Glenn Hoddle had possessed the man-management skills to go with his undoubted football intelligence. But then you could sum up my entire international career with those two sad words, 'if only'.

The fact is that Glenn possessed a great football brain, and still does – just listen to him as a pundit. He's a guy who can spot a player and read the nuances of a game. He was a very good coach who wanted England to play the right way, with intelligence, valuing possession.

When it came to strategy, he was excellent at laying out what he wanted, in a very detailed way. Perhaps he was a bit fixated with 3–5–2. Terry had always been flexible; Glenn wanted to groom us in one system. But, fair enough, Glenn knew what he wanted and why he thought it would be successful.

The trouble was, Glenn never had Terry's ease around the players. Terry had a natural authority but, perhaps because he was younger and less experienced, Glenn felt a need to exert control. I detected this change in tone right from the first squad meeting.

As usual we were staying at the Burnham Beeches hotel in Buckinghamshire and I went to book a car to go down to the shops to buy some magazines. An FA official told me it wasn't allowed under the new management. Then I tried to order a sandwich in my room. Again, forbidden. Glenn wanted to know exactly where we were, what we ate, and precisely when we went to bed. This was a culture shock. These may seem petty matters, but under Terry and our boss at United we'd always been trusted to be adults and to do the right things.

I didn't have any preconceptions when Glenn started. He'd been a talented player – maybe not the type I really loved, but you had to appreciate his skills. He used to show them off on the training pitch, too. I always got the impression Glenn was disappointed that we didn't have the flair and skill of European players. If you miscontrolled a ball, or a pass wasn't true, you could often hear a tut. There was one occasion when Becks was asked to go through a free-kick routine and didn't take it quite right. 'I'm not asking too much of you, am I?' Glenn said.

Still, we'd negotiated some testing and unglamorous trips to reach the 1998 World Cup finals. We'd endured a tour of Eastern Europe, with matches against Moldova, Poland and Georgia. The Moldova trip in the autumn of 1996 proved memorable for Becks, but not for anything on the pitch. At that time with England we shared rooms, me with Becks. We were lounging on our beds watching MTV when he first noticed Victoria.

The Spice Girls had come on the telly. 'Say You'll Be There' I think it was. Victoria was in that tight shiny catsuit and Becks just said, almost matter of fact, 'She's the one for me. I've got to go out with her.' And not long after he did. I think it took him about three weeks.

You could never fault Becks for his single-mindedness. If he wanted something, he'd go out and get it. He's always been that way, focused and determined, whether it's his football or, in this case, a girl he liked.

I would share a room with Becks but we were incompatible. I'd be in bed at ten, he'd be up until one a.m. I'd be up at six in the morning, he'd be up at eight.

It was when he started going out with Victoria that the publicity around Becks exploded, though it had been brewing for a while. There'd been the goal from the halfway line at Wimbledon, which showed his star quality. And just before that he'd signed with the agent Tony Stephens. Stephens only had a few big-hitting clients and he'd sorted some major commercial deals for Shearer and Platt. It was obvious that Becks would be appearing on adverts before long with his looks and his talent.

It just seemed logical: Becks was always going to be a star. That's very different to me, in the same way that he'd always wanted to play abroad, even as a kid, and it never really appealed to me. I never wanted to leave Bury.

Soon Becks was the face of adidas, though he could thank me for his first Predator boots. I was given a pair, one of the very first prototypes. All that technology to bend the ball was a bit wasted on me, so I handed them over to Becks, and I could never get them back. Becks would be out there every day practising his passing, his set-pieces, perfecting his spin on the ball. He was dedicated to his craft, and those boots gave him even more whip.

During World Cup qualification I was in and out of the team as Hoddle tried out different defensive line-ups. I could handle that, though I was disappointed to be left out of the final, crucial qualifier in October 1997, when we needed a draw in Rome to avoid the perils of the play-offs. The manager went with Gareth Southgate, telling me that he wanted more strength in the air.

We made it, thanks to the goalless draw in Rome which some write up as one of the great performances by England in the last couple of decades, which only goes to show how little we have to shout about. We were chuffed to have qualified but it wasn't as if we'd gone to Italy and played them off the park. We'd battled and defended well – Incey looked like he'd been through a war zone, ending up with a bandage round his head – but like the Greece qualifier a few years later when Becks got us off the hook with his free-kick, this wasn't a performance to get excited about if we were serious about being World Cup contenders.

I was never a massive shirt-swapper but there were a few players I held in awe, and Paolo Maldini was definitely one of them. Eric Harrison used to show us videos of the great Milan team he was a part of, the way the defence used to play high and catch opponents offside. I'd watch that Channel 4 show *Football Italia*, and I also loved Franco Baresi. He was the man. Everything about him was aggressive, on the front foot. He was a proper leader. He was hard, and nothing seemed to get past him.

That match in Rome was the first time I'd come across Maldini so I thought, 'Sod it, I'm going to get his shirt.' I went to the Italy changing room in the Olympic Stadium, humble and nervous. I knocked on the door not knowing what to expect, but Maldini couldn't have been more charming. He called me in to where he was sitting at the back of the changing room. With a few words of congratulations and good luck for the World Cup, he signed his shirt and gave it to me. A legend, and a nice bloke with it.

My experience up to that point had been that if you've lost a game, screw the opposition. But since then, whatever people say about me being obsessed with United and blind to anyone else's qualities, I don't believe I have been ungracious in defeat to opposing teams. Maldini showed me how to rise above disappointment.

I think of our defeat to Porto in the Champions League when a little-known bloke called José Mourinho knocked us out. I knew it was a huge night for Porto, a massive achievement, so I walked into their dressing room, congratulated the players and manager and shook them all by the hand. I think the boss did the same just afterwards.

Even against Liverpool I will shake hands when we've lost. I always try to keep my dignity however gutted I am. I wouldn't go searching for the opposition after every league game, but definitely after the decisive knock-outs. That's usually the case at United with the players and the manager. People might see the boss as someone who takes defeat badly but he knows how to congratulate the opposition.

If not among the favourites heading into the World Cup, we were regarded as dark horses – and rightly so. We had most of the players who had gone so close at Euro 96 plus Becks and Scholesy, who were now two of the biggest talents in England. And we had Michael Owen, the new whippet-thin, and whippet-fast, striking star at Liverpool. But still there were gripes between certain players and the manager as the World Cup drew near.

Teddy landed himself in a bit of tabloid bother just before the tournament. He nipped off to Portugal for a couple of days and someone took a snap of him with a fag in one hand and a bird on the other. These things never look clever but they are meaningless in the grand scheme of things; a good manager would have read the riot act in private and stuck by Teddy in public. That was always our manager's way at United: kill the story while dealing with the player. But Glenn made Teddy read out a public statement. It was like a full apology to the nation, and totally over the top.

I wasn't too thrilled with the manager myself when we played our last warm-up game against Belgium out in Casablanca. Admittedly we'd been very poor in the first half but it still came as a shock when he said, 'Gary and Phil, you're coming off.' The two of us were sat in the changing room without a word from any of the coaches. I'm not saying we deserved words of comfort, but a sentence of explanation would have helped. Communication was lacking.

We flew back to La Manga for final preparations. After some long, hard days, the manager allowed us a rare night out. We assumed we could let our hair down and go to the bar but we ended up locked in a private room by ourselves with a pianist playing old Sinatra songs. This was no one's idea of a relaxing evening.

As with any gang of lads, we wanted some fun, so as soon

as Glenn had left Gazza grabbed the microphone and belted out a couple of favourites. Martin Keown, who is more fun at a party than you might imagine, sang the worst 'Danny Boy' you've ever heard. We were starting to relax, have a laugh. Gazza brought me, Scholesy, Phil and Becks a pink cocktail in a martini glass with salt around the top. Coming from Bury, the only thing I put salt on is chips.

This was more like it; nothing harmless, just the lads letting their hair down. But it didn't last. At about ten p.m. Alan Shearer rang Glenn to see if we could go to the public bar and join the other drinkers in the hotel. 'No' was the firm answer. Soon after that the manager and the coaches came down and told Michael Owen and Rio Ferdinand, who'd been playing cards, to go straight to bed. An hour or so later, the rest of us were told it was time to go upstairs.

So much for party night, yet it was written up in the tabloids like we'd had a massive bender. The pianist sold his story of our 'wild night'. The FA had forgotten to get him to sign a confidentiality clause, which summed up the whole evening.

For most of us, La Manga was the place for final warm-weather preparations. For an unlucky handful it was where they would find out that they weren't going to France.

We knew the moment was coming; it loomed large at the end of the week, spreading anxiety among the squad. There's no easy way to tell a player they won't be going to a World Cup but Glenn appeared to have picked a particularly agonising method by making every player turn up for a five-minute appointment in his room. The meetings overran and at one stage there were half a dozen lads sitting outside, too nervous to speak. It was like waiting for the gallows.

Luckily for me, I was one of the first up. I went along feeling confident for myself and Phil. My brother wasn't first choice in the team, but John Gorman, Glenn's assistant, had given him the nod a few days earlier that he'd be in. There was little reason to doubt it.

'This is one of the easy ones,' Glenn said as I walked in. 'You've done well.' But as he explained how we were going to play at the tournament, with a back three and wing-backs, I became so worried for Phil I couldn't concentrate on anything the manager was saying. I could sense it was going to be bad news for my brother. I knew he'd be distraught.

When I left I saw Phil waiting outside, behind Ian Walker in the queue. I told him I was in, and then said I'd see him in a bit. I couldn't tell him my fears, but I probably didn't disguise them too well either.

Phil later said he could see it in my eyes, and I'm not surprised – I was stunned. I waited a bit and then walked down to Phil's room where the bad news was confirmed. Phil was sitting on his bed in tears. He was inconsolable.

As we hugged, I heard shouting down the corridor. I walked outside and one of the lads said that Gazza had been left out. He'd taken it badly, smashing a lamp in Glenn's room. I didn't blame him for blowing his top. The whole experience felt brutal.

That episode remains my worst moment in football, no question about it. I felt terrible, not just for Phil and Gazza but for Butty and Dion Dublin, who were also axed. There's no easy way to leave out a player, but this felt particularly distressing. They were given less than an hour to pack their bags and clear out.

I was so upset that I moved into Scholesy's room for the

night. I'd been sharing with Phil, and Scholesy had been with Butty so I moved down the corridor. We sat up till the early hours talking over the decisions and the way it had all been handled.

I'd have taken Gazza and Phil. Glenn had left Andy Hinchliffe behind too. But no Phil as well meant no cover for Le Saux. It was a strange move, one that would be exposed during the tournament. Rio Ferdinand had been picked but, for all his promise at nineteen, he was never a left wing-back. Rio wouldn't play at all in the tournament, and Glenn ended up bringing on Southgate for Le Saux against Argentina.

With Gazza, I always thought his talent was enough to change a game for us, even if it was just coming on as a sub. Glenn evidently thought he was going to be more trouble than he was worth and that he'd become a problem, particularly if he was left out of the team.

Everyone knew that Gazza was liable to have a few drinks, and he had indulged in La Manga. He'd led the party, or at least tried to until Glenn called time. But even though I'm completely the opposite in terms of character to Gazza, I would have tolerated his failings. I was never appalled by him. I'd witnessed players in the early days at United out on major drinking sessions and I wasn't going to judge them because I knew they'd still perform. And that's how I felt with Gazza. He could take the ball in any situation, even in the tightest of spaces. England had few players with that ability. It was a risk worth taking.

Butty was also on the plane home. Like Gazza and Phil he was given forty-five minutes to pack his bags and jump in the car taking them to the airport. Sitting in the hotel, I felt as upset for Phil as I'd ever done for myself. It wasn't just being left out, it was the way it had happened: the raised hopes, the colossal disappointment, the heavy-handed way of giving out the bad news.

I asked John Gorman the next day what had gone wrong. 'You told Phil he was in,' I said.

John, a totally straight and decent bloke, couldn't have looked more embarrassed. 'I know, Gary, and he was. I'm really sorry. Glenn changed his mind.'

I was gutted for Phil.

Then came another complication when Glenn told a press conference that he was leaving Becks out of the first game against Tunisia because he wasn't focused. Again, it was the way he did it, announcing it to the press and causing a storm. I think if Glenn had had five or six more years under his belt he could have been an excellent England manager, but he showed his inexperience.

Our manager was furious at the way Becks had been handled. But then he and Hoddle never got on great. One time when I'd had a knock on England duty I mentioned it to the boss who wanted me back at Old Trafford straight away. Hoddle wanted me to stay. Rather than be caught in the middle, I said they should speak. I was in the room when the conversation happened, and even standing five yards away from Hoddle I could hear the manager barking down the phone. 'That lad's coming home now!' Blood was draining from Hoddle's face. Eventually he came off the phone. 'Right, I'll let you go, but next time I'm not putting up with it. You'll have to tell him that.'

Somehow, I didn't think that was down to me.

Becks wasn't the only one who sat out the first game. Glenn

preferred a more defensive back three of Sol Campbell, Tony Adams and Southgate. But when we lost the second match to Romania, he didn't have much choice: he had to be more adventurous. I came in for Southgate, Becks replaced David Batty, and Michael Owen, who'd scored off the bench against Romania, replaced Teddy up front.

With this new line-up we beat Colombia 2–0 in our final group game, Becks nailing a free-kick. We'd progressed to the last sixteen but – and this set a pattern for much of my England career – we'd made life hard for ourselves by not finishing top of the group. Finishing second behind Romania set up a massive do-or-die confrontation with Argentina.

We knew it was going to be tough against a team featuring Batistuta, Simeone, Ortega and company, but I was confident. We had big players of our own; Shearer, Campbell and Ince were in their prime. It was all set up for a titanic clash.

Our first challenge was getting to the ground in St Etienne on time. Glenn never left anything to chance in terms of preparations but we were late because so many players were having injections. Glenn had been having our blood checked for months before the tournament for vitamin levels, iron levels, and so on. We'd taken a lot of pills every day – so many that it felt like a meal in itself. There were all sorts of different-coloured smarties. I know that creatine, the muscle-building protein, was included, along with antioxidants. When the tournament started, some of the players started taking injections given to us by Glenn's favourite medic, a Frenchman called Dr Rougier. It was different from anything we'd done at United, but all above board, I'm sure. After some of the lads reported that they'd felt a real burst of energy, I decided to seize any help on offer. So many of the players decided to go for it before that Argentina match that there was a queue to see the doctor.

Eventually we raced into the ground, and Glenn did his usual pre-match routine of moving around the players, shaking their hands and touching them just over the heart, a little pat on the chest.

As well as injections, Glenn believed in alternative methods, including Eileen Drewery, the faith healer, who'd visited the camp a few times before the World Cup. As a bit of a sceptic, I'd never gone to see her. If I had a bad leg, I wanted to see a doctor. I remember Scholesy having to brush off the manager when he tried to push him into seeing Eileen about a dodgy calf, but he never raised the issue with me. As long as it stayed that way I was happy to let Glenn believe in anything he liked.

We'll never know if the faith healing had any positive effect. But one of the masseurs told me after the Argentina game that Glenn had asked the staff, including the physios, to walk around the pitch anti-clockwise during the game to create positive energy for the team. Sadly it didn't do us much good on an epic evening.

We did well in the first, blisteringly quick forty-five minutes. We exchanged penalties through Batistuta and Shearer right from the off. Then Michael's sensational run from the halfway line put us ahead. In the maelstrom of a big match, you don't celebrate the brilliance of a goal. That's for later. I just felt a surge of belief that we could hurt Argentina if we kept running at them.

We might have done but for two horrible set-backs. First we were pegged back to 2–2 just before half-time. Fair play to Argentina, it was a brilliant free-kick routine, Javier Zanetti breaking off the end of the wall, and one that caught us completely cold. I don't know if they'd saved it for a special occasion but, for all our attention to detail, we'd been caught unawares.

We'd just lifted our chins from the floor when, two minutes into the second half, Becks was sent off after a tussle with Diego Simeone. 'Oh no, he's kicked out,' I thought. 'He's going to get sent off.'

There was no time to analyse it. You briefly go into shock, then you put the ball down, roll up your sleeves and get on with it. And we were magnificent as the game went into extra-time. I thought we'd won when Sol stuck in a header. So did several of the lads, who ran off to celebrate on one side of the pitch. But the referee had disallowed it for a push, and with half our team out of position I was on my own as Argentina's cavalry came charging back. It was four against two but somehow I got a tackle in and hacked the ball away.

We'd never formally practised penalties under Glenn, which some people felt was a mistake. All I'll say is that I've also been part of an England squad that did practise penalties every single day, at the 2006 World Cup, and still missed. Practice can help, but only so far.

Glenn came over to tell us who the five takers would be and asked me if I was happy to be the sixth. I nodded. 'Just concentrate, pick your spot and whack it or place it. Just don't change your mind.' It never came to that. When David Batty missed our fifth we were out and I never did get the chance to see if I could have kept my nerve.

Off we trooped to one of the quietest dressing rooms I have ever known, with Becks staring at the floor. I sat next to him on the coach as we drew out of the stadium. He had no idea about the brewing storm, and, to be honest, nor had I. We were just gutted to have been knocked out of the World Cup, and he was particularly upset because he'd been sent off, though I don't think anyone seriously thought it was a red card offence. He was daft to raise a foot but it was petty and hardly an act of violence. It simply didn't cross my mind that one player would be held up as a scapegoat, that he'd be vilified for months to come. But that just shows the mood in the country at the time. We didn't go for Simeone, who'd gone down like he'd been shot. We didn't criticise the bloke who'd play-acted and ended up getting Becks sent off. We didn't say, 'Get up and be a man.' Instead we hammered Becks for one silly mistake.

A few things conspired against him. There was all the anti-United stuff at the time, all those idiots singing 'Stand Up If You Hate Man U' even when we played for England. We'd all had it at Wembley since we'd started playing for our country. Our last game there before we left for the World Cup training camp, a friendly against Saudi Arabia, had been one of the worst occasions. Just to wear a United shirt was to be vilified.

Glenn had made things more difficult before the tournament when he said that David lacked focus, and this was now to become part of the vilification. With so much abuse coming from outside the squad Becks now needed people to rally round, but there wasn't a lot of support from anyone around the England hierarchy.

The trouble with England and the FA is that in times of trouble there is a rubber-dinghy management system: they chuck you overboard and look after their own. The attitude is 'as long it's not me, we're all right'. So Becks took all the flak. All the frustration that England had failed to win a tournament – again – was dumped on him, which was ridiculous.

We had a decent team in '98 and the biggest error had been a collective one – failing to finish top of our group and make life easier for ourselves. Whether we'd have had the class to beat Brazil, France or Holland, all very good teams at the time, is questionable. But why have that debate when you can dump it all on one player?

Becks would bounce back soon enough, showing immense resilience, just like I knew he would. He's incredibly stubborn and single-minded is Becks. The word 'courage' is maybe overused in sport, but he showed plenty of it in the way he answered his many critics. He has incredible focus when it comes to achieving his goals. He'd worked so hard to get where he was and he wasn't going to be deflected by abuse after the World Cup, however bad it got. He also knew he could depend on 100 per cent backing from the manager and everyone at United.

But Glenn was on the back foot, especially when we lost the first of the Euro 2000 qualifiers in Sweden, which I missed. I returned for the next game, the horrible 0–0 draw at home to Bulgaria.

People said at that time that Glenn had lost the players. I wouldn't agree with that, but it wasn't a happy squad. As I said, I think that if Glenn had had five or even ten years' more experience in club management and Champions League football, he could have been one of the best England managers. In hindsight, it all came too quick for him, and I think he'd agree with that.

Results were on the wane, but, in true FA style, his sacking came as the result of a newspaper interview that had nothing to do with football. It was typical FA: the football's not going great, the media are up in arms, throw the man overboard. If they'd wanted to make a change, they should have had the courage to do it on football grounds. Glenn's comments about religion were nice and convenient for them.

11

The Treble

Every player, coach and United fan will have their own high-light of the Treble season; there were enough unforgettable moments to share around. There were so many epic contests in that 1998/99 campaign, including the greatest game I ever played in – and I'm not talking about the Nou Camp where we clinched the European Cup so dramatically.

It was a ten-month period packed with spectacular foot-ball, but if I had to select one instant to take with me to the grave, it isn't anything that happened on the pitch. No, it's the memory of turning into Deansgate, on our triumphant bus ride after the Champions League final, and seeing a few hundred thousand people in the city centre. That was the moment when Manchester became my heaven.

I can still see the face of one United fan among the many thousands who lined the road. This guy was screaming so hard that the veins were popping out of his neck. This was joy that came from deep inside. The best moment of his life had arrived; all his dreams had come true. All our dreams had come true that season. Alongside him were others, blokes from Salford, Trafford, Middleton and Wythenshawe with tears streaming down their faces. I guess for the older ones, who remembered 1968, this was a return of the Holy Grail. For the younger fans it was sheer euphoria that we were kings of Europe at last. We'd been striving and failing for long enough. Now, finally, we'd reached the summit.

I had barely been to sleep. I was shattered at the end of a long season but the whole experience of moving slowly through the throng gave me the most amazing shivers down my back. People were hanging off lamp-posts, and out of office windows. This was euphoria. There was something special and shared about that bus ride. The glory was for anyone and everyone who loved United.

I wouldn't presume that holding those trophies mattered more to me, a home-grown lad and United fan, than to someone like Jesper Blomqvist or Ronny Johnsen. Winning the European Cup as part of a Treble is a wonderful achievement for anyone. But this was a day when I realised how blessed I was to have played for the club of my boyhood dreams. As a supporter, I'd sat and watched enough poor United sides down the years. Now, as a player, I'd been part of a team that had put us back on top. Now we could stand comparison with any United team in history.

And the greatest thing of all was that we deserved it. There'd been some unbelievably tense matches, some moments when it might have gone wrong, but this wasn't a streaky season. This was the culmination of all the hard work since we were kids, all the toil by the manager; the result of years of learning and improving and sometimes failing. We'd sweated hard for it.

It was even more special because if you'd asked anyone at the start of that campaign whether they expected history to be made, they'd probably have said yes – by Arsenal. They were champions of England. Real Madrid were champions of Europe. We'd not won a thing.

There were reasons to think we'd be more competitive. We'd bought Jaap Stam, that great hulk of a centre-half, from PSV Eindhoven. Roy was fit again after his bad knee injury. Dwight Yorke arrived from Aston Villa in September. They'd all prove to be world-class performers.

But not on the day we were stuffed by Arsenal in the curtain-raiser, the Charity Shield. We lost 3–0, and I was as bad as anyone. Overmars destroyed me. It was boiling hot and Petit just kept dropping the ball over my head on that big Wembley pitch. Even before half-time I was desperate for the final whistle. I looked over at Becks and said, 'I can't wait for this to fucking end.' I meant it. Jaap wasn't any better against Anelka. A lot of us were still unfit after the World Cup finals, but there were no lingering effects on Arsenal's players, and some of them had gone all the way to the final in Paris. We were terrible.

We started off the league season sluggishly too, with a couple of draws. I was so knackered that I ended up coming off at half-time against West Ham. The manager sent me off to Malta for a week and I lay there and did nothing. The campaign was only weeks old and already I needed a time-out.

We lost badly at Arsenal in September, another 3–0, with Nicky Butt sent off and the manager going crackers afterwards. There was no denying it: domestically, Arsenal were the team to beat.

It was in Europe that we were starting to show our true capabilities, even though we'd been drawn in a group of death that included Bayern Munich and Barcelona. Even against top opponents we were starting to show a cutting edge to complement what we'd always had at United, an attacking spirit.

Yorkie took to Old Trafford like he was born to play there, and with Coley, Teddy and Ole already on the books, we could score goals whoever was paired together up front. And we scored them by the dozen, including eleven in two matches against Brondby.

We went through scoring twenty goals in six games and without losing a match, knocking out a fantastic Barcelona team that boasted Cocu, Luis Enrique and the flair of Rivaldo, Luís Figo and Anderson. Our two 3–3 draws against Barcelona were fantastic games. At Old Trafford it was like the Blitz. In addition to Figo's class, Rivaldo was on top form, and I don't know how we kept it down to three.

Figo was a great player. I was established, I'd been to a World Cup, I'd won championships and I thought I could cope with pretty much anything thrown at me – and then he came along. He took me down the line on his left foot and when I went to block he pulled it back and left me on my arse. It was effortless and graceful, even though he wasn't a small guy.

The next time he ran at me I thought, 'I'm not going to buy it this time. I'll stop him turning back on to his best foot.' But he just ran past me and whipped in a perfect cross with his left. So he could go both ways, cross with both feet, and he was quick, strong and perfectly balanced. Ginola and Del Piero were similarly two-footed but, of that bunch, Figo was the pick.

Six group matches, twenty goals scored, eleven conceded. Whatever happened that season, we weren't going to be boring. We were letting in plenty in the league as well – fourteen conceded in a run of seven games at one point. We lost 3–2 at home to Middlesbrough a week before Christmas – 3–0 down at half-time at Old Trafford – when the manager was away at a funeral. Eric Harrison had been drafted in for the day as assistant manager. Aside from the boss, Eric could make the most brutal comments of any coach I've come across. At half-time he turned to the defence and said, 'We've had to stick three in midfield because, by fuck, don't you lot need protecting.' It felt like we were back in the youth team being bawled out, but it had the desired effect. We wouldn't lose another game between then and the final day of the season.

Plenty of times we cut it desperately fine. Facing Liverpool in the FA Cup fourth round, we were 1–0 down at Old Trafford in the eighty-eighth minute. We were on our way out. We'd hit the post, we'd hit everything except the back of the net. Then Dwight got one back for us, and seventy-three seconds into injury-time Ole Gunnar bagged the winner. Two goals in the dying minutes to rescue a match that seemed dead – and not for the last time.

Being a cup tie, there were about eight thousand Liverpool fans at Old Trafford who'd been singing songs about me all afternoon so I ran over to their fans to celebrate – it wouldn't be the last time that happened either.

The FA Cup was the least of the three trophies in terms of

prestige but it gave us momentum. After beating Liverpool, in March we drew at home to Chelsea in the quarter-final and beat them 2–0 away in the replay. These games, particularly coming sandwiched between huge European ties, helped boost that sense of invincibility.

It was all coming together, and that spring we began to sense that we were creating a rare opportunity to pull off something special. Little things were clicking into place. Momentum continued to build.

Behind the scenes, Kiddo had left for Blackburn Rovers, which could have been disruptive given that he was an excellent coach and had such a strong bond with those of us brought through the youth ranks. For a while the manager was forced to take a more active role in training. We never ran so many laps mid-season.

In early February, as we prepared to face Nottingham Forest in the Premiership, this bloke walked into the hotel restaurant the night before the game. Like everyone else, I thought, 'Who's that?' I'd never seen him before, never heard of him. It was Steve McClaren, and the next day he led the warm-up on the pitch.

By the end of the afternoon we'd won 8–1, with Ole scoring four times in twelve minutes.

I'm sure Steve wouldn't claim credit for that, but he fitted in seamlessly. He was lucky to take charge of a squad blessed with great players and great hunger, but there's no doubting his coaching skills. He put on great sessions, some of the best I've been involved in – sharp, intense, full of purpose, but also fun. Tactical plans were important, but he also knew how to lighten the mood as we moved from one massive game to the next. We used to play the Rest of the World against Britain on a tight pitch. They were fantastic, fiercely competitive matches. The spirit and intensity around the club was unbelievable.

Peter didn't get on great with Roy, Roy and Teddy were hardly best pals, and Andy Cole and Teddy didn't speak because of some old feud. But they were men and it never came between them on the pitch. If anything, it created a positive edge in training. The five or six of us who had come through the youth ranks probably knitted it all together. I'm sure a successful team can be built without a gang of close mates – there are enough examples – but it was a massive factor for us. We weren't a clique but a focal point for the dressing room. There was just a great sense of camaraderie.

In his first season, Yorkie was a big influence in terms of morale. He was new and had this carefree attitude which was at odds with how we'd been educated, but it made for a good mix. We knew he'd go out and have a drink. He'd be out until three a.m. Yorkie wasn't exactly the most invisible bloke in the world, wearing his baseball cap back to front, balancing cocktails on his head and leaping behind the bar to help the waiters. With his network of contacts, the manager would hear things. 'I know where you were last night,' he'd say. But in that first season even the manager turned a blind eye to it as long as Dwight delivered.

The partnership of Coley and Yorkie was a joy. Coley was always quiet, which some people misinterpreted as arrogance or moodiness, but once you got to know him he was great in the dressing room. And now he was loving his football, Yorkie helping to bring the best out of him. At the same time, every time Teddy or Ole were involved, they seemed to have a match-winning impact.

With Yorkie taking to United as fast as any player has

done, Jaap like the Great Wall of China, Keano at his peak and half a dozen young lads who were maturing together, we had a really strong, balanced eleven. At last we had a spine to compete with the best teams in Europe, with Giggsy and Becks as effective and hard-working as any wingers in the world. And we had a sense of adventure, a confidence to go on the front foot that surprised even the best opposition.

Perhaps we could be too gung-ho. It wasn't the most sophisticated type of football. None of us would pretend we reinvented the game or outwitted opponents tactically. Mostly it was 4–4–2 (or 4–4–1–1) but played at an incredibly high tempo with real quality.

But we were learning to control games better, and there were a couple of tactical tweaks. Faced with Inter Milan in the Champions League quarter-finals, we knew that Roberto Baggio would float into a tricky position as a deep-lying forward just off-centre. Del Piero used to do it brilliantly and Giggsy learnt to do it too, floating in what seems like no-man's land. It gives the defending team a difficult choice. Does the centre-half come out, does the full-back move inside, or do you deploy a midfield marker? Fail to deal with it properly and as soon as you lose the ball a player of Baggio's class will cut you in half.

Every time we had the ball and went forward, I moved into midfield to pick up Baggio rather than stay back as a natural right-back. It would detract from my attacking play. There would be very few overlaps from me past Becks. But Baggio didn't get a kick in the game, and Denis Irwin did the same to Youri Djorkaeff on the other side. We won 2–0, blitzing them in the first half, hitting them with crosses they couldn't handle. We were hanging on a bit at the end. Schmeichel made an unbelievable save from a Zamorano header – a world-class player making a difference. But we'd proved we could cope against a top-class Italian team, and we'd be smarter than them in the second leg, too.

In the San Siro we were pelted with oranges as soon as we went on the pitch for a warm-up. I'd not heard noise like it since Galatasaray. The manager must have wondered if we'd stand up to that sort of pressure but he'd already taken pre-cautions. He picked Ronny Johnsen in central midfield instead of Scholesy, and it proved an inspired choice. Ronny was everywhere, taking the sting out of the game.

The boss had told me and Denis that we'd have to be brave, we'd have to show for the ball, because otherwise we'd be under too much pressure. 'Take the ball, take the ball,' he kept saying in the dressing room. He was giving us the confidence to play in a testing environment. And it worked.

Nicola Ventola came on for a half-fit Ronaldo and scored but, despite being under the cosh, we came through, helped by Scholesy's late equaliser. I looped a ball into the box – I wouldn't flatter myself by calling it a cross – Scholesy did the rest, and we were through.

Tactically we were becoming so much more aware as a team, and as an individual I was feeling right at the top of my game. That match at Inter was a night when I felt total con-fidence in my ability. It was like a utopia moment when you can do nothing wrong. You feel completely in control. Your dummies come off and every pass seems to fly to feet. I felt great, and why not? We were top of the league and through to the semi-finals of both the FA Cup and the Champions League.

*

We relished the looming challenges, so much so that Jim Ryan, who had now become first-team coach alongside Steve McClaren, started a countdown – as if he was counting down the steps to greatness. 'Twelve to go, boys,' he'd say when we came in after another victory. And then we would knock another one off and it would be eleven to go, then ten. Ten games in which to make history, though the mighty Juventus stood in our way.

We'd lost to them three times out of four in the last couple of seasons. We had ghosts to banish. Since the men-against-boys beatings of 1996 we'd felt like we were closing the gap; it had reached the point of now or never. Juventus were still a great team with Montero and Pessotto, Conte, Deschamps, Davids and Zidane, but we'd won trophies, we'd grown as players. They were good, but we weren't frightened.

At home, we lived on the edge once more. At 1–0 down we were clinging on a bit in the first half. But we battled and deserved to get our goal. Giggsy scored with seconds to go, a huge strike in terms of the balance of the tie and for keeping our unbeaten run going. That now stretched to more than three months and twenty-one matches.

It was a fortnight until the return in the Stadio delle Alpi and we had the small matter of an FA Cup semi-final against Arsenal. When that finished goalless, we knew our mental and physical reserves were going to be tested to the limit. Now the depth of squad was to prove invaluable because we started the replay at Villa Park with Teddy, Ole and Jesper Blomqvist which allowed Coley, Yorkie and Giggsy to spend some of the evening on the bench.

This wasn't the first or last time that the boss would leave out big players in a big game, showing the courage that makes him such a great manager. The truth is that he pioneered the squad system in England. He had the foresight to start using the Carling Cup to blood younger players. He took a lot of stick for it at the time, but now every club does it – for all the right reasons. People have looked at teamsheets and said he's mad for leaving out certain players, but the boss recognised that the demands on players had changed. He adapted. And he's been brave.

What a game that replay was – quite simply the best I ever played in. Two great teams giving their all, battering each other to a standstill. Of course reaching the FA Cup final mattered, but this went deeper than that: after losing to Arsenal in too many games we had to show to the world and to ourselves that we were the better team.

I feel knackered just thinking about it. Becks scores, then Bergkamp equalises with a deflected shot. With seventy-odd minutes gone, Roy gets sent off. Then a penalty to Arsenal in the last minute and the chance for Bergkamp to finish us off, to knock us out of the cup, to end our run and our Treble dreams, to give Arsenal momentum for the rest of the league season. But Schmeichel saves it brilliantly.

On we go to extra-time. Patrick Vieira hits the pass of a tired man across midfield. Giggsy, fresher than most having started as a substitute, goes on a mazy run before arrowing a shot into the roof of the net. He went through one of the best defences in the history of the English game and smashed it past England's number one – the FA Cup's greatest ever moment, surely. It was also the night when the world found out that Giggsy had an Axminster rug on his chest.

It was an incredible match, the most dramatic of my

career. The pitch invasion afterwards was like a scene from football in the sixties. We were swamped by fans, most of them reeking of booze. 'Christ, lads, what have you lot been on?' I'd never had so many kisses, sadly all of them from pissed lads.

After wriggling out of the clutches of our fans, I made it down the tunnel to find Lee Dixon and Tony Adams waiting by our dressing-room door. They'd been standing there for ten minutes just so they could say, 'Well played, all the best.' It was a big, generous gesture, reminding me of Maldini. That's how to lose with dignity.

Inside the dressing room there was champagne everywhere, except down our throats. It was being sprayed around, but with games coming thick and fast we only had a swig each. Luckily I was experienced enough to know that you put a towel over your suit if you don't want to sit on the bus home smelling of stale booze.

We had some special games at Villa Park in that era and I loved the ground, my favourite one away from Old Trafford. It's got history and tradition, and you drive up to that great big brick stand – a proper English football stadium. It holds a special place in my memories.

They were a great team, Arsenal, but our momentum was now unstoppable. Every time we should have lost a game, someone – Schmeichel, Becks, Giggs, Keano, Yorkie – made a match-winning intervention. The manager summed it up after that victory at Villa Park: 'We never gave up. The time to give up is when you are dead.'

We'd need to prove our resilience again a week later at Juventus for another make-or-break match against a top-class team. Every game was now like this, even in the league.

Arsenal were giving us a run for our money, as you'd expect from a team led by Tony Adams with all their big-hearted competitors. We couldn't afford to relax for a minute.

Our confidence was sky-high, which was just as well as we found ourselves 2–0 down in the first ten minutes in Turin. Had we climbed within touching distance of the summit only to slip all the way down again?

I was responsible for the first goal. Zidane whipped a cross in and I was convinced it would never reach me at the far post. Then it did. Filippo Inzaghi nipped ahead and scored as I tried to rugby-tackle him.

Then Inzaghi got down the side of Jaap, shot, and the ball bounced up off Jaap's foot and looped over Peter. Two goals down to Juventus in Italy – ninety-nine times out of a hundred that's game over. But a few minutes later we created a chance and suddenly they looked a bit shaky. Becks turned to me, clenched his fist and said, 'We can do this, you know.'

When we did score a couple of minutes later, Roy heading in Becks' corner, the old spirit stirred. Look back at the tape and see how Roy scores and then turns and sprints back to the halfway line. Forget the celebrations. He's waving everyone back to the restart. We've got plenty of time on our side, an hour to play. Come on! We can win this!

We were level by half-time thanks to Yorkie's diving header – a fantastic comeback, though still not enough to satisfy the manager who had an almighty dig at the defence at half-time. 'We're playing great football but you lot had better sort yourselves out.' He was as hyped up as the rest of us.

Juventus had their chances in the second half, but when Coley stuck in the winner I sprinted down the flank to join the celebrations. To have played the greatest game ever the week before and then come back like this was unbelievable. To have overcome such great opponents as Arsenal and then Juventus with all their experience, their world champions like Zidane and Deschamps, and their streetwise Italians, not to mention the scary pitbull, Edgar Davids.

One of my favourite photographs is from the end of that game – me and Becks holding our shirts out to show the United badge, screaming our heads off. We had reached the European Cup final after all those agonising near misses. That was a mindblowing thought – even without the FA Cup final and the six games to tie up the championship.

There was one significant downer: the bookings for Keano and Scholesy, which meant they would be absent from the final in the Nou Camp. The way it was reported, Roy had been even more heroic following his booking – in contrast to Gazza crying at the 1990 World Cup in the same stadium – but I didn't see it that way. He'd done his job, outstandingly. Emotion hadn't come into it.

It was bound to put a dampener on celebrations. These were two of our best players. It was a massive disappointment for them personally and for us as a team. I told them I was gutted for them, but what more could you say? You learn pretty quickly playing professional sport that stuff happens – injuries, bad breaks, suspensions. You have to get on with it.

Missing our central midfield was going to be a massive problem for the manager to get his head round, but before then we were still on our Premiership countdown with six games left to clinch the league. Just to test us further, the championship race was proving a nail-biter.

We drew 1–1 at Leeds United at the end of April – not a bad result in the light of all the tough matches we'd been through, but not enough to keep us on top. Arsenal were ahead. It was a sprint to the finish. Into the final week we went and it was advantage United when Arsenal lost at Leeds on the Tuesday night – Nelson Vivas made a bad mistake to let in Jimmy-Floyd Hasselbaink. Watching at home on the telly, I was thrilled. 'Win at Blackburn tomorrow and we're there,' I thought.

But at Ewood Park we drew 0–0. More drama. Now we had to beat Tottenham at home in our final game to be sure of being champions. All this graft, all these massive games, and we still hadn't got our hands on a trophy.

When Les Ferdinand scored to put Spurs 1–0 up, Old Trafford filled with nerves, and that transmitted to us. We might have been on the brink of a Treble but we could still lose the lot. We were anxious and in need of inspiration when Becks produced an unbelievable goal, whipping the ball into the top corner. Anyone who needs reminding of what a great footballer he was at United should replay that goal – a top-class piece of skill produced under massive pressure when doubts were creeping in.

We still needed another goal, and the manager brought on Coley at half-time in search of it. Five minutes into the half I pulled the ball back on my left foot and floated a pass over Sol Campbell's head. Coley brought it down and dinked it over the goalkeeper. We were 2–1 up and on course to be champions, although only after another nervous forty minutes. I kept looking over at Graham Poll screaming, 'Blow the fucking whistle!' I've never known time drag so slowly.

The manager had always said that to win the league at Old Trafford on the last day cannot be bettered. And the celebrations were huge. Relief that we'd not blown it was mixed with total joy that we'd won back our title from Arsenal. We had our hands on the first of the three trophies.

The FA Cup final six days after that Spurs match was the easiest game of the entire run-in, and just as well. I was knackered. Becks and I had played the most games, and I was heading into my fifty-third for United plus my games for England. The manager kept asking us if we needed a rest but he probably knew the answer, even though I was struggling with my groin.

Fortunately, everything fell into place at Wembley against Newcastle United. Even when Roy had to go off very early with an ankle injury, his replacement, Teddy, scored almost as soon as he had arrived.

I had such a good feeling that day, like I could do no wrong. Alan Shearer bore down on me at one point and I turned inside to throw him a dummy. He bought it, and the fans gave a big 'Olé!' That wasn't a familiar sound to a Neville. I was in a place where everything seemed so simple and natural. I guess it was what golfers call 'the zone', where they're not thinking about their swing, just letting it flow. If only it could have lasted a lifetime.

After securing the title we'd celebrated with a big night in Manchester, at the Marriott hotel, into the early hours with all our families. The evening after the FA Cup final we didn't drink – except for Keano and Scholesy, who probably had a skinful. We had the European Cup final to think about, and we flew out to Barcelona the next day on Concorde. Supersonic wasn't exactly necessary for the short hop to Spain but we didn't get to play a game of this stature every week.

We were laden with bags and it seemed like we were in Barcelona for ages. We had time to sit, chat and think about what we were involved in. On the Monday night, on the balcony of our hotel, me, Phil, Butty, Becks, Giggsy and Scholesy talked about the chances of being in this position again – not just in a European Cup final, the first one for an English team since 1985, but in the Nou Camp, and going for a Treble.

The atmosphere over the next couple of days was one of nervous excitement. I had known the mood before big England matches to be horribly tense – that feeling that the world will end if you lose. In Barcelona the stakes could not have been higher but the mood was focused. We didn't want to lose, we loathed the very idea, but we weren't afraid of the consequences.

The manager must have had concerns, though. He'd lost Roy, our most influential player, and our playmaker Paul Scholes, though the replacements probably picked themselves. Nicky would come into the middle and Becks was needed there too. That just left the wingers to decide on, but it was obvious it would be Ryan on one side and Blomqvist on the other. The only other option was to play Ole Gunnar wide right, but he hadn't been used there all season.

It is fair to say that the team shape didn't work great, but I don't think the manager could have done much different. It was just a tired performance by us against Bayern. My groin had been deteriorating and now it started playing up. As a team we had been sprinting so hard for so long. We were trying to summon one last performance without two of our main men.

In the Nou Camp, I looked up at all the United fans with

twenty minutes to go, and the scoreboard showing 0–1, and thought, 'We can't go home without giving them something to shout about'. Our supporters weren't even singing. Bayern were cruising. They'd hit the post, the crossbar. It looked like it was game over.

The manager had made a speech at half-time about walking past the cup if we lost and not being able to touch it. They were inspiring words which many remember as game-changing, but, if I am being honest, they hadn't produced much of an instant lift. That only came when the boss made his substitutions.

We needed a spark, and it came when Teddy replaced Jesper, allowing Giggsy to move back to his best position on the left and Becks to the right. Yorkie dropped into the hole, and suddenly we started flowing like a team. We shifted up a gear.

We could never have started with that line-up; it would have been brave going on suicidal. A final twenty minutes of desperation was another matter. Suddenly we started overlapping for the first time. Bayern were under pressure. On came Ole for Coley, so more fresh legs to get at them.

You know the rest, though I'll happily relive it any day of the week. The clock was ticking past ninety minutes. I know because at that very moment I glanced over and saw the fourth official hold up the board to signal three minutes remaining. And that's when we won a throw-in at the far left corner of the Nou Camp.

I was absolutely knackered. We'd all been tested, physically and emotionally, to the limit. But from somewhere I found the energy to sprint from right-back to the left-wing position to take the throw-in.

I've wondered a few times since, 'Why did I do that? What was I doing running all that way?' And it's simple, really: it's what I'd been taught to do since I was a kid at United. You keep playing, you keep trying, you keep sprinting until the death.

Out on the left flank I took the throw, and I was still stuck out there when the ball came back out of the box. In my one and only cameo as a left-winger, I went down the line and crossed, hitting a defender and forcing a corner. And that was my contribution to football's most famous comeback. From that corner, with big Peter using his size to cause mayhem in the box, the ball was half-cleared to Giggsy. He miscued his shot and Teddy was there to sweep it in.

Pandemonium for a few seconds. We're back in the game. Now we have to win it.

Forward we go again, and Ole wins another corner. By now we're fresher than the first day of the season and Becks runs over to whip it in. Teddy flicks and Ole stretches out a boot. I collapse to the floor.

The rest of the players rushed over to smother Ole, who was sliding on his knees towards the fans, but I didn't go. I literally couldn't run that far. I was back on the halfway line, lying there on the ground thinking, 'Oh my God, we've done it!' There was just complete and utter disbelief that we'd won the game – and the way we'd pulled it off.

I was thrilled for myself, thrilled for my club, and thrilled for everyone associated with United. And I was really thrilled for Ole. You couldn't have picked a nicer bloke to score the winning goal in the European Cup final than him. I sat next to him for eleven years in the dressing room, him on one side, Scholesy on the other, and he's one of the most genuine guys you could ever meet. Everything he did was for the team, which isn't true of all goalscorers – and Ole Gunnar was one of the very best. He was so unselfish and he deserved his moment of glory.

I'm honestly not sure how much of the celebrations I actually remember or whether they're in my mind as a result of watching the highlights again and again. I can see Samuel Kuffour, the Bayern defender, running around like he'd just got home and found his house ransacked. I can see David May clambering above the rest of the players on the podium. I can see the whole squad lining up on the pitch singing 'Sit Down' by James. We made a tunnel for Roy and Scholesy to come running down with the trophy, eager for every single member of the team and the staff to feel part of this unbelievable victory.

I definitely remember not sleeping, walking round Barcelona as the sun lit up the city. Who would want a night like that to end? I was still ambling along the streets at six in the morning with some mates, not wanting to go to bed, never wanting the day to finish or the high to fade away. No English team (or Spanish or Italian up to that point) had ever pulled off the Treble, and it had been such an incredible journey, full of narrow escapes and epic victories, that I couldn't see how any team could repeat it. This was surely a unique feat, not just in terms of trophies but in the twists and turns, the sporting drama that created almost unbearable tension right up to the very last few kicks.

That season was all about never giving in, about coming back from the dead. People talk about the quality of our attacking play, and I think we scored a hundred-odd goals, but it was the fighting spirit that won us that Treble. It wouldn't have been half the story if we'd thrashed Bayern 3–0.

There are so many memories to cherish: Giggsy scoring his wonder goal against Arsenal; Keano's heroics in Turin, hauling us back from defeat; the European Cup final itself, which is enshrined as one of the game's greatest ever comebacks. Were we deserving champions? We weren't at our best in Barcelona, but I've never wasted a second worrying about our performance in the first eighty-nine minutes.

We didn't win the Treble because it was a substandard season – quite the opposite: the opposition was so tough we knew we had to raise our game. In the FA Cup we'd had to beat Liverpool, Chelsea, Arsenal and Newcastle, not Coventry City or Plymouth. In the Champions League we'd had to face down Barcelona and Bayern Munich, and that was just in the group phase; then along came Inter Milan with Ronaldo and Juventus with Zidane. In the league we'd been chased right to the last day of the season by the Arsenal side of Adams, Keown, Petit, Vieira and Bergkamp, as good a domestic rival as I'd meet in my career.

As for the way we won in Barcelona, I'm not sure I would have it any other way. It was perfect. It captured the very best of Manchester United. We never knew when we were beaten.

12

The Hangover

There's no denying that United failed to build on the Treble, at least where the Champions League was concerned. What a mistake that was – one of the biggest in my time at the club. I can see why it didn't feel essential to go out and buy more players. We were champions of England and Europe. But we had the chance to build a dynasty, and we squandered it.

We were linked with a few big names, like Gabriel Batistuta and Ronaldinho, but none came, not for a couple of seasons. It's a great strength of the club that it has rarely bought players at the top of the market where there's little value for money. But any squad needs competition to keep the players fresh. Roy went public and said some slacked after the Treble. He was probably right. There would have been less chance of it happening if we'd had an injection of fresh blood, a couple of big names to keep us ahead of the competition. It would be another nine years before we were back in the final of the Champions League.

The record books show how hard it is to juggle the twin demands of chasing domestic titles and European success. Not a single team has successfully defended the European Cup in my time. Clubs weren't winning two or three in a row like they'd done in the past. But that doesn't mean we couldn't have done more to defend the European title we'd worked so hard to win.

Our goalkeeping fumbles were the most obvious sign of slipping standards. We had an inconsistent few years after Peter Schmeichel departed, who timed it perfectly by bowing out at the Nou Camp. The problems between the posts lasted fully six years, until Edwin van der Sar signed in 2005.

Mark Bosnich was the first to try to fill Peter's boots, and although I got on fine with Bozzy, he rubbed others up the wrong way. He was just a bit too laid back for the United regime. On the first morning it was obvious he was carrying a few pounds. The manager was straight on to him.

'Bozzy, what are we going to do about your weight?'

'Boss, I'm just the weight that I like to be.'

'Well you're not the weight I'd like you to be. Lose some.'

I'm not saying Bozzy didn't work hard, but he trained in his own way, doing his own exercises rather than running and stretching with the rest of us. He was his own man, and you have to be one heck of a player at United to get away with being so individual.

We were flying high in the table but we really missed Peter – any team would, because he was an automatic selection for a World XI at the time. There was no one comparable, and we didn't just miss his technical ability but the confidence he spread through the rest of the team.

At a top club like United you need a goalkeeper who doesn't have insecurities. By that I mean a keeper who can stand around for half an hour and not feel like he has to prove himself. There is nothing more dangerous than a goalkeeper anxious to get involved. It makes him rash, reckless. Edwin was happy if he never touched the ball for ninety minutes. That's a rare quality.

Bozzy had his problems with distribution and concentration. Then came Fabien Barthez, who definitely had that desire to get noticed. Massimo Taibi, Ricardo – they all wanted to do something, to show they were good enough to be number one at United. Any team wanting to win the big prize needs a top-class goalkeeper.

In the outfield positions, Mikael Silvestre and Quinton Fortune were the only arrivals in 1999. In the short-term this wasn't a problem because domestically we were winning easily. Too easily. Opponents were rolling over. They didn't know how to mentally cope with the fact that we were on the attack all the time. We stuck five past Newcastle United, five past Everton, seven against West Ham United. Which was all great fun, especially for the forwards, but we weren't being challenged.

Edge is a massive thing in top-level sport, something you can't just turn on and off. It comes from having to stretch yourself. In the Treble season we'd had something to prove every game. We were on a lung-bursting run to the finish line. Every match was the biggest test of our lives. Then the next one felt bigger still. But we won the league so easily in 1999/2000, and again in 2000/01, and when you are that far ahead it's hard not to become a little complacent.

If it is possible to be bored as you win the league, then we were bored in those two seasons after the Treble. In 1999/2000 we finished eighteen points ahead of Arsenal – a ridiculous gap that said more about how far they'd fallen than our excellence. It was the poorest league I ever played in, and my own form suffered. I was still first choice for club and country but I was having my own personal nightmares.

Bizarrely, that season after the Treble was the most unsettling of my whole career. It was the first time I lost my form for a sustained period. And it culminated in Euro 2000, which was the most miserable of tournament experiences for me, my brother and the whole family.

I missed the first few months of the season with a groin problem. All those matches in the Treble season had taken their toll. I'd had an injection soon after the European Cup final and I'd tried to let it settle down, but my groin was still not right when I came back. I was late getting into the season, and though I was initially glad to be back and seemed in good form, it all changed with a trip to Brazil.

It was the season of the World Club Championship, and it was an ill-fated trip from the start. The tournament clashed with the FA Cup third round in January, and it still annoys me that United get accused of undermining the old trophy by flying off to South America. The truth is that the manager sat the whole squad down and asked us if we wanted to put a team in the Cup, even if it was the reserves. We all said, 'Yes, let's give it a go.' The decision was taken out of the club's hands by the FA because they were bidding for the 2006 World Cup and didn't want to upset Fifa. They said concentrate on the tournament in Brazil. It came down to politics, so don't blame United.

Off we went to the sunshine of Rio. It was the first World Club Championship and we didn't really know what to expect, although that's no excuse for how poor we were. We drew the first game against the Mexican side Necaxa, when Becks was sent off. Then things got really bad. In the second game we lost 3–1 to Vasco da Gama in what was probably my worst performance of my whole United career.

I made a terrible backpass for the first goal, a real horror, laying it straight to Edmundo who squared to Romario to score. Great Brazilian strikers weren't going to pass up that sort of gift. Not long after that I gave them another one, chesting the ball straight into the path of Romario, one of the game's greatest finishers, arguably the best I played against. Two goals, both defensive horrors, and both down to me.

I was all over the place, and just to improve my mood I came off the pitch to find a text message from Scholesy who was back in England recovering from injury. He'd been watching on the telly. His message: 'Fiasco da Gama'.

The rest of the lads managed to shrug off our early exit and enjoy the sunshine in Rio. We had a few days of hanging around, literally in the case of Butty and Keano, who decided to go for a hang-glider ride off Sugarloaf Mountain. We couldn't believe it when we heard these shouts from up in the sky and saw two maniacs floating past. The manager was sitting by the pool, half asleep in the hot sun.

'That had better not be any of my players,' he muttered.

I managed to raise a laugh, but that was about all I had to smile about. I'd never been the greatest player in the world but I'd always taken the ball knowing I could pass it simple, move and keep the game flowing. But now, for the first time in my life, I was thinking, 'What do I do with it?' In some games I just wanted the whistle to blow, for it to be all over. In the past there'd been the odd match like that, but never for weeks and months on end.

I was very conscious of my own anxiety. I would be stood on the pitch thinking, 'This is what it's like to be nervous, this is what it's like to be affected by a mistake.' And I didn't have a strategy to cope with that. I'd never experienced a period when I couldn't trust myself to pass the ball even over short distances.

Steve McClaren knew Bill Beswick, a sports psychologist who'd been invited to speak to the United players as a group and as individuals. I decided to go and see Bill on my own – the only occasion when I turned to a psychologist for help.

Bill was a good man, and if there was one piece of advice I took to heart, and have repeated since to other players, it's that if you have a long career in sport, you have to accept there will be a downturn like this. You have to try to be ready for it, not shocked by it. But while I knew Bill was talking sense, it was going to take time for me to get out of the rut. I'd feel better walking out of his room, but then I'd go on to the pitch and still feel like I was low on confidence and under-performing.

I really wasn't enjoying my football but I was getting away with it because, as a team, we were dominating the English game to such a ridiculous extent. We'd gone to Brazil a few points off the top of the table and it was pretty much the same when we came back.

We were the best team in England by a mile, with a psychological grip on every opponent, but that meant European defeats came as a nasty shock. We were in the middle of a free-scoring run of eleven consecutive league wins, clocking up thirty-seven goals, when we had to face Real Madrid in the Champions League quarter-finals.

Somehow I managed to produce a half-decent game in a goalless first leg in the Bernabéu. In fact the manager went out of his way to say I was the one player who had performed. Was I coming out of my slump? If only.

In the return at Old Trafford the nightmares returned. A long ball was played across that a pub player could have intercepted, but it sailed over my head to Roberto Carlos who raced away on yet another attack. What was happening to me? I couldn't even time a jump right.

The atmosphere had been electric at kick-off, but Madrid battered us, 3–0 up inside an hour – an own goal from Keano then two from Raúl. Henning Berg got mugged by a fantastic Redondo backheel over near the touchline. It was a brilliant piece of skill, but that was my area to cover. If I'd been on form, I'd have been back behind him.

We struck back through Scholesy and Becks but our European crown had been ripped away and it wasn't much consolation that Madrid were a classy side who would go on to win the trophy. We'd been found wanting. We'd needed an injection of world-class talent to improve the team and to make sure no one could sit on their laurels, and we paid for the lack of high-profile signings.

Three days after Real took us apart, we went to Southampton, won 3–1 and clinched the title with four games to spare, but I can't say I enjoyed the experience. There's a photo at the Carrington training ground of everyone celebrating. I'm there jumping up and down but I was putting it on, pretending to be ecstatic. The truth was that I felt hollow. Three trophies in 1999 had become one a year later. And my contribution was way below what it should have been. I could only put it down to some sort of hangover from the Treble season.

As well as my own struggles, Becks had issues with the manager. The Spice Girls were huge news so his fame had reached a new stratosphere.

Becks and Victoria had been married near Dublin in 1999 and I was thrilled, and terrified, to be his best man. I honestly don't think I've ever been more nervous. I'd never really done a public speech before, and though this was only in front of the wedding guests, I knew every word of it would get out in the press. Mess it up and I'd be a laughing stock all over the front pages.

I wrote the speech myself, though I got the wedding

organiser, Peregrine, to have a read through the night before. I was quite pleased with my gags but he seemed to think the one about George Michael in a toilet was a bit near the knuckle. That one came out, probably for the best. He left the one in about the Spice Girls hoping the entire Bayern Munich squad would turn up. Which girl wouldn't like men who could stay on top for ninety minutes and still come second? Well, it was funny back then.

Becks likes to tell the story that he found me on the morning of the wedding standing anxiously in front of a full-length mirror with a can of deodorant in my hand, pretending it was a microphone. And I can't deny it.

The wedding ceremony itself, with around thirty family and close friends, was a lovely occasion in a little folly. It was a very emotional event, with plenty of tears. Then we gathered for the main dinner and my big moment. I'd had a stroke of inspiration and borrowed a sarong from Victoria. David had been in the papers for wearing one so I slipped it on just before I had to go up. So that was one laugh guaranteed.

Becks' closest mates have always been guys he's known from way back – me, Dave Gardner, and Terry Byrne, one of the masseurs from the England camp who'd go on to be his personal manager. They were all there at the wedding, but there were obviously pop stars too, through Victoria. The occasion inevitably attracted massive publicity.

Then, in February 2000, Becks rang the club one morning to say he was going to be late for training. He said he'd had to look after Brooklyn, who was unwell; but Victoria had been pictured out that night at a party, and the manager assumed that Becks had been at his house down south. When Becks finally turned up and came out on to the training pitch, the boss sent him straight back in.

Becks was made to travel with the team to the big game at Leeds that weekend, but he wasn't even on the bench. He had to sit in the stands – which of course only brought more attention, with all the photographers at Elland Road taking pictures of Becks seething in his seat.

After the game we went straight off on international duty with England. We were playing Argentina at Wembley on the Wednesday. At least it gave things a few days to calm down, and Becks and I could chat about how he was going to work this out. We decided that I should be the mediator.

When we got back on the Thursday, I went and had a word with Steve McClaren.

'Look, I've had a chat with Becks and he wants to clear the air with the manager. But I think we need to help them find a solution.'

So we decided to have a meeting – me, Steve, Becks and the boss. To make sure it went smoothly, I sat down with Becks before the meeting and wrote down on a piece of A4 paper a list of commitments – pledges that he would stick to. The big thing for the boss was the travel, the shuttling up and down the motorway, so I wrote down that Becks would not go to London for the three nights before a game, that he would tell the manager about his movements, and that he would limit his travel. Knowing the manager, he's probably still got that piece of paper in a drawer somewhere.

To everyone's relief, the meeting was civil. They shook hands and agreed to put it behind them. The manager wasn't daft – Becks was a massive player for us, one of the best right-wingers in the world, and one of the hardest workers. And Becks was at his dream club with the chance to win trophies every season. Of course they had to patch things up.

13

Kevin

There was a chant, 'If the Nevilles can play for England so can I', that became very popular for a while. At the worst moments during Kevin Keegan's reign as England manager, I'd have happily swapped places with the clowns on the terraces.

I always took great pride in playing for my country, even though United always came first in my heart, but things got so bad during Kevin's reign that it was a relief to be left on the sidelines or injured.

It wasn't all Kevin's fault. His time in the job happened to coincide with my most miserable period as a player, when I lost all my confidence. I wasn't playing well at all for club or country. But the bottom line is that the England job brutally exposes any manager's failings. His weaknesses are put in the full glare of the media and then picked apart by the fans. And Kevin, as he'd eventually admit with admirable honesty, fell short of the level required.

We'd seen a lack of strategy during qualification for Euro 2000 with some strange decisions, like putting Sol Campbell at right-back in the play-off against Scotland. He'd chopped and changed between a back four and wing-backs. None of us was certain of our best eleven or the overall pattern.

There was still no sense of direction when we travelled out to our base in Belgium for the tournament, and I had bad vibes right from the start. I know it's a privilege to play for your country. You shouldn't complain. But we were staying in a really drab old hotel in the town of Spa. I wasn't in the best frame of mind, and as I put my bags down in my bedroom my mood darkened. 'This is going to be a long few weeks,' I thought. The tournament hadn't even started.

My form was poor and the team was desperately short of spark or imagination. I think Kevin's overall strategy was to make us a typical English side, based on power and high tempo. But you need youth and legs even to think about that, and we were so one-paced. Too many players were like me – solid and unspectacular. We had Ince and Batty in midfield but neither was the most creative. Becks had real quality, but on the left we had Dennis Wise ahead of Phil which was suicidal. We didn't have a single left-footer in the entire team, no one who could penetrate down that wing.

Kevin was unlucky on a few counts. Steve McManaman started the tournament and quickly got injured. Steven Gerrard, though young, was already a star in the making, but he got injured too. The player who should have been the exciting young talent, Michael Owen, was at odds with the manager. We could all see that from their curt exchanges. Michael came back from the 1998 World Cup as the big name but he just couldn't agree with Kevin's reading of his game. It was a professional issue that became a personal one. Kevin wanted Michael working deeper, with his back to goal. Michael thought that was a waste of his talents.

Not only did we have Michael in a bad mood, but we had the slowest England team in history. Two Nevilles, Keown and Adams, Batty, Ince, Wise and Beckham, with Owen up front and Shearer, who was retiring as soon as the tournament was over. We could have played for thirty years and we'd never have succeeded. We weren't good enough, not by a million miles. My brother would take terrible stick for the way we went out, but he did us a favour by sparing us any more punishment.

As well as the problems with the team, I was never thrilled about the gambling culture off the pitch. Too much of anything is bad, and the amount of time spent on horse racing or cards was ridiculous. It was all very old school, completely different to what I'd become used to in terms of discipline, focus and preparation at United. We'd have a ten-minute coach journey down to training and players would get the cards out. We'd lose a match and the gambling school would start up again.

There'll always be players who gamble, but this was too much. At United, we'd play cards, but never for big money. Even if we'd wanted to, the manager would have found out and stamped it out. Gambling is a cancer in a changing room.

I remember the only time I got suckered into a heavy card game. We were on a pre-season tour with United in Malaysia and I ended up with Yorkie, Keano, Butty, Giggsy, Scholesy and Teddy playing for a few hundred quid a hand. This was big by my standards and it got right into my head. I went to bed thinking about the Jack of Hearts, the King of Spades.

Gambling blows your mind. I can see why players fall into it. You've got money and you're spending a lot of boring hours in hotel rooms. But losing fifty grand and playing for ten hours until two a.m. can't be good for anyone's concentration. And at Euro 2000 the players definitely weren't gambling in moderation.

Socially it's divisive, too. If you have ten players in a room watching the racing or playing cards, it splits the camp. During Euro 96 a few of the senior players ran a book, but that was on the football matches. We watched the games together. That was sociable, and good homework. But some of the players at our hotel in Belgium were locked in rooms losing thousands on the turn of a card. If something goes to excess it can never be good. To be fair to Glenn Hoddle, he would never have allowed it.

You might have been fooled into thinking we were going to be contenders for Euro 2000 when we rushed into a 2–0 lead in our opening game against Portugal. That was as good as it got. They battered us in the second half. Luís Figo scored a screamer from thirty yards, straight through Tony's legs, for the equaliser, and then for the third I was in a bad position to cover Tony. It was typical of how I'd been playing for the previous five months. From 2–0 up we were lucky to only lose 3–2.

Germany, the old enemy, were next up, and I can't believe there's ever been a worse game played between the two countries. We scrambled a 1–0 win but, honestly, I don't know how. In the dressing room afterwards the players were euphoric and Kevin suggested that if we won the next game he was ready to snub the press after all the stick we'd been taking. But there'd be plenty more criticism.

I was already thinking about how much longer we'd be stuck out in Spa. I hate admitting that, but I knew that this team wasn't good enough and my own form was the worst of my whole career. It was obvious that we were going to be found out as a team.

As a man-manager, Kevin was great getting round the table and talking to players. Morale had been low when he took over from Glenn, and he was always great to deal with one-to-one. He's a good guy, full of enthusiasm and a real love for the game. But there was no strategy, no plan in our heads of how he wanted us to play. If you mixed the best of Kevin and Glenn together, you might have a good England manager. But, in very different ways, the demands of the job found them both out.

Under Kevin, we didn't learn. There were seven, eight coaches, all decent people, like Peter Beardsley, Derek Fazackerley, Arthur Cox and Les Reed, but there was no tactical nous being passed down to the team.

That was summed up one day when Les gave one of his lectures about our next opponents – and Kevin fell asleep. He was sitting on the front row and we could see his shoulders sagging, his head nodding forward. He woke up with a start and all the lads burst out laughing. It's unbelievable to recall that now, even though it was funny at the time.

We went into the last group game against Romania needing just a draw to reach the quarter-finals, but we were chaotic in defeat. We fell behind before Alan equalised from the penalty spot. Then we went ahead through Michael before we wobbled again. We were riddled with nerves and couldn't string more than a few passes together. We couldn't control the game at all. Then Viorel Moldovan burst towards the byline in the eighty-ninth minute and Phil stuck out his leg. It wasn't the greatest tackle in the world. He should have stayed on his feet. Ioan Ganea scored the penalty and we were out.

As Phil sat devastated in the dressing room afterwards, I told him repeatedly that he had nothing to feel bad about. 'We were shit, Phil. We were going home soon enough anyway.'

I was as much to blame as the next player. I'd been lousy. But England fans love a scapegoat and the sinking feeling I felt when Phil made that tackle was as much out of a feeling of protectiveness towards my younger brother as despair for my country. I'd seen the appalling stick Becks had suffered after the '98 World Cup. Phil was never going to endure that level of abuse, but he got it bad enough. When he arrived home there was a burning shirt on his gates and graffiti on his garden wall. It was probably a set-up by a newspaper because I can't believe anyone in Rossendale would have been stupid enough to do it. Either way, it was out of order.

I wish I'd made the tackle rather than Phil, but whichever of us had done it the stick for the Nevilles was guaranteed to climb another few decibels. I'd joke with Phil after Euro 2000 that he was to blame for all the abuse, though he's entitled to claim that I've made it a whole lot worse for him down the years.

At club level, I've always believed that you have to take the stick – especially if you give it out as I've done. I've never complained, however bad it's got. As long as we were winning on the pitch, a bit of chanting couldn't hurt me or my family.

But abuse from England fans when you are wearing the England shirt has always been plain idiocy. It's hard enough playing for your country without feeling that the supporters are ready to get on your case. As a young player it can really hurt you. It was pretty constant from around 1998 for a good few years, and obviously Phil's tackle didn't do much for the popularity of the Nevilles.

I expected Kevin to carry on after Euro 2000. He cared about England, and about his job, and he wanted to leave on a better note. But I couldn't see how things were going to improve.

In the end, it was a more depressing climax than even I'd feared: defeat at the hands of Germany in our opening World Cup qualifier – at home, in the rain, in the last game at the old Wembley, with another shocking performance.

Germany weren't much better. They were rubbish, in fact, just not as rubbish as us. Kevin had put Gareth Southgate in central midfield, even though Incey was on the bench, and it didn't make any sense.

I was as bad as anyone. Physically I wasn't right so it was a relief when the manager took me off at half-time. We needed some pace, and at least we would get some from Kieron Dyer.

But we couldn't get back in the game and it was a miserable, silent dressing room that Kevin entered after the match. I was already showered and changed but most of the lads were sitting, staring at the floor, when he started speaking. He began by talking about the game, just as normal.

'Lads, you've given your all, much better in the second half. I can't complain about the effort you've put in.'

Then, after a pause, he dropped a bomb on us.

'Anyway, I've taken it as far as I can. That's me finished.'

We were all stunned. I'd watched the second half from the mouth of the tunnel so I'd heard the fans getting wound up.

I'd heard the chants of 'What a load of rubbish!' and some of the abuse Kevin got as he walked off. It was obvious he was under massive pressure. But I hadn't seen this coming.

Arthur Cox stepped in. 'Whoa there, Kevin. You need to have a think about this.'

Tony Adams tried to say the same thing.

Kevin wouldn't be swayed. 'No, I've made my mind up. Thanks for everything you've done. You've been brilliant. But I have taken it as far as I can go.'

Before we knew it, all the suits were rushing into the dressing room – David Davies, Adam Crozier, the PR people. They were off in huddles, talking in groups. Yet another FA crisis.

It was a sad end to a sorry day – the lowest point of my England career. At United life was brilliant. We were winning trophies every year, playing great football, scoring goals galore. With England I was playing in a poor team and taking loads of grief. The only relief on the day was that I'd never have to play again in that crap old ground.

I hadn't expected Kevin to quit but I respected him for the way he handled it. It's not easy to admit when you aren't good enough, especially live on national TV. Kevin was probably right: he had taken it as far as he could and he was falling short. But there's plenty of managers who would have carried on taking the money, waiting for the sack. Kevin had the guts to front up in public.

With Kevin gone, the FA had to put someone in place for the trip to Finland a few days later. So in came Howard Wilkinson – the second time he'd been caretaker. On both occasions I had to drop out on the eve of the match. Howard probably thought I was chucking it in. I wasn't, although knowing his training methods I can't say I was itching to play for him. Before the France game in 1999 he wanted to practise free-kicks near the halfway line. His instruction was to stick the two centre-forwards and the two central defenders on the edge of the box and punt it forward. Against the world champions at Wembley we were going to resort to chucking it into the mixer.

It's fair to say that I hadn't heard anything like it in all my time at United. When I think of the quality of Spain, France, Real Madrid and Barcelona over the last decade, it goes to show how the English mentality was so far behind. And Howard was the FA's technical director.

14

Still the Boss

I've heard it said that a manager can't do anything once the players have crossed the white line. And it's bollocks. Anyone who says that has never had a good manager.

Our boss has a massive effect on the team whenever a match is on. You can feel him in your head. At the back of your mind – sometimes at the front, too – you'll be thinking, 'Christ, I've got to go and face him at half-time. I'd better start playing better or he might rip my skull out.'

Don't get me wrong, you aren't living in a state of fear. Mostly you are concentrating on your game. But you know, deep down, that you are puppets at the end of his string. He's in control. He makes or breaks your career. He decides whether it's going to be a great Saturday night – 'Well done, son' – or a sleepless weekend. It's down to him whether you get to enjoy your Chinese meal and your glass of wine with your family after a match or sit there in miserable silence. He controls your destiny.

Managers helpless on the sidelines? You won't hear that from any United player who sees our boss on the side of the pitch shouting his head off. You'll see him out of the corner of your eye, you'll know he's coming after you so you'll try to make it look like your concentration is elsewhere. You pretend not to see him – Giggsy's become a master of it down the years – or you start a totally unnecessary conversation with a teammate to fool him that you're busy. But you know he won't let it slide. You know it's coming at half-time or after the game unless you get yourself out of a hole sharpish. That has a massive effect on you. It makes you regret any lapse and work twice as hard to put it right. You could argue that it's the manager's greatest talent – to always make you feel his presence.

He's there all the time. At the training ground he's never been one to lead the sessions. He must have done a handful in all my time at the club. He's always been strictly manager, not coach. But somehow he never misses anything.

He'll suddenly appear, walking up and down the sidelines, chatting to the coaches or talking into his mobile, but always alert. Everyone knows he is a workaholic, into the training ground before the milkman. And there's nothing his eyes and ears don't pick up before he leaves.

He's a constant presence, but it's on match day he really comes alive. From 1.30 p.m. until two is the manager's team talk. This is his moment, his most important thirty minutes of the week. He'll tell us the team, how we are going to play, the strengths and weaknesses of our opponent. In later years we had a video to watch too, but the manager always spoke from his handwritten notes. There might be half a dozen points to make, some to the team, some to individuals. He might mention a danger man, or the need to avoid conceding set-pieces. He might say, 'Let's get behind their left-back because he can't run.'

He doesn't shout, he just delivers his message, like a general before battle, clearly and confidently. Every word is said for a reason. It's mostly serious, though sometimes he'll lighten the mood, often unintentionally. We'd always look forward to playing Aston Villa just to hear him mangle Ugo Ehiogu's name. 'Make sure you pick up Ehugu, Ehogy, whatever his name is.' We'd always chuckle at that one. He never got it right.

In the dressing room before the match, he'll not say too much, though occasionally he'll feel it's the time to rouse the players. He's got a squad of different nationalities, different ages, different characters, kids from Brazil and local lads like me, and he wants to make us all feel like we're in it together. Part of a team.

Three or four times a season he'll make the same speech – and it never fails to work. 'Look round this dressing room,' he'll say. 'Look at each other and be proud to be in this together.' He'll point to an individual. 'I'd want him on my team. And him, and him.' By the time he's finished, you can feel the hairs on the back of your neck standing to attention. Your skin will be covered in goosebumps. Your heart will be thumping.

Sometimes he might latch on to a specific incident, like when a Chelsea groundsman took a swing at Patrice Evra. 'Look at Patrice, he's four foot tall and he's not afraid of any-one. He's not giving in to anyone. He's a fighter. Now, what about the rest of you?'

Then, just before you go out, he'll stand at the dressing-room door. No player leaves without him being there pre-match and at half-time. You walk past him and he shakes the hand of every player and every member of staff. He doesn't have to say anything. He's the boss, probably the greatest manager ever in this country. What more motivation do you need?

The influence and intensity of our boss has never dimmed for a nanosecond, even as he approaches seventy. So it's amazing to think he was planning to quit in 2002. What a waste that would have been. Just think of all those championships and trophies he'd have missed out on. Count all the rivals he's seen off since then.

As we went into the 2001/02 season, there's no doubt that we were counting down the days until his retirement. He'd confirmed that this would be his last campaign, even though we'd won the last three championships. We'd been a machine trampling over our rivals, but now every week brought another story about the club's future, about who might take over and what role the manager would play.

I couldn't specifically say how all this chatter undermined the team. Most of the talking went on outside the club, but its unsettling effect was indisputable. There was no waning of the manager's authority – not by a fraction – but I guess sub-consciously you start to waste energy thinking about what lies ahead. And you can't afford even the slightest distraction when you are in the business of chasing trophies.

Fearful of what the future might hold once the manager had gone, Steve McClaren departed to Middlesbrough, and he wouldn't be properly replaced that season. We could have done with his tactical insight given that the team was in transition.

Jaap Stam was sold, which was a bombshell as big as Sparky leaving, even for the players – especially for the players. We were as mystified as anyone. All kinds of conspiracies swirled around because Jaap's exit came on the back of his 'controversial' autobiography; but I've always believed that the book was a minor factor, perhaps irrelevant. I know the manager wasn't thrilled about the book, and nor was I at being called a 'busy c***'. Jaap had called me that to my face many times, and I know it was meant affectionately, but it didn't look quite so clever spread across the front of the *Daily Mirror*.

He was very apologetic, because he was a big softie at heart, a big playful bear. Phil, Butty and I used to wind him up by flicking his ears or tapping him on the back of the head so he'd run after us, like a father chasing after a naughty kid. He didn't mean any harm with the book, he'd just not thought through the consequences of serialisation, when little passages get blown up into big stories. As I explained to him, you can say Ruud van Nistelrooy was selfish when he was near goal but the headline won't explain how that selfishness was part of his brilliance.

People came up with their conspiracy theories for Jaap's exit, but all that counted was that the manager had lost confidence in him – a mistake, as he'd later admit. He thought Jaap had lost a bit of pace, and was dropping off. But even if that was partly true, he remained an immense presence for us in defence. He was missed.

Understandably, Jaap was in a state of shock when I bumped into him coming out of the manager's office.

'I'm out of here. I'm flying to Rome tonight to sign for Lazio.'

'You're under contract. You can stay.'

'No, he wants me out. There's no point staying where I'm not wanted.'

It was a strange one, made more bizarre when Laurent Blanc, a class act but clearly past his best, arrived as replacement. There aren't many big decisions you can point to and say the manager called that one wrong. This was one.

On the positive side, we made some marquee signings. A year later than planned, Ruud van Nistelrooy arrived. What a class striker he'd prove, as good as any I played with.

And then came Juan Sebastian Verón, bought from Lazio for £28 million. Like everyone, I was excited about Verón coming. He'd had success in Italy. Perhaps a bit of South American flair combined with our British doggedness would make a perfect mix as we strived to reconquer Europe.

Sadly, that's not how it worked out. We'd see Seba in training and he was fantastic. He could pass and shoot, he had vision and athleticism, and he was a hard worker. But it proved impossible to integrate Seba into the side. Using him alongside Roy meant pushing Scholesy further forward, as a second striker behind Ruud. He wasn't happy now he was being asked to play with his back to goal. We had a squad of great players, but we weren't clicking.

I could understand what the manager was trying to do. We needed to control games better in Europe, to dictate and vary the pace rather than try to outgun every team. Champions League defeats to Madrid and Bayern had taught us that. But now we were caught halfway.

We still had wingers but they were delivering balls to a

centre-forward in Ruud who didn't like to use his head. We'd try to go through the middle but Scholesy and Seba were getting in each other's way. We'd needed to move on, but it wasn't easy to change our habits. In December we found ourselves down in ninth place after three consecutive league defeats. This was not the way the manager had wanted to say farewell.

There were rumours that the club was trying to lure Sven-Göran Eriksson at this time – and it made sense, given the instant, positive impact he'd had with England. Perhaps another manager, maybe Sven, could have come in at United and led us on to many triumphs. But I'm glad we didn't have to find out. Following the boss is going to be a huge job for someone one day – probably requiring a manager with José Mourinho's track record and self-confidence – but I couldn't imagine playing under anyone else. I was thrilled when in February the boss revealed that he wouldn't be retiring after all.

He gathered all the players in the dressing room to tell us. There was no great emotion expressed on either side – that's not how it works in a dressing room – but we were all very happy deep down. I say 'all', but Yorkie's face dropped because he was being left out by the boss and he could maybe start afresh under a new manager. The boss had barely left the room when Keano piped up, 'Well, that's you fucked, Yorkie.'

The manager's decision to stay was a massive boost, ending all the uncertainty, but it came too late to save a domestic season that was full of inconsistencies. The upside was Ruud's form. He had made up for lost time by scoring twenty-three goals in thirty-two league games in his first season. He was a proper goalscorer, obsessed with hanging around the penalty area, which was both a great strength and, occasionally, a huge frustration. He's the only teammate I've almost come to blows with.

We were playing away at Middlesbrough and I hit a ball down the channel. Ruud threw up his arms in the air, as if to say 'What am I meant to do with that?'

I ran forward. 'Run after it, you lazy bastard.'

I was thinking that Sparky, Andy Cole or Ole Gunnar Solskjaer would have chased it all day. But not Ruud. He wanted to save his energy for the penalty area.

I forgot all about it, but after the game I was sitting in the corner taking my boots off when he came flying towards me, swearing his head off. 'Don't fucking shout at me on the pitch!'

I stood up and tried to push him away. The lads jumped in and separated us.

It was handbags, really, though Ruud had properly snapped. Things simmered overnight, but we shook hands the next day.

Partly I could take his point. Ruud played within the eighteen-yard box. That was his strength, and he's probably the greatest goalscorer United have ever had. In terms of ratio of goals to chances, he was unbelievable. He was right up there with Shearer, probably just above, with that steely mentality that he was born to score. There was an arrogance about him. He probably thought I was a hairy-arsed English right-back while he was the heir to van Basten. Chasing the channels wasn't his strength, and in some ways he was right. In McClair and Sparky's time, they would chase wide and hold the ball up, laying it off to a full-back. But that had become too predictable. The game has changed, and changed for the better. It's become more sophisticated.

Despite Ruud's goals, 2001/02 was notable for being our first trophyless season since 1997/98. We'd lost too much ground in the league to Arsenal early in the season, and of all our defeats in the latter rounds in Europe, perhaps our least forgivable was at the hands of Bayer Leverkusen.

We were knocked out in the semi-finals by a team there for the taking – and I broke my foot in the second leg and missed the World Cup finals. I'd been feeling pain in my foot and had actually gone for a scan the day before we played Leverkusen. I was told it was just bone bruising. Then during the match I went for a tackle and something went. After a few minutes of limping around, I knew I had to come off. Within an hour I'd be in hospital in an X-ray department and the doctor would be telling me I'd broken my fifth metatarsal.

'What about the World Cup?'

'Sorry, no chance.'

It was going to be eight to twelve weeks. Even with my maths, I knew that ruled me out. It was a disaster, really, because I was at a peak moment. I'd recovered from the debacle of 2000 and was back in top form.

I'd resolved to change my lifestyle. I used to read the papers, probably too often. I'd note down all the bad articles. I was too intense. So after Euro 2000, and my own crap season at United, I decided I had to loosen up. I decided to be tabloid-free.

I moved home, too, from a house outside Manchester into a nice penthouse flat on Deansgate right in the heart of the city. I wanted to have more of a social life. This wasn't Gary

Neville becoming a party animal – far from it. I was still tucked up early a couple of nights before a game. But I might at least go out for a meal and a glass of wine on a Thursday night rather than lie in bed at 9.30 thinking about my opponents. I was finding more balance in my life. About time, too.

I'd also consciously challenged myself to become a more progressive right-back, working hard on my attacking and crossing. I knew I didn't have much choice if I wanted to stay at United. I had to become an all-round full-back, capable of making penetrating runs and not just defending. My determination to improve had kicked in again, and I was really feeling the benefits.

So I was gutted to miss out on the 2002 World Cup, not only because I was back enjoying my football, but we were on a roll under Sven, who'd taken over from Kevin and made instant improvements. I liked Sven from the start. I would have reservations by the end of his reign, but the first few years were as enjoyable as any in an England shirt, up there with the spirit and the purpose of the Venables era. I certainly never had a problem with having a foreign manager of England. We'd all like a home-grown leader, but I just wanted a good one, particularly after previous disappointments. I still believe that. English might be preferable, but the best man for the job is the priority.

And Sven was a good boss. He inherited a team with its chin on the floor and within months led us to the ecstasy of that 5–1 victory in Munich. It wasn't rocket-science, just sensible decisions about team selection and simple but effective communication. He gave us the sense that everything was under control; that if we held our nerve everything would turn out fine. At a time when my own game and confidence had been suffering, his calmness and light touch were just what I needed.

He seemed blessed in those early days. Even when we made very hard work of drawing against Greece in our final World Cup qualifier, a chaotic performance was forgotten in the euphoria of Becks' last-minute free-kick. I was standing close by when he sized it up. Teddy asked if he could have a go, but to take a set-piece off Becks was like stealing his wallet.

I turned round and looked up at the clock high on the edge of one of the stands at Old Trafford. Time was up. Becks must have known it too, and that's what separates the really great players from the rest: when the chips are down, when everything is on them, they can produce.

I knew it was in from the moment it left his boot. It capped an astonishing performance. I'd never seen him run so far. He was a hard-working player anyway, but the England captaincy really brought out the best in Becks.

He loved wearing that armband, though in April 2002 I thought I might get to slip it on when Becks missed a friendly against Paraguay. Sven sat me down at the front of the coach on the way to the ground.

'Gary, I'm going to make Michael Owen captain tonight.'

Typical Sven, he tried to be diplomatic. He practically told me that I was a more natural captain than Michael. He was almost apologising to me. So why didn't he give me the job?

Nothing personal against Michael, but there were other players, like Rio, Steven Gerrard, Frank Lampard and me, who were more obvious contenders. But Michael was the bigger name, and Sven could be a little weak like that. The decision wasn't going to win or lose us matches but it was a strange choice. I accepted it, but I should probably have objected more strongly. That little sign of weakness in Sven would be repeated.

What I wouldn't blame Sven for is defeat by Brazil at the 2002 World Cup finals, a game I watched from a TV studio. Danny Mills got the right-back spot. I've never been his greatest fan, but I couldn't be too hard on him or any of the lads for the way they went out in that quarter-final.

True, they didn't keep the ball well, but they were up against a top-class team in baking heat in Japan. They were knackered, chasing after the ball. I couldn't be too critical because I'd been there with England a few times myself, being outplayed by quality opposition.

15

Farewell, Becks

When Carlos Queiroz arrived as the boss's right-hand man, I suppose it was logical that he would want to make an impression, shake things up a bit.

From the start of the 2002/03 season there were a few occasions when Carlos would pull me and Becks and ask us to do things differently, to play in different ways. He was on to us quite regularly, particularly after our defeat by Liverpool in the Carling Cup that season. He had a go at both of us for not getting close enough to Steven Gerrard. When he showed us the video the next day, we could see he was right. We were to blame.

Maybe Carlos thought it was time to change things around, to inject a little more pace down that right flank. He was trying to move the team on. That's what he had been hired to do. The mood of change was unmistakeable.

Nonetheless, as a team we were on our way back after

surrendering our title to Arsenal the previous season. We'd made a £30 million signing, Rio Ferdinand from Leeds United, in the summer. All that money on a defender, but what a classy one.

And the manager had solved the problem of Verón by resolving not to build the team around him. Seba would have to take his games where and when he could – on the left, on the right, filling in when needed. He'd not let us down, but it represented a demotion of sorts – not exactly what he'd been signed for, for all that money.

Moving Seba out of the centre allowed Scholesy to slip back into his preferred deeper position, with Ruud either joined by Ole or Diego Forlán or spearheading the team on his own in a 4–5–1 formation that would become increasingly familiar. The team was evolving – a sign of Carlos's influence.

We were looking strong, but however hard the manager drove us, even in the most successful campaigns, there always seemed to be a game when it all went horribly wrong. A nightmare match that reminded you that success never comes easily. It was as if we needed to lose a game badly to teach us that we couldn't afford to lose any more. That season it came at Maine Road in November.

It was scheduled to be the last Manchester derby at the old stadium, and I was captain for the day in Roy's absence. What an honour. Except we turned it into a City carnival. Or rather, I did.

At 1–1 the ball was played over my head. I'd say that ninety-nine times out of a hundred I'd have cleared it to safety, but I dawdled and then decided to lay it back to Barthez, knowing he was comfortable on the ball. Disaster. I scuffed the pass, and Shaun Goater pounced. As errors go, it was a bad one in any game; in a Manchester derby it was unforgivable. So much for a captain's performance: the manager subbed me after an hour.

We lost 3–1, and the boss was steaming as we came into the dressing room. You could see him looking around, ready to explode but not yet certain of his target. Then Ruud walked in with a City shirt slung over his shoulder. He'd been asked to swap on the way off and hadn't thought anything of it. But the manager did.

'You don't give those shirts away. Ever. They're Manchester United's shirts, not yours. You treasure those shirts. If I see anyone giving a shirt away they won't be playing for me again.'

Losing is bad, losing shambolically is unacceptable, and losing that way to Liverpool, City or Arsenal was a hanging offence in the manager's eyes. And it wasn't any easier to stomach for the supporters, who'd booed us off, raging that they'd now suffer humiliation at the hands of City fans.

'I should let them in here, the lot of them,' the manager went on. 'They can tell you what they think of that performance. Absolute shambles.'

I didn't need telling. I drove home for one of the loneliest nights of my life. I opened the front door, walked straight to the fridge and just sat there with two bottles of beer on the go. I needed to drink to forget.

Part of your brain is trying to remind you that there will be another game in a few days' time. You tell yourself that in the crazy rollercoaster of professional sport you're going to have massive highs and lows and it'll all look better in the morning. But this was one of those nights when I couldn't find any comfort wherever I looked.

I kept going over the game in my head, and the manager wasn't in the mood to let me forget it quickly. A few days later we were up against Bayer Leverkusen, but I was dropped to the bench. Very harsh, I thought. I'd made a mistake, a bad one, but I'd been playing well. Steeling myself, I decided to go and see the boss and make that very point. I should have known better. He told me he couldn't accept that performance without making changes. And it would be another three games before I was back in the team.

I returned for our trip to Anfield – the game when Diego Forlán, despite his struggles at United, would guarantee himself lasting affection from our fans. He scored twice in a vital win. Then, a week after beating Liverpool, we faced the champions, Arsenal, at Old Trafford. We were without half a team so Phil was drafted into central midfield, alongside Scholesy. He faced a massive job against Patrick Vieira, but it was our best display of the season so far. We hustled them out of the game, and Phil was superb. Scholesy and Seba scored, and we finished the afternoon knowing we were back in the business of winning championships.

Ruud was brilliant that season. He scored twenty-five goals in the league, none better than his second in a hat-trick against Fulham in March. He beat about five players in a run from the centre circle. That win took us top of the league, and, with our experience, we could smell the title. 'Something's happening,' Becks said to me as we walked off the pitch. He meant the championship, but it was also clear that his time at the club could be coming to an end.

In February we'd been knocked out of the FA Cup by Arsenal, but it wasn't the result which caused a massive stir.

In the dressing room, the manager blamed Becks for one of the goals – and Becks disagreed. He answered back, which was always liable to escalate things. And the manager erupted, spectacularly.

He wheeled round, saw a boot lying on the floor, and in his fury kicked it like he was blasting for goal. He was facing Becks but there is no way he meant to kick the boot into his face. I've seen the boss in training; if he tried it a thousand times, he couldn't do it again. But the boot flew up and hit Becks just above the eye, cutting him. He put his hand up to his forehead and felt blood. So suddenly he was standing up too, shouting and raging.

For a second the gaffer was dumbstruck, which isn't like him. I think he knew that hitting a player with a boot, even by accident, was a bit extreme. He apologised straight away: 'David, I didn't mean to kick the boot in your face.'

Becks wasn't having any of it. A few of us had to stand up to keep them apart.

We left the ground and went out that evening. Becks was clearly wondering if that was the end for him at United.

With another player, the story might not have leaked out. But, of course, it was Becks, and the incident was quickly all over the front pages. On and on it went. The press followed him everywhere.

Becks carried on training and being professional. But as the matches got bigger and bigger towards the end of the season he was left out of key games. The papers started to speculate about his future. He was being linked with Europe's biggest clubs, from Barcelona to Milan to Madrid.

Change seemed inevitable. The boss and Becks were at odds, and Carlos seemed to think we'd run our course after eight years together. He felt that neither of us was quick enough, even if Becks had bundles of stamina. Perhaps we'd become too predictable. Perhaps it didn't suit how he wanted to play if we were going to use Ruud as a lone striker. Whatever the reason, it was obvious that Carlos had his doubts, and he was the manager's closest adviser.

I think all the players saw strengths and weaknesses in Carlos. There's no doubt he was instrumental in helping us evolve as a team, becoming more sophisticated and patient in Europe. He had us playing different formations, weaning us off our traditional 4–4–2. Tactically he was excellent, but his day-to-day training could be very dry. Some days things would feel very bogged down in specifics, stopping the play to rerun one pass. Rene Meulensteen, the first-team coach in recent years, was much more into flowing training sessions, Steve McClaren too. Carlos was different from any coach I had at United and he'd be quite open that he didn't want us playing small-sided games all the time. It was as if he didn't want us having too much fun in the week so we'd be hungrier on Saturday.

The transfer rumours around Becks gathered more momentum in April when he was on the bench as we thrashed Liverpool, and then again when we travelled to Arsenal. He was also a substitute when Real's 'Galácticos' came to Old Trafford, defending a 3–1 lead from the quarter-final first leg. Roberto Carlos, Luís Figo, Zinedine Zidane and particularly Raúl had done for us in the Bernabéu. It was Ronaldo's turn in the second leg.

I was suspended but, sat in the stands, I couldn't fail to join the standing ovation as the great Brazilian came off after his hat-trick. It was a unique moment as we realised we were in the presence of one of the great players of the last twenty years. What was it, sixty-two goals in ninety-seven games for Brazil? What a talent, even with all his injuries, and what a character. I remember a game against Brazil with England in 1997 when Ronaldo and Romario were standing on the halfway line having a joke, cracking up, while the game was going on. I don't know if they were taking the piss, but I guess I'd have been that confident if I was as gifted as them.

Ronaldo was the star of the night, but, typically, Becks wouldn't be kept out of the headlines by anyone. He came on and scored twice, and he would help us secure the two more victories we needed to clinch the championship. I was chuffed for him that he finished on a high. That 2002/03 title was one of the sweetest because we reclaimed it against some people's expectations. It's always a great feeling winning it back because all year you'll have felt like you had something extra to prove. That's a great motivation.

We'd got our trophy back, but it was the end for Becks. As we walked around the pitch after beating Charlton in the last home game of the season, waving to the fans, Becks told me that a move was in the offing. 'They've had talks,' he said. Our little chat would get picked up by lip readers on *Match of the Day*.

It was the first time he'd actually confirmed to me that he was probably off. All the talk about his future had alerted Real Madrid and Barcelona. The latter wanted him in the Nou Camp, but his heart was set on the Bernabéu.

It wasn't the way he wanted to leave but Becks had always had this urge to go and play abroad. He hadn't chosen its timing, but the move could be sold as something good for him as well as for the club. United would get £25 million for a player who'd served them brilliantly and cost them nothing, and Becks would get to play for arguably the only club in the world as big as United, where he would be a huge star alongside some of the greats like Zidane, Figo and Roberto Carlos.

It went down as an acrimonious split but I know Becks has huge respect for the manager, and vice versa – something confirmed in the many warm words they've said about each other since. It was a wrench for Becks to leave United, but he's not exactly done badly since, playing for both Real Madrid and AC Milan.

I knew I'd miss my mate. We'd roomed together, sat next to each other on the team bus for the best part of a decade. To the rest of the world he might be David Beckham, superstar, but to me he was still the best mate I'd known since the age of fourteen. We'd been through so much together. We'd played together every week on that right side for club and country to the point where we became almost telepathic. We'd learnt to play with each other since we were kids and could react instinctively. I'd see a pass played into Scholesy in midfield and before the ball had even left his boot I'd be setting off on the overlap, knowing for certain that it would soon be arriving at Becks' feet. The opposing winger would already have been left behind, caught unawares, and now the full-back wouldn't know whether to come with me or close down Becks. It sounds so simple, yet it caught out opponents game after game, for years and years.

We knew each other's games, and we learnt how to handle each other's temperaments. I can barely remember a cross word. We didn't need to get on each other's case because we trusted each other to be giving everything. Becks had a phenomenal work rate during his time at United; he had a capacity to run and run. In the physical tests there were few players who could match his stamina. There's the infamous bleep test in training, a running exercise designed to make you sprint until you drop. Becks and Yorkie were the only two players in my time who managed to run it all the way through, to beat the machine. The rest of us would be on the floor.

His technical excellence hardly needs restating. Name anyone from the two decades the Premier League has been in existence more likely to land a cross on someone's head. And he had what I call great 'game intelligence'. To be honest, I think all of us – me, Becks, Butty, Scholesy, Phil – had that. There's not enough intelligent English footballers who understand the game, who don't need to be told where to move or what pass to make. Becks was one of the very best for decision-making. Neither I nor he was blessed with the greatest pace so we worked out a way around it.

On top of all that, he had a fantastic big-match temperament. He wanted the ball all the time. That's the courage the best players have – to take possession, to take the heat off a teammate however tightly marked. It wasn't just those celebrated passes and set-pieces but his ability to hold the ball that marks him out as having a very special technique.

Becks had ambitions from a young age, and when he left United he was well on his way to achieving them. He was more than just a footballer, and he had become a globally recognised figure. That's opened a whole lot of fantastic opportunities for him, from his academies to helping London win the 2012 Olympics.

His career has gone the way he wanted it to go, and looking back on a glittering twenty years you have to say that he hasn't let it affect his football. Just consider what he's achieved, with all his trophies and his 115 caps for England. Unlike a lot of players who get wrapped up in a showbiz lifestyle, there was real substance to David. He is a model for any aspiring footballer – driven to succeed with a beautiful talent.

Becks is one of the United greats, but I could understand why the manager – particularly our manager, who was so used to controlling his players – was put out by the attention from the press on one player. It was time to say farewell to my best mate.

16

Strike!

It was the affair that earned me the nickname Red Nev, the episode which seems to get brought up as often as any of my on-field achievements. I'll always be the one who takes the blame over the Rio strike. I'm forever to be seen as the leader of the rebellion.

'The most hated footballer in the country' was how the *Sun* branded me, and the strike made the front pages of every paper. It even led the *Ten o'Clock News*, so God knows what recriminations there would have been if we'd actually followed through and refused to play for England.

Would I have walked out? Would I really have refused to represent my country over someone else's missed drugs test? I can say now that I came closer than anyone imagines.

At the height of the talks, I swear I was ready to grab my bags and leave the England hotel. I knew the consequences would be drastic. At twenty-eight, I would never play for

England again. I'd be slaughtered by the media and fans up and down the country. I'd definitely become England's most hated footballer – if I wasn't already. But that's how strongly I felt about it. And only one telephone call stopped me.

From the start I was convinced right was on my side – I still am. We can argue all day about the threat to go on strike, and whether that was the best way to make our point. But I still believe, passionately, that the FA badly mishandled Rio's case and someone had to stick up for a point of principle.

At United, it was no great secret that Rio had missed a drugs test. We knew he'd screwed up and that he was due to have an FA hearing. I assumed Rio would continue playing and be given a fine and some kind of warning or suspended sentence. I assumed justice would take its natural course. How wrong I was.

It was the week of England's final group qualifier for Euro 2004 and my dad had just picked up me and my brother to take us to Manchester airport to fly down to London to meet up with the squad when I took a call: Rio had been dropped over the drugs test. My initial reaction was that it was a joke. 'How can they drop him? He's not even had his hearing.' I have been brought up with a strong sense of right and wrong, and from the start I thought this stank.

Before we reached the airport I rang the boss. 'We've got to do something about this. Rio's been left out and he hasn't even been charged with anything.'

The boss said the matter had been discussed the previous night when the club had been urging the FA to pick Rio, but they'd got nowhere.

I rang Gordon Taylor, chief executive of the players' union, and made exactly the same point to him. I wasn't just going to stand aside and let the FA hang Rio out to dry.

This was never a case of trying to get Rio off the hook. He was wrong to miss the drugs test. At the very least he was daft and forgetful. He was going to get punished for it. My point – and this was what I kept hammering home – was that the FA must wait until the hearing to punish him. For me, it was a clear case of judging before the evidence had been heard. He deserved the chance to explain himself.

I don't think Mark Palios, the chief executive of the FA, had much interest in listening to those arguments. He hadn't been long in the job and he'd already set this agenda of cleaning up the game. I saw this as being his chance to prove that he was a strong man. He wasn't going to back down.

At Manchester airport, Scholesy and Butty felt the same way about Rio's position. They thought that it was a disgrace. As United players, we had been raised to stick up for each other, so that's what we decided to do.

But this was not a case of just looking after our own. At the time, Rio was not a particularly good mate of mine. There were plenty of players in the England squad – David James, Kieron Dyer, Frank Lampard – who knew him better. I like to think I would have acted the same way whoever was in trouble, whether they played for Arsenal, Liverpool or Chelsea.

We arrived at Sopwell House and insisted that the four of us, the United lads, had a meeting with Palios. It was the first time I'd really spoken to him.

'You've been a footballer,' I told him. 'You've actually been in a dressing room, you know what it's like. You know that some lads sometimes do something silly, step a little bit out of line. What do you do, hang, draw and quarter them? Or do you think, "No, they're entitled to a disciplinary process"?'

'I have to do what's right and proper,' he kept saying, but this wasn't law, it was just his opinion. No one except the FA seemed to think it necessary to ban Rio. Not Sven, not Uefa, nor our opponents the Turks. They all came out and said they had no objections to him playing. It was a policy decision by the FA. As far as I could see, it was about one man's image. Having made a decision, it seemed as if Palios needed to look tough.

'You're being judge and fucking jury,' I told Palios. 'You've just come in here and you've wanted to make a point for yourself, the new sheriff in town.'

That hit a nerve and he snapped back. I reckoned there and then that he didn't have the temperament for a big job like running the FA.

There had been a feeling that under Adam Crozier, his predecessor, it had all been a bit too carefree, particularly when it came to money. Palios was brought in to tighten the belt. He might have been a top finance man but that's what he should have stuck to – punching numbers into a calculator. Being chief executive of the FA is about being able to manage people, to deal with a crisis – about being the front man for the biggest organisation in British sport. To me, he seemed out of his depth.

'We're going to go and talk to the rest of the players, but we want Rio reinstated,' I said. 'This is fucking out of order.' And off I went to see Becks, the captain.

Becks called a team meeting in the hotel. Sven was there for that first one. He was supportive and said he backed what we were doing, but he didn't want to set himself against the FA publicly, which was a disappointment. I can understand why he felt in an awkward position, but if we'd had Alex Ferguson in charge, I think Rio would have played. Sven was always a diplomat. He avoided confrontation.

So it came down to the players. I spoke for most of the meeting. 'Look, this could be you next week,' I said, 'and this doesn't just relate to missing a drugs test. This could relate to anything. If we think Rio is getting a raw deal, and I do, we've got to defend him.'

We were on a roll now and another meeting was demanded with Palios involving the players' committee – Jamo, Michael Owen, Sol Campbell and Becks – as well as the lads from United.

Palios kept banging on about how 'we never leaked this out' and 'we never breached Rio's confidentiality'. And I kept replying, 'You're not picking this up. What part of you thinks that you wouldn't breach his confidentiality when you left him out of the squad? You might as well have announced it on the *News at Ten*.'

Palios made it plain we weren't going to get anywhere with negotiation, which is when we decided to go for the secret ballot on the Tuesday evening about whether to strike. Was that the clever thing to do? I don't think anyone would ever say, 'Yeah, that went brilliantly.' But would I do the same thing again? I think so, and at the time I certainly couldn't see any other way. We had to show the FA that we were serious. And we had to find out if everyone else in the squad felt as strongly as the lads from United.

We gathered in a room and tore up a sheet of A4 paper into enough pieces for ballot papers. 'Yes' to strike, 'No' to go along with Rio's ban, with all the papers in a bucket so no one would know which way you had voted.

There were twenty-three players in the squad and there wasn't one 'No'. It was unanimous. So Becks and I stood there at the front and said, 'Right, so every single one of you has voted that we're not going to play this game unless Rio is reinstated?' There was not a murmur.

By Wednesday morning, news of our vote was out in the papers and it was all kicking off. We were being labelled a disgrace on the front pages and during phone-ins and I sensed a few of the players wavering, now the full consequences of a strike were becoming clear. The FA was saying that we could be thrown out of Euro 2004, which was obviously putting the wind up some of the lads. The media weren't exactly rushing to support a load of millionaires threatening to go on strike. I could sense a few players wobbling.

They had their reasons, but I didn't want to be party to a climbdown. I'd staked my reputation on it. The situation felt unstoppable, like a runaway train. I couldn't be sure how it was going to finish, but I felt I'd gone too far to stop now. In my mind, I couldn't see any alternative. Unless the FA backed down I was going to have to walk out of the England camp, even though the consequences would be grave.

My brain was frazzled after all the meetings. My head was banging with the pressure. But the more I thought about it, the more I could only see one way out – through the exit. Thoughts of international retirement swirled around my head. I spoke to my dad and warned him. 'I think I'm going to have to go. This is just wrong.' He knows how stubborn I can be. He knew I meant it. In the privacy of my room in the team hotel I said the same to Scholesy, Butty and Phil. I was ready to leave.

And I would have gone had it not been for a telephone call

from the man who has been the biggest influence on my life outside my family. Without the boss, things could have been very different.

It was just when I was on the edge of a momentous decision that he called. I was with some of the other players. 'Go upstairs to your room, we need to have a talk,' he said.

Once I was in my room, he got straight to the point.

'Look, you've trained too hard, you've played too hard, you can't throw everything away. You've made your point, you've taken it as far as you can, now you've got to go and play the game.'

'Boss, it's fucking wrong.'

'I know that, you know that, but you can't ruin your career over it.'

'But I've gone too far with it. I can't back down.'

'You just need to calm down and think that your England career could be over in one hit. What effect does that have on you as a player, as a person? Does that affect United? I can't let you do that.'

It was when the boss mentioned all these consequences for club and country that I knew the strike was over. I knew I had to back down. If I was going to be bringing pressure and massive aggravation on my own club as well as everything else I couldn't go ahead, simple as that.

It was written at the time that Rio had talked the players round, but I think I only had one quick chat with him during the whole episode. It was the boss who stopped me gathering my kit together and walking out of the door.

There is a big part of me that wishes I had seen it through to the bitter end, but I know that the manager was doing the right thing by me. It's hard enough being a professional footballer and staying at the top. He knew that I'd be walking into a whole new world of pain if I'd walked out on my own. I'd be associated with this one decision for the rest of my career. He didn't want one of his senior players up to his neck in controversy.

I sat on my own for a couple of hours, reflecting on what the manager had said, acknowledging, reluctantly, that I had to follow his instructions. If I walked out now, and defied him, I'd be risking everything.

I went to see Becks and said we'd taken it as far as we could. The FA weren't going to bring Rio back in, that was fairly obvious. With only a few days to go before the most critical game of England's season – an automatic place at Euro 2004 was still at stake – I'd go along with the rest of the lads who wanted to back down.

We put out a statement, although even that took a lot of discussion. I'd written a version myself and passed it to Michael Owen and the committee. Michael and Becks showed it to their agent, Tony Stephens, who was desperately trying to get it watered down. I was trying to beef it up, to at least leave something on the FA and Palios.

The statement was eventually released on Wednesday evening. Part of it read:

> It is our opinion that the organisation we represent has not only let down one of our teammates, but the whole of the England squad and its manager. We feel that they have failed us very badly. One of our teammates was penalised without being given the rights he is entitled to and without any charges being brought against him by the governing body of the game.
>
> Rio Ferdinand was entitled to confidentiality and a fair

hearing in front of an independent commission. We believe the people responsible for making the decision did not give Rio Ferdinand that due process and that has disrupted and made the team weaker against the wishes of the manager and the players.

If there was one line in it which I disagreed with, it was a sentence which suggested that the strike threat was a bluff: 'In our minds, there has never been any question as to whether we would play in this game.' That might have been true of some of the squad, perhaps even the majority, but it certainly wasn't the case for me.

Now we had to get on with the job of trying to get a draw in Turkey to qualify for Euro 2004 knowing that the country were right on our backs, the fans were banned from travelling because of previous trouble, and that the opposition were no mugs.

To make matters worse, we trained on the Thursday morning and were shambolic. 'I'm not sure we can win this game,' Becks said. 'It's taken so much out of everybody.' I shared his worries. The lads were dead on their feet. We'd been having meetings until late for two nights running. And when we weren't talking, I'd been staring at the ceiling, thinking about the consequences of what we were doing.

In the end, getting out of the country was probably what we needed. Escaping that environment helped us focus on the game. We were a bit better in training on Friday, and on Saturday we produced a battling performance. I still don't know where it came from. It was a real team effort under huge pressure. Becks missed a penalty and there was a fight in the tunnel at half-time, but we came through for a goalless draw which ranks as one of my most satisfying games for England.

If anything took the edge off it, it was when Palios came into the dressing room to congratulate the players. He wasn't comfortable in there. He couldn't even look me in the eye.

I don't know if he believed that he had 'won' by keeping Rio out of the squad, by forcing the players to stand down. But it all came back to bite him on the backside a month later with the whole Alan Smith/James Beattie debacle, which emphasised just how right we had been to take him on – and how ill-suited he was to be the FA's leader.

A month after the Turkey game we were playing Denmark in a friendly at Old Trafford. On the day the squad was due to meet up the FA suddenly announced that Alan had been dropped because he'd been arrested. 'Arrested' is a terrible word; it makes you think, 'Something must have gone on there.' But it was over nothing. A bottle of water had been tossed on to a pitch. He'd tossed it back. The police had arrested him for questioning as a matter of procedure, but it never came near a charge.

It was enough to get Palios back on his high horse. He deemed that Alan was no longer fit to wear the England shirt. So that was Alan out. But in his place the FA summoned Beattie, who was serving a drink-driving ban – something Palios didn't know until it was too late. Cue red faces.

I'd told him he was making a rod for his own back when he waded into the Rio affair. He'd set himself up to be whiter than white, which is inadvisable at the best of times. And then he went and got himself all over the front pages over a private affair.

Under normal circumstances I would never suggest that

someone should have to resign over a personal issue. But with his stance on behaviour, Palios had made his own position untenable. The man who had come to clean up football had given himself no real alternative but to resign. He's not worked in football since.

Rio received a £50,000 fine and an eight-month suspension, which ruled him out of Euro 2004 as well as massively undermining United. I thought it was very harsh. It was definitely inconsistent: a lad at Manchester City, Christian Negouai, had also missed a drugs test but got a £2,000 fine and no ban. Rio had paid a high price for the case becoming such a cause célèbre.

He'd not been helped by his legal advice, going into the hearing with all guns blazing. Knowing that the FA were out to make a stand, I told Rio he should walk in with his mum and a simple handwritten apology: 'Look, I've cocked up, I've done wrong, I didn't realise how serious it was, I forgot.' But he went for the expensive barrister and was punished for it.

I've never doubted that Rio was genuinely forgetful. I detest drugs, and if Rio or anyone had tested positive – and you've got to remember he did a hair follicle test which showed him to be clean – I would have been the first to argue for a lifetime ban. Personally, I believe football is a pretty clean sport. I've not had any reason to be suspicious about any of my opponents.

But I can also understand why there's a need for testing. Thanks to Rio a shambolic system was overhauled, so at least one good thing came out of it. From that point on, players would no longer be able to leave the training ground through forgetfulness. We'd be the same as athletes, followed by the testers while you have a pee.

We saw the rigidity of the new system some years later when we played at Arsenal and conceded a last-minute winner. You can imagine the foul mood of the players and the manager even before we walked into the dressing room to find three drugs testers waiting for samples. They got a right earbashing from quite a few of us. It wasn't fair on them – they were only doing their jobs – but it was an issue that always made emotions run high at United.

I've no regrets over the Rio affair, or any other time I've stuck my neck out – like another threatened strike in 2001 when the PFA was fighting for a share of the Premier League's billions. Rightly so.

The league was trying to drop the share of payments paid to the PFA at a time when they were making more cash than ever. I was part of the management committee which decided that we had to show we were serious – and a strike was the only way. As I explained to the players at United, 'I might never need the PFA, and nor might you. We won't need the benevolent fund or community support. But there are plenty of footballers, and ex-footballers, who do.'

We weren't arguing for Rooney and Neville but for the teenager whose dream is destroyed by injury at eighteen and needs retraining. Or a player from yesteryear who gave his all to the game but now suffers from ill health. We were seeking to protect a union going back a hundred years to Billy Meredith. It was a cause worth fighting for.

I was outspoken on that, just as I was over Rio, and just as I have been on a number of issues to do with the game. Not everyone seems to like it. Put 'Gary Neville' and 'wanker' into Google and you'll get about ten thousand results.

I don't understand the hostility, to be honest. We constantly hear about footballers being cut adrift from the real world, caring only about the money, but then we slaughter them when they have strong opinions. I'm not saying you have to agree with me, but I thought we wanted footballers who were passionate about their club, about the game.

It's always been in my nature to stand up for what I believe in. I was brought up with a strong sense of right and wrong, and I've always been willing to argue my case – whatever trouble I've landed myself in.

I think it comes partly from being the older brother. I've always wanted to take responsibility. As a teenage apprentice at United, I was made foreman. Later, I'd be captain. I'd help the young players negotiate their contracts. I was the unofficial social secretary. I like to organise, to be in control. Or to stick my oar in, as my critics would argue.

When I am right – or when I think I am right, which might not always be the same thing – I will never give in. I'll fight my cause to the bitter end. Sometimes that has got me into trouble. But I'd much prefer to be known for being loyal to a fault than for being flaky.

Occasionally I've stopped and wondered how it came to this, but I've never worried about it. I could have had an easier life but I'm glad that I stood up for people, for the club, for the things I believed in.

You grow a thick skin after a while. You need to if you want to succeed, particularly if you aren't blessed with looks and talent. You have to brace yourself for a barrage of abuse, particularly if you're a high-profile player for Manchester United and England. A fan will walk past you in the street: 'You were fucking shit yesterday.' You turn on the radio: 'Gary Neville isn't what he was.' You pick up a paper: Neville, captain of the Ugly XI. Phone-ins, newspaper articles, TV shows . . . you are playing for one of the biggest clubs in the world and you are going to get that scrutiny. You have to learn to let it wash over you, pick yourself up and go again. That's probably been one of my biggest strengths. I've never let anyone get to me that much. It's the only way to survive. Being called bolshie Red Nev has never bothered me. Far from it.

To be honest, once the boss has ripped you apart a few times and you've had a captain like Keano put you in your place a few times, you can handle anything that comes from fans or media. There's only a few people in the world you need to impress. That's something very important that you learn with experience.

17

England Blow It, Again

No one can doubt that Rio was punished severely, forced to miss eight months of football including Euro 2004 in Portugal. And we stood a really good chance in the tournament.

We had Wayne Rooney. He'd burst into the English consciousness when Sven picked him for his full debut against Turkey in April 2003 even though he'd only played a handful of times for Everton. But I'd already had a secret glimpse of the hottest young talent in the country.

Six months earlier, at the Halton Stadium, Widnes, of all places, I'd played against Everton reserves on my way back from injury. There was this stocky bull of a kid, just sixteen years old, rolling the ball under his feet like he was the main man. He was that good I came in at half-time and asked our coaches, 'Who the bloody hell is that?' It wasn't just his skills but the physique and the confidence to throw his weight around. He sent one of our lads sprawling. I was tempted to ask for his passport. He couldn't be sixteen.

As I said, he'd barely played in the Premier League when Sven called him up, but he took to international football like a veteran. That first game against Turkey was a difficult, feisty match, but he juggled the ball in the middle of the pitch, almost taking the piss. It was like seeing Gazza at his peak.

Wazza's emergence was the joy of that England campaign, and although there had been some bumps on the journey, notably the 2–2 draw at home to Macedonia, we approached Euro 2004 believing we would be genuine contenders. Rooney had given us goals and unpredictability; Frank Lampard had emerged as a significant player at Chelsea; we had Becks, Scholesy and Steven Gerrard.

If I had a worry, it was that Sven had created a fixed first XI. Everyone knew the names: James, Neville, Cole, Ferdinand, Campbell, Beckham, Gerrard, Lampard, Scholes, Rooney, Owen. While it is always helpful to have a settled team, it doesn't keep players on their toes.

The problem would be made worse by Sven's reluctance to make changes and to trust the reserves. He was sticking with that first team, whatever the evidence. Of course he wanted his big names on the pitch, but he could have used the subs much better. Kieron Dyer played for seven minutes in the whole tournament. We had Joe Cole on the bench and he didn't even play for one minute, even though he could have given us some variation. We needed him, particularly with Scholesy unhappy now that he'd been shoved out to the left wing.

We started brightly enough against France in Benfica's Stadium of Light. A massive game against Zidane and Henry. A huge test. We were excellent in that first half, with Rooney giving Silvestre and an ageing Lilian Thuram nightmares. Lampard scored with his head and we had a great chance to go 2–0 up, but Barthez saved Becks' penalty.

Then, being England, we committed suicide.

We conceded a needless free-kick, up stepped Zidane, and he caught Jamo out of position. 1–1. Then Stevie G made a blind backpass, and Jamo hauled down Henry. 2–1. Next thing I see, the French are being knobs, skipping around the pitch in celebration. We'd let ourselves down, again.

We'd still progress from the group. Wazza scored four goals in two games, the victories over Switzerland and Croatia, to cement his status as the rising star of European football. He was playing with a belief that anything was possible. He was magnificent.

But instead of cruising through, we ended up flogging all our best players in the group stage. I thought that was the wrong approach, and said so to Steve McClaren, Sven's right-hand man. I thought we should rest players for the third game, against Croatia, especially key men like Becks, Scholesy and Stevie G.

It would be a risk, but we needed freshening up if we were going to beat Portugal, the hosts and a dangerous team under 'Big Phil' Scolari, in the quarter-final. We were never a team to dominate possession and we'd wear ourselves out chasing the ball. We should have been brave and changed the team around, but my view is that England have never been brave enough in major tournaments.

The failure to rest players was not the prime reason we went out – losing Rooney with a broken foot after twenty-seven minutes against Portugal was the turning point – but it was a significant factor. Our match-winners were not fresh when we needed them most.

We started well enough against the Portuguese, but once Wazza had gone off it soon became a tired performance. Only Frank of the midfield four was at his sharpest. Scholesy was unhappy with his role out on the left, Becks had not enjoyed a great run-up to the tournament with Real Madrid, Stevie G has admitted that he was preoccupied with a possible move to Chelsea. We were undercooked in midfield.

As the game went on, we started to lose control of it and were forced to defend for our lives on the edge of the penalty area. Helder Postiga never did anything in the Premier League. He was the sort of player you wouldn't even notice at club level. But we allowed him a free header for Portugal's equaliser to take us into extra-time.

We'd done a decent job on their wingers. Luís Figo was hooked and Cristiano Ronaldo kept swapping sides, looking for a way through us. But we couldn't see it over the line, just as we'd failed to do against France.

Scolari made three attacking changes – Deco ended up at right-back – while our substitutions were cautious. Owen Hargreaves replacing Steven Gerrard wasn't going to help us take the game to Portugal, and my brother came on for Scholesy. As Phil won't mind me saying, he's not a game-changing player.

In the tiny margins of international tournaments we'd fallen short again – the familiar combination of not quite enough top-quality players, a few misguided decisions, and an inability to take penalties.

Becks and, fatefully, Darius Vassell were the players to miss as we went down 6–5 on spot-kicks. I was already pissed off when Steve McClaren came up to me afterwards. 'Why didn't you take the seventh penalty?' he said. 'Why didn't you or Phil take it?'

'Well, Steve, for one thing I'm not a centre-forward. If you want me to go up first next time, tell me and I'll do it. I can handle scoring or missing but it's not what I'm best at. Sticking the ball in the net – that's a striker's job.'

I'd never taken a penalty in my life. I had about five shots a season. Don't get me wrong: if Sven had asked me, or ordered me, I'd have taken one. But as far as I was concerned, you can take bravery to the point of stupidity. You might say David Batty was brave taking one in 1998 against Argentina; he wasn't a penalty taker, and you could see that when he ran up. Afterwards he admitted that he'd never taken one in his life. So what was he doing taking one to keep us in the World Cup?

Maybe I could have taken one better than Darius. But that's easy to say afterwards. As I said, like Batty, I'd never taken a penalty in my professional career.

Scholesy retired from international football the day after Euro 2004, which I found a terrible shame for the English game. He came down in the morning and said, 'That's it, I've had enough.' Typical Scholesy, no big drama. He'd thought it through privately and decided he wasn't enjoying it.

He hadn't been used correctly by Sven, and while he'd swallowed his frustration at playing on the left side of midfield during the tournament, he knew that wasn't the best use of him. I also think he'd started to resent that England was increasingly becoming a huge media circus. The WAGs business was just taking hold, though it wouldn't really be picked up by the media as a negative for another two years.

Scholesy can't stand that stuff any more than I can. He hates all the showbiz frenzy. To him, there's literally nothing that should be of any interest to fans apart from what he does on the pitch.

I tried to talk him out of retirement because he was exactly the sort of player who suited international football. If he didn't perform as well for England as he might have done, that's because the team wasn't set up right. We should have played 4–3–3 far more than we did, and then Scholesy would have fitted in perfectly instead of being shoved out to the wing. We should have been playing a more compact midfield.

He was moved out to accommodate Frank, but, with all respect to Frank, Scholesy's a higher class altogether. He's got a vision that's probably unmatched by any English player of the last twenty years. Ask the top players in the world, like Zidane or Henry, and they'll tell you the same. We drool over Xavi and Iniesta, and rightly so. Scholesy could have fitted into that Barcelona team without missing a beat.

The classic English failing is an inability to keep possession and control the tempo of a game. Scholesy should have been doing that for two decades for England but we never found the right midfield combination. So he quit international football with seven years left in his playing career.

When he said he was going to retire, I knew there wasn't much chance of talking him out of it. He's tough like that. At United, he once refused to travel to a Carling Cup game because he thought the boss was punishing him unfairly. He turned the manager down flat. That takes balls.

I told him to wait a month with his England decision, but he wouldn't be swayed. I was gutted. I wouldn't just miss him in midfield but in the hotel, on the team bus and in the dressing room on those long international trips.

People think Scholesy's shy and quiet but he's one of the most cutting people I know. Example: the day Diana Law, who worked in United's press department, was chatting with the players.

'Gary, you remind me of my brother for some reason,' she said.

'Why?' Scholesy replied, quick as a flash. 'Is he a knob too?'

Scholesy has plenty of opinions – it's just that he doesn't waste words. Now that he's retired from club football too, I have no doubt he'll make a top coach, passing down his knowledge. He understands the game, he's got a great eye for a player, and when he says something, it's always worth listening.

He could be an absolute pain in the arse, though, constantly nicking your car keys, your wedding ring, your phone. The time I must have wasted looking for something he'd hidden.

Sven tried to talk him round, but he wasn't having any of it. He wasn't even thirty and he was walking away from England. He'd never come back, not even when Capello made a late bid to get him to go to South Africa.

Scholesy just didn't want any further part in it. But I can't say I'd lost my belief in England at the end of Euro 2004. I still had faith in Sven and we had a squad of very good players – great players in Rio, Becks, Ashley Cole, Gerrard and Wazza, and all at a good age. We could look at Wazza's injury against Portugal and wonder how much was down to bad luck.

But, as it turned out, I was fooling myself.

18

Beating the Invincibles

There are all sorts of ways to win a football match, and there were plenty of occasions when Manchester United, for all our gifted players, relied on a bit of brute force. Physical toughness is an essential part of the game, though you wouldn't have thought so sometimes when you heard Arsenal's bleating.

Arsenal's 'Invincibles' were a truly brilliant football team but their attitude wound me up. They acted as though the rest of the world was meant to sit back and admire their beautiful football. Sorry, count me out. Some of us had a mission to stop them by all legitimate means.

At Aston Villa last season Robert Pires did an interview and he was still banging on about how annoying I could be. He talked about me tripping him, insulting him, standing on his feet, and being a general pain. 'I thought more about having a row with Neville than playing football,' Pires said. Music to my ears.

What did he expect? When Arsenal were in their pomp, I had him and Ashley Cole rampaging on the left flank and Thierry Henry doing those blistering runs from inside to out. It was like marking the Red Arrows.

Stopping Arsenal was a job that required a defender to reach for all the tricks. Especially on the afternoon in October 2004 when the Invincibles rode into Old Trafford, hoping to notch up their fiftieth league game unbeaten.

We were under massive pressure. Arsenal had stolen the title back from us in 2003/04 with their incredible run, finishing fifteen points ahead of us. They'd not lost a league game; we'd lost nine. We'd finished in third place behind Chelsea.

We'd won the FA Cup thanks to our 3–0 victory over Millwall in Cardiff, and we'd celebrated properly, as the manager always told us to do. A trophy was a trophy. Most teams in the country would have killed to be in our boots. But even when Wayne Rooney rejoined us after his Euro 2004 injury it was clear we were on the slide and the fans were growing agitated.

It went without saying that we had something to prove when the Invincibles came to Old Trafford. We couldn't bear another humiliation. The idea of Arsenal celebrating fifty Premiership matches unbeaten in our back yard was unthinkable. It was all set up for the match forever to be remembered as Pizzagate, or the Battle of the Buffet.

It's the only match when I've ever been accused of brutalising an opponent. So let me first make it clear that in almost twenty years at United the manager never asked me to kick anyone. I've no idea if other managers have issued instructions to 'take out' a player, but I can promise you that wasn't our boss's style. But did he tell us to get tight, put a foot in and let Arsenal know they were in for a battle? Of course he did.

The manager's belief was that too many opponents had stood off Arsenal. They had allowed them to play, to strut around. I'm not taking anything away from a great team. They were brilliant. Technically they were as good as anything we've seen in England in my time. But there are all kinds of attributes that make up a football side and they didn't like it when the contest became physical. You could never say that of the 1998 Arsenal side. We knew the Invincibles had all the skill in the world, but they also had a soft centre.

'If you let them play they'll destroy you,' the manager told us in his pre-match talk. 'So you'd better be right up against them. It's a football match. You're allowed to tackle. And no other team tackles them so let's make sure Mister Pires and Mister Henry know that today's going to be hard. Today's going to be different.'

That didn't mean going over the top. It didn't mean reckless two-footed challenges. Who wants to get sent off? That would be self-destructive. But we knew a lot of them hated aerial challenges, so what did we do? Clattered them in the air at every opportunity.

My job was to nullify the threat of Antonio Reyes. My thought process was simple: 'He's a great player, a pacy, tricky winger. If I stand off him and don't tackle, he'll run rings round me and made me look an idiot. He's got more skill, he's got more speed. I might have more stamina but that's not going to be much good if he's ripped me apart in the first thirty minutes.' You are like a boxer trying to work out whether to jab and run or get into close contact. And while I could try to intercept, using my experience and my positional abilities, I knew that above all I had to get tight, get physical. I had to makes Reyes lose his confidence. If there were question marks about him – justified by what turned out to be a short spell in England – they were over his temperament. It was my job to expose that weakness.

Some say I crossed the line. How? Reyes was subbed after seventy minutes, and it wasn't for his own protection. He didn't have a mark on his leg. Yes, there was a time in the first half when he knocked the ball through my legs and, chasing back, I went through him and tripped him. It wasn't pretty, but it's something any defender does dozens of times a season: you concede a foul high up the pitch rather than risk worse trouble around the penalty area.

People said we ganged up on Reyes, but Phil's collision with him was a nothing tackle. He got there a bit late and pushed Reyes off the ball, which wasn't hard to do. I'm not going to deny an element of intimidation, but only because Reyes wasn't tough enough to take it. Cristiano Ronaldo would get that sort of treatment all the time, until defenders realised it didn't put him off, it just made him more determined. That sort of courage is part of being a great player. Ask Diego Maradona, Pelé; they had the physical courage to withstand being kicked. Reyes couldn't properly handle the rough and tumble, which is why Wenger ended up selling him back to Spain. He had the skills but he fell short of being a top player because he couldn't take a bit of stick.

Brilliantly talented as Arsenal were, there was a mental fragility about quite a few of their players. Still is, to be honest. Wenger is always liable to start complaining about a physical approach, but it's sour grapes because his skilful players have been outfought. He described Darren

Fletcher as an anti-footballer once, which couldn't be more ridiculous.

Physical toughness is part of the game, and our boss has always known it. At Old Trafford we couldn't believe the naivety of people complaining about Stoke and Blackburn having a physical approach to the game. Anyone who talks like that is advertising a weakness. We learnt right from the days of Nobby Stiles and Eric Harrison that the first lesson of football is that you compete. We had obvious tough characters, like Sparky and Keano and Butty, but the whole team has always been able to handle itself. How many defenders do you see rough up Giggsy? He'll get kicked but he'll never get physically dominated by a defender. He'll simply not allow that to happen. The manager won't allow that to happen. Look at the way Giggsy went through Lee Bowyer at Birmingham last season after Bowyer had put in a bad tackle. It was a challenge that carried a message: 'Don't think we're gonna get bullied.'

Every team can be outplayed, but the idea of walking into the dressing room if you've been pushed around – well, that's just unthinkable. Our early games against Juventus were hard in that sense. I think of the 1998 Arsenal side and Chelsea under Mourinho as big and powerful. Strength isn't enough on its own, but there's no doubt Arsenal have underestimated the importance of being able to compete physically.

Rough up the Invincibles and they'd act as though it was an affront. They believed – and this must have come from their manager – that their beautiful, intricate passing game deserved to be admired, not challenged. They had a superiority complex. Henry would look at you as if to say, 'How dare you try to tackle me!'

United have never really tolerated prima donnas. You get kicked, you get up and get on with the match. Look at how Ronaldo cut out a lot of his histrionics – that's because we told him to stop rolling on the floor. He benefited massively from the toughening-up process that came with playing in England.

In the end we beat Arsenal 2–0, with a bit of help from a dubious penalty when Wazza went over Sol Campbell's leg. But we deserved it because we'd thrown them off their game. And the way they reacted afterwards told you everything about their inability to see football as a battle of skill and courage. They had become bad losers, and they threw a really big tantrum.

I was still walking off the pitch when it all went off outside the dressing rooms. I'd wanted to savour one of the best atmospheres I'd known at Old Trafford so I was clapping the fans when the pizza was lobbed from the away changing room, one slice landing on our manager and splattering his jacket with tomato and pepperoni.

Apparently it had all gone off in a hail of pizza and sausage rolls, but I missed the fun. When I got to the dressing room, a few of our lads were arming themselves and planning to launch a raid back. The manager quickly put an end to it.

It was all set up for a feisty return at Highbury four months later, and the contest lived up to expectations. This time there was almost a fight before kick-off. I'd been out for the warm-up and was heading back to the dressing room when I heard Patrick Vieira running up the tunnel behind me. I don't know if he'd been waiting for me, but he wasn't in the best of moods.

'Neville, you won't be kicking anybody out there today.'

'What the fuck are you on about? You need to calm your-self down, pal. The game hasn't even started yet.'

The next thing I knew he was coming at me, looming over me. A policeman stepped in to separate us.

I went off to the dressing room where I was sat next to Roy.

'Fucking hell, Vieira's wound up,' I said. 'He's just come at me in the tunnel.'

This got Roy's juices flowing. He couldn't stand Vieira any-way. So when we got out into the tunnel ahead of the game and Vieira started on at me again, telling me who I was allowed to tackle, it all got very lively. A policeman tried to intervene again, and when Roy saw what was happening he was straight back down the tunnel into the thick of it.

'You, Vieira, come and pick on me.'

That's when Vieira squirted him with water out of his bottle. And that's when Roy got seriously angry.

I know we are grown men, and this was now a water fight to go with the pizza-throwing of a few months earlier. You'd shout at your kids if they behaved like that. But we were revved up before a massive game and we weren't going to back down for anyone.

Roy started jabbing his finger at Vieira. By now the temperature in the tunnel was at boiling point. Wisely, Graham Poll and the rest of the officials stepped in to stop things escalating. They pushed us back into line, ready to go out on to the pitch, but Roy was still giving Vieira stick. He started laying into him about his split loyalties, about how he played for France even though he was always talking about his charity work back in Senegal.

Out we went on to the pitch, and when Vieira walked down the line to shake my hand I made sure I looked him right in the eye. Playing for United had taught me not to be intimidated.

And we weren't going to be cowed by Arsenal, even when they raced into an early lead through Vieira – a goal that prompted Ashley Cole to run past me, screaming in my face. They were wound up beyond belief.

It made it all the more satisfying when we hammered them 4–2, even though Mikael Silvestre was sent off twenty minutes from the end. Defeat must have hurt them double. To be honest, I think they'd lost it even before the game. There's a fine line between being wired up for a match and losing the plot. As far as I was concerned, Vieira had crossed it.

I've had my own red-mist moments, but, whatever Reyes might say, I've never been a dirty player. In February 2004 I was shown a red card in the Manchester derby for a supposed head butt on Steve McManaman, but I didn't even mean to nut him.

He came towards me shouting his head off, calling me a diver after I'd gone down in City's penalty area. He was raging and I was convinced he was going to shove his face in mine, the way you see footballers banging foreheads. We'd never been mates. I shoved my head in first thinking he was coming for me. Unfortunately he'd pulled out so it looked like I'd done him. I couldn't blame the referee for sending me off, but at least we won the game.

As a team, we've had our tantrums and our losses of control, but the way some people talk you'd think United have been a disciplinary nightmare under the boss. Our record is not bad at all. There have been a few high-profile cases, and I'll accept we overstepped the mark when we hounded Andy d'Urso on that infamous occasion. It was bad behaviour and it looked terrible. The boss told us we'd gone too far, and rightly so.

But it's inevitable you'll lose the plot sometimes playing top-level sport. Everyone wants this perfect world, but the mentality you've been engrained with is to fight and scrap for everything, to win every little battle and every little decision. Especially when you are young, you feel like you are fighting against the world. Occasionally you lose your head, even if you wish you wouldn't.

I'm sure if you ask a lot of referees, they wouldn't have liked me during the earlier years of my career. I was gobby. It landed me in trouble when Paolo di Canio scored a ridiculous goal to knock us out of the FA Cup in 2001. He looked about half a mile offside, everyone stopped, and he rolled the ball past Fabien Barthez. In my mind I saw total injustice and had a right go at the officials afterwards. 'A fucking disgrace' is what I think I said to them. I thought they'd made a shocking call, made worse by the FA's decision to ban me for two matches and fine me £30,000. That was totally over the top, and it was reduced to £7,000 on appeal.

Eventually I'd ease off refs, especially with the responsibilities of being captain. I also think the referees improved, or at least they got rid of the worst ones.

These days players are increasingly aware that there's a camera on them all the time and every little incident is going to be picked up. I can see it reaching the point where players won't be allowed to talk to refs at all, and maybe that isn't such a bad thing. I can say that now I've finished playing, but, I'll be honest, it is hard for a lot of players to stay level-headed when they're fighting for their lives on the pitch.

We've had our run-ins with officials at United but we've never been a filthy team or a cheating team. We play within the rules, as much as any club does, though of course most try to push the laws to the limit. People are naive if they think it's otherwise. It makes me laugh sometimes when I see a media outrage about a 'crime' that is commonplace. There was a massive storm when Becks admitted he got himself deliberately booked playing for England – but plenty of footballers have done that, including me. You'd see a big game looming so you'd get a caution by tripping a player, and get the suspension out of the way. As I said, it's naive to think that's not happening fairly regularly.

There's a level of gamesmanship which every team tries to get away with – and anyone who says otherwise is lying. Players will go down too easily to get a foul. You are a defender, you are at the far post and you know you are in trouble, that the striker's about to beat you in the air. You feel a small nudge in the back and you go down, gambling on getting the free-kick. Strikers will say the same about tumbling under the slightest challenge to win a penalty. It's not blatant diving, but they'll go down if they get half a chance. I'd be a hypocrite if I called them cheats.

This sort of behaviour becomes second nature, just like appealing for decisions that you know aren't yours. 'Offside, lino!' even though you know the striker is onside. Cheating? If you want to be pedantic, but it happens in every sport – batsmen not walking, rugby players sticking their hands in a ruck when the ref isn't looking.

The higher you climb, the more you feel you have to scrap for every little advantage. You think that if you don't influence the referee then you can be sure that the other team will. It's not always pretty. But top-level sport is about winning.

19

Captain

All this time while we and Arsenal were slugging it out as bitter rivals, Chelsea were racing ahead of both of us. José Mourinho had arrived in 2004 with his coat and his charisma and his talk of being a Special One. And, to be fair, he was living up to his own billing.

I'd never had a problem with Abramovich splashing out millions. At a club as big as United we weren't going to be intimidated by a new kid on the block. Money could buy Chelsea success. Mourinho had organised them superbly, and they had a strong, physical team with top-class internationals like Didier Drogba, Frank Lampard and John Terry. That early Mourinho team, 4–3–3 with Damien Duff and Arjen Robben, was formidable. I don't think they've been as good since.

They had bought a top manager and some top players, and we had to accept that Abramovich's wealth had created a major new rival. But I wasn't going to lose sleep over it, or worry about United's place in the game. All the money in the world could never buy our history, our tradition, our fan power or prestige. It never will, not in a hundred years.

Peter Kenyon seemed to think otherwise. He moved from Old Trafford down to Stamford Bridge and now he was chirping away every five minutes about how Chelsea were going to be the biggest club in the world. Total nonsense.

They were making good progress, as we had to admit, losing one league game all season in Mourinho's first year. They were due at Old Trafford in the penultimate game and we formed a guard of honour to welcome Chelsea on to the pitch as champions. It was the right thing to do, an honourable gesture, though it stuck in my throat. I have respect for the champions of England, whoever they are, but it always hurts to see someone else with the trophy.

People said how unhappy I looked. I think someone wrote at the time that it was like me having to clap burglars into my own home. Spot on. As far as I was concerned, that was our trophy. How do you want me to look?

After the Invincibles and Mourinho's Chelsea, we'd gone successive seasons without a title for the first time in more than a decade – and two seasons would become three. We'd failed in Europe again in 2004/05, beaten by AC Milan in the first knock-out round without scoring a goal. We lost the FA Cup final to Arsenal on penalties. We were hurt, and the wolves were at the door.

All the fans could see was an era of Chelsea domination. You couldn't blame them for their pessimism. United had set the bar high and now we were getting stick for falling below those standards.

We were in the throes of what I call, perhaps a little unkindly, the Djemba Djemba years. We'd had more goalkeeping problems. Barthez had been loaned out after one mistake too many and now we were moving uncertainly between Roy Carroll and Tim Howard. Either could have made a respectable number two but they had no claim to be the next Schmeichel.

As well as Djemba Djemba, we had others in Kleberson, Forlán, David Bellion and Liam Miller who were struggling to play at a championship-winning standard. None of them were bad players, or bad lads – and some thrived elsewhere – but they weren't good enough to be first-team regulars at United. I felt sorry for them more than angry.

We all knew Cristiano Ronaldo was going to be a special player, but it was going to take several seasons for him to fill out and fulfil the potential the lads had seen when they first played against him in a friendly against Sporting Lisbon. I was injured for that game but I saw his skills on the television and the lads were raving about him when they came back. There was no way the club were going to miss out on him, but we were signing an eighteen-year-old who would need time to adapt to a new country, a new language, a new environment.

We'd captured Wazza, the best young English footballer in the country, who'd make a typically spectacular debut with a hat-trick against Fenerbahçe in the Champions League. But all the youthful promise of Rooney and Ronaldo wasn't going to buy us time with the fans. They were growing sick of one embarrassment after another. They were used to better.

The manager might be able to see all the potential in Rooney and Ronaldo and a promising kid like Darren Fletcher. On the training pitch, so could I. But there was frustration on the terraces, and in the dressing room too, as we slipped behind Chelsea.

My brother was feeling it, and in the summer of 2005 he decided he'd had enough of being left out of the big matches. He'd not even made the squad of sixteen for the FA Cup final. This had been brewing for a couple of years. He'd play thirty-odd games but be left out when it really counted. He wanted to play more, and he'd heard that some decent clubs and good managers – David Moyes at Everton, Steve McClaren at Middlesbrough – were interested. Rumours were swirling around about whether United would let him go and it was getting tough on Phil. So I told him one day that we'd ring up the manager and get it sorted face to face.

'Boss, can we come round?'

Half an hour later we were drinking tea in his sitting room. It remains the only time I've been to his house in all my time at United.

The boss got straight to the point. 'Phil, I don't want to sell you, but if it's first-team football you want, I won't stand in your way if someone pays the right money.'

I think they both knew it was time, and Phil had a great option at Everton. He was impressed with Moyes, as you would be. Everton were in the north-west, a good club going places. There was still plenty of time for Phil to enjoy a second wind to his career. But I knew I'd miss him, and I did.

I missed the little rituals – sitting together a few hours before a game, chatting about the match. It's nice to have the comfort, the familiarity. I was sad at him leaving but I also felt lucky to have spent a decade playing with my brother, and mates like Becks, Butty, Giggsy and Scholesy.

It must have been strange for a Neville to be driving into Merseyside for his first day's work. I never had to adjust to a fresh environment, a new set of players, different methods. But Phil, being the most diligent pro that's ever been born, was such an instant hit that he soon became captain at Everton.

Respect to Phil, he threw himself into being an Everton player completely. Any lingering doubt about his loyalties was banished when he clattered into Ronaldo in a match against United at Goodison Park. I secretly admired him for it, even though I wanted my team to win. As ever, Phil was doing what he had to for his team.

If Phil had grown frustrated, that was nothing compared to the anger brewing inside Roy. He wasn't tolerant of under-achievers at the best of times. And now he was seething.

There were two Roys that I knew at United. I couldn't give you an exact date when one transformed into the other but there is no doubt that there was a change, a dramatic one, in the way Roy went about his daily work around the 1998/99 period.

You probably couldn't spot it from his performances, but Roy would probably tell you himself that he reached the point where he realised he had to look after himself better – drink less, eat the right foods, stay out of bother. His body fat must have shrunk from 12 per cent to about half that – the lowest in the club. Doing his weights, or his yoga, he became a machine.

He became an inspiration, not just in his performances but the way he pushed himself off the pitch, working like a dog even though he was already one of the fittest players at the

SQUADS FOR THE FINAL

ENGLAND
CHRIS DAY
GARY NEVILLE
KEVIN SHARP
DARREN CASKEY
CHRIS CASPER
SULZEER CAMPBELL
MARK TINKLER
NICHOLAS BUTT
JULIAN JOACHIM
JAMIE FORRESTER
PAUL SCHOLES
ROBERT BOWMAN
ANDREW MARSHALL
ROBERT FOWLER
KEVIN GALLEN
NOEL WHELAN

TURKEY
TURKSOY MURAT
ARSLAN ILHAMI
YIGIT SAMET
KARAMAN DURSUN
DEMIRCIOGLU SINAN
NURI EVREN
ALTUNTAS TEMEL
ALKAN TARKAN
DERELIOGLU OKTAY
KOCABEY MUSTAFA
TRAS ENDER
SAYGILI MUSTAFA
SAZLOG TEKIN
OZER HASAN
RECBER SERKAN
CAN HAKAN

SQUADS FOR 3rd AND 4th PLACE PLAY-OFF

PORTUGAL
NUNO SAMPAIO
RUI GAMA
JORGE MADUREIRA
JOSE SILVA
PEDRO HENRIQUES
HUGO RIBEIROS
CARLOS MORBEY
NUNO AFONSO
JOAO PEIXE
NUNO LUIS
FREDERICO FERNANDES
PAULO MORAIS
JOAO ESTEVES
RUI GUERREIRO
NUNO RIBEIRO
LUIS CASSAMA

SPAIN
JAVIER LOPEZ
JOYCE MORENO
AURELIO SANTOS
RAMON GONZALEZ
LUIS CUARTERO
CESAR PALACIOS
GERARDO GARCIA
EMILIO CARRASCO
JOSE GALVEZ
CARLOS SIERRA
JAVIER MORENO
DANIEL GARCIA
JOSE SANCHEZ
ENRIQUE MEDINA
MARCOS VALES
OSCAR VALES

Above left: My first England call-up came for an Under-18 international against Switzerland at Port Vale.

Above right: In July 1993, we won the European Championships, beating Turkey in the final with a penalty from Darren Caskey after Julian Joachim was brought down.

Above and below: Along with the United contingent of Scholesy, Butty, Casp and me, Sol Campbell (*back row, fourth from right*) and Robbie Fowler (*front row, third from right*) were also in that victorious team.

Above: My England debut came against Japan in the Umbro Cup at Wembley on 3 June 1995. (*Back row, from left*) Shearer, Batty, Collymore, Flowers, Scales, Anderton; (*front row, from left*) Neville, Beardsley, Platt (capt), Pearce, Unsworth.

Above: Teddy Sheringham and I celebrate Gazza's goal against Scotland at Euro 96.

Right: With Becks after his last-minute free-kick against Greece at Old Trafford in 2001 saw England qualify for the World Cup finals.

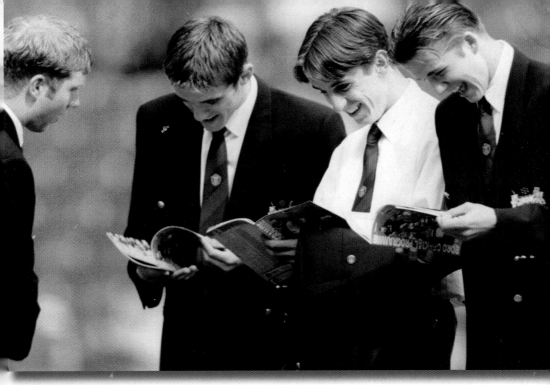

Above: First-team regulars – although I often had to battle my own brother for a place in the starting line-up.

Below: With Becks at Wembley for the FA Cup Final; Eric Cantona gave us a famous victory against Liverpool in 1996.

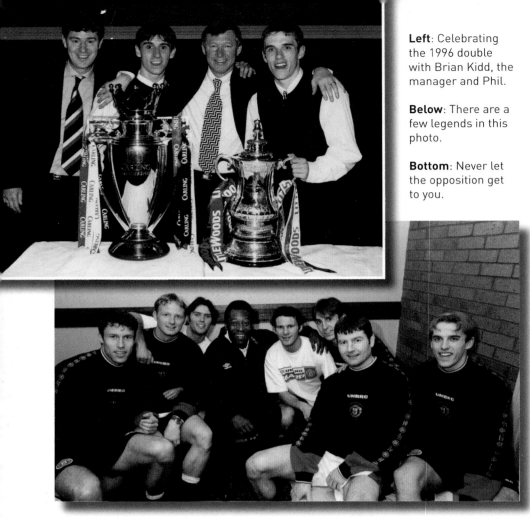

Left: Celebrating the 1996 double with Brian Kidd, the manager and Phil.

Below: There are a few legends in this photo.

Bottom: Never let the opposition get to you.

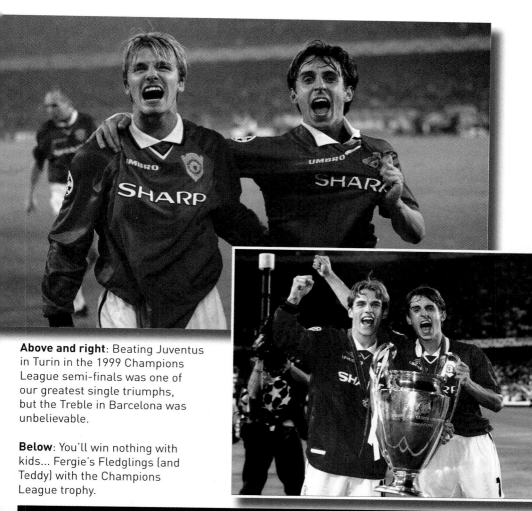

Above and right: Beating Juventus in Turin in the 1999 Champions League semi-finals was one of our greatest single triumphs, but the Treble in Barcelona was unbelievable.

Below: You'll win nothing with kids... Fergie's Fledglings (and Teddy) with the Champions League trophy.

Left: The manager and I parade the Carling Cup in 2006 – my first trophy as United captain.

Above: Wazza's two goals in Cardiff signalled the start of a new era of success.

Below: Saving the best till last. With Edwin van der Sar, Scholesy and Giggsy after securing another Premier League trophy in 2009.

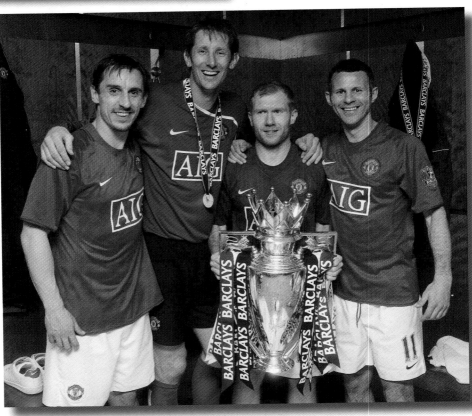

I was still recovering from injury when we won the Champions League trophy for a second time in Moscow in 2008, but that didn't stop me celebrating.

Above: A proud day: I walk out for my testimonial at Old Trafford on 24 May 2011 with my girls Molly and Sophie.

Right: Becks says goodbye, for now.

Below: We'd come a long way together.

club. I loved training with Roy in the gym because you knew you'd be pushed to the limits.

Off the field he changed too, because even the most driven of us mellow a little over time. In Roy's first four or five years at Old Trafford I didn't speak to him much apart from the usual brief exchanges before and after games, or at training. But in those last few years, me, Ole Gunnar and Giggsy would have great chats with him about the game, about what was in the papers, about who was saying what. Roy was always worth listening to. To be in his company was challenging, just as it was on the pitch. Say something unfounded and Roy would be the first on to you to say, 'That's bollocks.' He didn't like lazy thinking any more than lazy footballers.

But you could say that intolerant streak in Roy was his undoing.

No one wanted the split to happen – not Roy, not the club – but a problem had been building up in the dressing room, and something had to give.

A few of the younger players in the team – Rio, Rooney, Fletcher and O'Shea – were in awe of Roy and I don't think they knew how to handle him. It wasn't Roy's fault. I'd played with him for ten years and you learnt to live with his direct approach, when to give it back and when to shut up. But the younger gang tiptoed around him. You can see why they were intimidated by this hard man.

A natural changing of the guard was brewing, in the same way that me, Scholesy, Giggsy and Butty had taken over from Ince, Hughes and all the big names who had terrified us initially. The younger players need to be allowed to come out of their shells. But it was hard to see what might bring change about – until that infamous programme at the end of October 2005 on the club's own channel, MUTV.

I was actually down to do the 'Play the Pundit' show that day. Roy and I were both injured at the time but, fatefully, we ended up switching. On a Monday morning, you would go through the tape of the match just played – in this case a 4–1 hammering at Middlesbrough which left us trailing in the league again to Chelsea. I was first in that morning and then Roy arrived. Just me and him in the changing room.

I knew the match had been a horror-show and I could guess that Roy would be brutally honest given the way he was feeling.

Roy was up for it. He was wound up because he felt the younger players were falling short. He'd see them on their gadgets like their PlayStations and he couldn't get his head around it. He didn't have time to go through several seasons of rebuilding. You don't use a word like 'transition' around Roy Keane.

Roy had used MUTV before to get things off his chest – to complain about some of the young players slacking. But we knew he must have gone further when the Middlesbrough programme was pulled by the club. Clearly worried by the strength of Roy's opinions, someone had shown it to the manager and David Gill. They had blocked it.

The story leaked out of the club within hours and the press were all over it when the team, without me and Roy who were injured, flew to Lille in the Champions League. There was speculation about what Roy had said. The manager prides himself on unity, on keeping troubles behind closed doors, on not letting your enemies detect any weakness. But Roy had aired his grievances and the fans, already disgruntled at how the team was playing, were on the team's back in Lille. It was the worst possible outcome: a poor performance, a 1–0 loss, and the fans singing 'one Roy Keane'. The chants continued as the players made their way through the airport on the way home.

This was becoming divisive.

With everyone back at the club, Roy talked to a few of the players. I don't think any of them had confronted Roy about it. For someone like Fletch or Kieran Richardson, that wasn't what you did where Roy was concerned.

Then the manager called everyone up to his office to clear the air. We were all sat in there. The place was crammed, twenty of us sitting on chairs, on the desk, with standing room only at the back. We watched the tape, and, as Roy would claim, parts of it had been blown out of all proportion. And as the manager would argue, some of it wasn't exactly the message you wanted broadcast on MUTV at a time when the team was struggling.

Roy had gone for it, but in his eyes only in the way that he always speaks his mind. The difference was this was on tape and obviously a source of embarrassment to the club at a time when the team was under pressure and the fans were agitated. Moreover, it had been pulled which had led to huge media headlines.

Anyway, the tape finished and the talking began – which is when things got really bad. It didn't take long for the conversation to get heated. Very heated.

Some time during the exchange I realised it was all over. Now that he's been a manager, Roy would understand himself that there was no coming back.

Roy being Roy, there was no embarrassment about that. He

was willing to live by the sword and die by it. He'd said his piece, he'd got it off his chest, and he'd take the consequences, however drastic.

Things went quiet for a few days, and there was the happy distraction of beating Chelsea, which at least kept the fans at bay. But the calm was misleading. Roy and the manager weren't speaking to each other, and it couldn't go on like that.

As Roy prepared to make his comeback with me in the reserves, one of the backroom staff told him he wasn't playing. He must have known the end was imminent.

The next day, the boss wanted everyone out on the training pitch, even those like me who were injured. Shortly beforehand, he pulled me and Quinton Fortune aside and said, 'Look, Roy has left the club.'

Even having witnessed everything, the words still came as a shock. 'Did it have to come to that?' I said.

'Yes, it's best for everybody. We've both agreed, it's done with.'

Roy had gone and he wouldn't be back. I texted him: 'I'm really sorry what's happened.' And I genuinely was, because there wasn't a player at United who could match Roy's influence in my time at the club. If I'd been a young kid growing up as a fan in that era, Roy Keane would have been my hero. I feel blessed to have played with him.

He was a great player, beyond question; a midfielder of extraordinary tenacity and box-to-box dynamism, with a ferocious tackle and an underrated ability to use the ball astutely. But perhaps his greatest gift was to create a standard of performance which demanded the very best from his team. You would look at him busting a gut and feel that you'd be betraying him if you didn't give everything yourself.

When he became a manager, you would hear about some

furore when he dropped a player for bad timekeeping, but I would think, 'Well, why not?' He's not asking players to be Pelé, he's asking them to turn up on time. And that is the sort of basic standard we had drummed into us.

Of course Roy got into a few scrapes in his time and the manager did give him a bit of latitude because of the player he was.

Roy didn't get on with all the players. There were clashes of personality – with Teddy Sheringham, among others. Occasionally he went too far. He went for Phil at Middlesbrough one day. Phil had made some small mistake and Roy went up and shoved him. But at least he apologised afterwards. Roy could say sorry. He was seriously intense but never arrogant or overbearing.

He's one of those rare characters you meet who is like a pan of boiling water, constantly simmering for twenty years. It's like they are constantly on the bubble. The manager is similar. I look at men like that in awe and wonder how they aren't having heart attacks. You're exhausted just looking at them, but they are the highest achievers.

The manager has said that he saw Roy as an incarnation of himself out on the pitch. But it would be selling both short if you limited the comparison to eruptions of anger. They are both bright, sharp men who have never stopped changing and learning. They are quick-witted. Their minds are alert.

Roy's got a great, dark sense of humour. You never knew what was going to come out of his mouth. He kept you on your toes. He used to make me laugh all the time. One day I was texting around a new mobile phone number. Roy replied straight away, 'So what.' Typical.

People say he overstepped the mark on occasion; he

criticised our own fans with the prawn sandwich remark, he slaughtered his own teammates on a few notable occasions. But if people found that shocking, it's only because it is so rare to find anyone in football willing to speak his mind. I didn't always agree with the way Roy was but I had huge respect for the footballer and the man. He is one of the true greats of this, or any, era.

A few weeks later the manager sat me down and offered me the armband. Captain of United. I've never been one for overstating the importance of captaincy. It wasn't going to make me a better player, or a different person. But it was a massive honour for a lad who'd spent his youth sitting in the K-Stand.

There's no particular task that comes with being captain. It's not as though you have to make a pre-match speech. That's the manager's job. Mostly it's just an honour, a great honour. My only regret was how I got it.

So we moved on, like we always do at United. Another legend out of the door. It happens even to the very best of them.

Things would get worse before they got better. My first game as captain was in December, away at Benfica in the Champions League, and it couldn't have been more traumatic. We needed to win to stay in Europe, but in that big, noisy stadium we went down 2–1. Ronaldo was hauled off after a stinker.

It was our worst performance in Europe since I'd been in the youth team. People were openly questioning whether the manager had finally lost it. The doubts were getting to all of us. Giggsy and I chatted about whether we would ever find our way back. We weren't panicking, but it wasn't easy to see us winning another title, never mind a Champions League.

Further embarrassment followed in January 2006 when we drew 0–0 at Burton Albion in the FA Cup. The manager had to throw on Rooney and Ronaldo in the second half as we struggled against no-hopers.

About all we had to celebrate was a victory over Liverpool, with a late goal from Rio, which is why I went berserk in my celebrations, running towards the travelling supporters over in one corner at Old Trafford. It was a release of so much pressure – a respite from all our problems. The FA saw it differently, and charged me with misconduct.

It was ridiculous. Since when had celebrating a goal become a crime? As I wrote in my column in *The Times*, 'Being a robot, devoid of passion and spirit, is obviously the way forward for the modern-day footballer.'

The whole thing became even more laughable when I ended up giving evidence to the FA disciplinary panel via video link from an office in Manchester. I couldn't believe my ears when some old blazer asked me whether there had been any 'sexual connotations' in my pumped-fist gestures to the Liverpool fans. Sexual connotations?

I was fined £5,000.

The punishment was a joke, but I'd pay the money again and again to have that feeling. That's what I played the game for, those moments when you erupt in joy. A last-minute winner for United gives you the most unbelievable high.

The FA could fine me all they like but I'd never lose the edge that came with playing against Liverpool and I never wanted to. I know the manager felt that it had affected my game in a couple of matches, believing I'd made mistakes trying too hard. In one team talk before we went to Anfield in February, he went out of his way to tell me to chill out. 'It's all right this "Gary Neville is a Red and he hates Scousers" stuff but it's no good if you make mistakes, if you give goals away. Relax, do your job, and play it like it's any other match. No one's going to die out there.'

A month after my goal celebration, we walked out at Anfield. I expected plenty of abuse but I hadn't foreseen Harry Kewell, of all people, clattering into me almost straight from the kick-off. Kewell was trying to get in with the Liverpool crowd who'd never warmed to him and he'd decided to get stuck in for the first time in his life.

'Fuck me, you're a right hard-man now,' I said, picking myself up off the floor. 'Has someone given you a courage pill?'

Defeat to Liverpool that day knocked us out of the FA Cup. We'd been kicked out of the Champions League before Christmas for the first time and Chelsea were waltzing away with a second title under Mourinho.

We were reduced to the Carling Cup if the season wasn't going to end trophyless. For a club of United's stature and expectations, this was a long way to have fallen in a couple of seasons. But history would show that the green shoots of recovery sprouted with that 4–0 victory over Wigan Athletic in Cardiff.

For Rooney, who scored twice, it was his first taste of silverware. It might not have been the trophy he'd dreamt of, but it was a step towards building a new team. And there were more signs of improvement when we won eight of the next nine matches. It was a return to the sort of form we'd come to expect at United.

Lads like Fletch, O'Shea and Wazza were becoming noisier. They were throwing their weight around, and they'd come to take over the dressing room. Old ones like me and Giggsy would have to take a back seat.

There was another important indicator that the young brigade was taking over when Ruud departed. The manager had left him out of the Carling Cup final, preferring Louis Saha, which signalled the beginning of the end.

Ruud had been unsettled for a while, getting angry in training. He was having a go at a few of the younger players, and he was certainly having a negative effect on Ronaldo. Ruud had often been frustrated at Cristiano not delivering an early ball. He'd throw his hands up in the air. One day the final straw came when he gave Cristiano a shove in training. However justified his complaints about this young, erratic talent, you could see it affected Cristiano.

He'd always had this selfish streak, Ruud. He'd tell you straight himself: if the team won 4–0 and he didn't score he'd be pissed off. That was part of his make-up, part of what made him such a great striker. But Ronaldo was the coming man.

Ruud was the greatest goalscorer I'd played with; I rated him better than Shearer. Both of them were superbly accurate, rarely wasting a shooting opportunity, but I thought Ruud had better feet. He could tie up a defence even when he played in isolation. Knowing Ruud, he probably preferred to be on his own up front so no one could nick his chances.

But now he was gone, in the same season as Roy, marking

a massive shift in the team. The manager, once again, had shown that he was willing to make the big, brave decisions that kept the club moving. He'd cleared the space for Rooney and Ronaldo to thrive. But whether we'd improve enough to catch Chelsea and end a run that now stretched to three seasons without the title remained to be seen.

20

Sven

It's gutting to look back on the 2006 World Cup finals as my last international competition. This was no way to go out, at a tournament that will always be remembered more for WAGs than for football. And for yet more penalty misses.

How we allowed the WAGs stories to dominate I will never understand. It was the one farcical issue of Sven's reign. What people overlooked was that this situation had been brewing in 2004. Wives and girlfriends had been regular visitors to the team hotel in Portugal. If it was a minor irritation to me then, it had grown into a monster by 2006.

The whole issue of celebrity wives was something I couldn't get my head around. There were people who saw a tournament not as a series of football matches but as a photo opportunity. Sven wanted a relaxed atmosphere, and that's how it started, but by the time we arrived in Germany it had become ridiculously carefree.

I'd never exactly been a fan of the whole *OK!* and *Hello!* culture, and here we were right in the thick of it. Particularly for someone brought up at United, where the manager always insisted on private and professional lives being kept well apart, to walk around Baden Baden was a joke. The families were staying in the same hotel as some of the press, which was ridiculous to start with.

I went round there to visit on the first day and saw a dozen paparazzi hanging outside. I swore then I wouldn't go back. I wasn't in Germany to have a lens shoved in my face when I was trying to have a sandwich with my family.

The more I saw, the more annoyed I became that my own family were there. I made them aware of my concerns, and my reservations about the motives of quite a few of the travelling party. As the manager, Sven had to take the blame for allowing this situation to get out of hand. But it didn't say much for the players, or their families, that it had gone so far.

It's hard enough playing for England without distractions. You need to be clear-headed. At the end of the day it's not a bad life with all the perks that come with the job. There are downsides, and one of those is spending a lot of time away from your family, but the rewards are huge for the top players. That's the compensation for being on the road all the time.

It put me in a bad mood every time I heard players talking about how they had to catch up with their wife or girlfriend or kids. I hope many of them are embarrassed looking back. You are away for a month, and it's not easy. I can understand people missing their kids. But there is a time and a place during a tournament for visiting families, and I'd say strictly for one afternoon only after each match.

There was one player a couple of days before the

quarter-final against Portugal saying that it was his daughter's birthday and he had to go to the family hotel because she'd made a cake. Two or three other players took that as an opportunity to sneak out too. It got so bad that a couple of us went to see Sven and said, 'Look, we've got to stop this, we've got a World Cup quarter-final coming up.' The mentality was ridiculous. It would never have happened at United.

My worries about the focus within the squad were confirmed in the massage room one morning when I heard one player whining about a harmless piece in a newspaper that had criticised him. I had real misgivings. If one of our best players was fretting about some stupid article, what chance did we have when it came to the real business?

As well as the WAGs, I was worried that the team had become stale under Sven. I'd thought it was right to continue with him after Euro 2004. We'd been through a few managers in quick succession with Venables, Hoddle and Keegan. None of them had lasted more than one tournament and the FA were looking for stability. Right up to the moment when Rooney broke his metatarsal against Portugal at Euro 2004, there had been only positive momentum.

But we were still way too reliant on an automatic first XI. The big names were guaranteed to play rather than the best team. The experiment during qualifying, when Becks was used in the 'quarterback' role in central midfield against Wales and Northern Ireland, proved the point. The team was put out of shape to accommodate the big players. I had no problem with a three-man midfield – in fact I wanted it – but this seemed to me like a fudge to get around the issue of how to keep Becks, Gerrard and Lampard in the same eleven.

I missed those qualifiers through injury, but I was watching on telly and I could see the frustration among the players. None of the performances leading up to the tournament were great. Too many players were concerned about their own role rather than how it all gelled together.

We had a midfield quartet of Beckham, Gerrard, Lampard and Cole, with Owen and Rooney up front, and they all wanted to be the match-winners. They probably didn't realise it themselves. But the problem wasn't being addressed because there was a first XI, and that was how it was going to stay.

I expressed my concerns to Steve McClaren, Sven's right-hand man, in the run-up to the tournament. 'We need to build a team. We need to get players in there that are going to gel this together. We can't all be generals.'

Our over-reliance on an established first XI was summed up when the whole country fretted over Michael and Wazza as they both raced back from injuries. Michael had barely played for five months while Wayne, who'd broken his metatarsal as late as April, was never going to be able to start the tournament. It was understandable that the manager should give two big players every chance to recover, but it did emphasise how little faith he had in their understudies.

When Sven named his squad, there was another problem, this time self-inflicted. He left out Jermain Defoe – an odd decision that looked foolish when he was superb in pre-tournament training. In Defoe's place was Theo Walcott, a kid I'd barely heard of. He was seventeen and hadn't even played a game for Arsenal. Part of me was excited about the idea of a precocious kid with explosive pace, because that's exactly what the team needed. But at training it was clear that he was still just a kid. The World Cup wasn't the place to throw him in.

Sad to say, most of my fears were realised. We played poorly in the opening victory over Paraguay, slow and laboured. Next we beat Trinidad and Tobago, but the team was ponderous, with Rooney still racing to be fit.

I injured my calf in training, which gave Sven a problem at right-back. It showed alarmingly muddled thinking when he considered Becks at full-back. The plan struck me as a halfway house. He wanted to get more pace on the right flank from Aaron Lennon, which was the right call, but he didn't want to drop Becks.

Sven was clearly worried about leaving out one of his big players, whether that was Becks, Lampard, Gerrard or Owen. But it had to be done if it would benefit the team, and I definitely believed it would help keep the side on their toes. But because we'd become so used to this first eleven playing all the time, to leave out one of the stars had become a big deal.

I thought we needed to freshen up both the line-up and the formation. Playing three in midfield, and using the whole squad, would have meant seeing more of Michael Carrick. He's a player who rarely gets acclaim even from his own supporters at United, but I felt he could have made England tick. He's unselfish that way. People will argue about his calibre until the day he retires but I've played with him and I know he could have done a good job for England. He's like Darren Anderton, the type of player who can take to international football because he is not hurried in his game. Of course many people valued Lampard and Gerrard more than

Carrick, but as a pair they'd rarely performed well together. We had to be adaptable and find a functioning team.

We should have seen more of Owen Hargreaves, too. Carrick and Hargreaves could have provided the platform for our two world-class talents, Rooney and Gerrard. If that meant leaving out others, so be it. Rooney and Gerrard needed to be the focal point of the team. They were our match-winners.

These would have been brave decisions, and that's what the very best managers like Mourinho, Capello and Ferguson do. They don't worry about getting it wrong.

I had all these thoughts, and passed some of them on to Steve. Whether he discussed it with Sven I don't know. That was his call. It wasn't my job to go banging on the manager's door despite my mounting worries.

But things just got worse. We finished top of the group by drawing 2–2 against Sweden but lost Michael to a snapped cruciate ligament. Now we'd really pay for the decision to leave Defoe behind.

We struggled to a 1–0 victory over Ecuador in the last sixteen, this time with Hargreaves at right-back, but we were up against it as we faced a quarter-final rematch with Portugal. I was back in the team, but I wasn't convinced by the eleven selected. In a 4–5–1, Rooney was isolated up front. Gerrard and Lampard were in poor form and not in great moods by now. Hargreaves had a magnificent game in central midfield but it was another laboured performance. We lacked pace and penetration.

Walcott hadn't played all tournament, and Sven didn't think now was the time to bring him on, even though with twenty minutes to go we were crying out for fresh legs, the element of surprise.

Then Wayne was sent off.

He's not exactly the hardest person in the world to wind up is Wazza. He reacted to a heavy challenge by Ricardo Carvalho and stuck a boot in. There was no arguing with the decision. A big fuss was made afterwards about Ronaldo winking, as if to say, 'Good job, boys, we've got him sent off.' I didn't see it, and it wouldn't have made any difference if I had. No complaints. Wazza had kicked out, wink or no wink.

So we came to penalties, again, and in the light of our poor form and our past record I can't say I was confident. When you go to spot-kicks, you try to get that sense of whether a team believes in itself. And as a group of players we'd been in this nightmare scenario before and been beaten. I knew exactly what was going to happen and, sure enough, we missed a couple and, inevitably, Ronaldo smashed his in.

It was over. My last shot at the World Cup. I never get too upset at the end of football matches. The disappointment normally hits me later. But I stood on that pitch in Gelsenkirchen feeling desolate. That's it, another chance gone. It's never going to happen now. Same old story. Why don't we ever get it right? Regrets, regrets – and the biggest of all, even more than the defeat itself, was the way we'd gone out in Germany.

It's the worst possible type of defeat, knowing you could have done more. At United we never leave anything in the changing room. We give our all. We've had some big defeats, disastrous nights. But if I have a vision of United losing it is with ten men in the opposition penalty box, the keeper coming up for a corner, guns blazing like Butch Cassidy and the Sundance Kid. You might still lose, you might go home in tears, but you've given it your best shot. With England it's a damp squib. I was gutted as I walked off the field in Gelsenkirchen. More than that, I was angry.

It might sound contradictory given the mistakes I've outlined, but I was sad to see the back of Sven. I liked him and I would have been delighted for him if he'd enjoyed success with England. His final campaign was a massive disappointment, and he should have made braver decisions. But I don't go along with the idea that Sven should forever be remembered for blowing a 'Golden Generation'. Three quarter-finals is a respectable record, and I'm not convinced we ever quite had the depth in our squad to win a major tournament.

Those who have hammered Sven for his mistakes should also give him the credit he deserves for turning us around in the first place. Playing under him, it was easy to see why he had enjoyed success around Europe. The players liked him and respected him. But, like us, he'd just fallen a bit short.

Sven had given us stability and he'd given us decent results. Not great, but acceptable. Three quarter-finals – I'm not exactly proud of it, and I think we did have a squad at Euro 2004 that should have made the final four. But to dismiss Sven as a failed England manager isn't remotely fair to him.

Sven was a bit wet around the eyes when he gave his farewell speech in Germany. He wasn't the only man standing down. Becks had decided to quit the captaincy. It was a big decision for him because he loved the job. He adored it, in fact, and it had made him a better player. But things had also reached the point where he needed to get the pressure off his back. He needed to be liberated. People were asking whether the armband made him untouchable. It was detracting from the fact that he was still a great football player who was in the squad on merit.

We'd talked on the coach back to the hotel after the game. I told him to take his time, but I think he'd already made his mind up to stand down.

He had to fight back the tears when it came to reading out his statement. Becks has always cared about his country, passionately.

21

Ronaldo – Phenomenon

It's a very subjective judgement to name the best player of my time at United. I'd not hesitate to declare that Scholesy is as good as any, but how do you weigh up his class against the longevity of Ryan Giggs and the desire of Roy Keane? The brilliance of Peter Schmeichel and the charisma of Eric Cantona? I've been lucky enough to play with quite a few true greats of the game. But if it's sheer match-winning quality we are talking about, Cristiano Ronaldo shades it.

He's a great lad, Cristiano. Some see him as a prima donna. And it's true, you've never seen a guy spend so long in front of the mirror. He'd never arrive, or leave, without making sure he looked immaculate in his tight-fitting Dolce & Gabbana T-shirt. If he wasn't a footballer, he'd definitely have been a model. If you preen yourself like he does, you'd better be good. And he is a phenomenon.

In the dressing room, he'd have all the players transfixed

with his skills. He'd spend twenty minutes most days taking the piss with his tricks. He'd do stuff so good I couldn't even work out how he did it – like pretending to kick a ball in your face and, as you dived for cover, dragging it back on to his foot so you looked an idiot. He could disco-dance and juggle a ball at the same time. He loved the ball, he loved the game. He'd have fitted right into our old youth team because he relished hard work and practice. And you don't become a great player like Cristiano without a serious work ethic.

Take free-kicks. He didn't have a dead-ball technique when he first came to United but he developed that incredible dipping shot off the laces of his boot, toes pointing downward, through hours and hours of hard work and perseverance on the training ground.

And he was brave. He always wanted the ball, even when he was being booted up the arse by a defender.

The only thing that annoyed me about Cristiano was that I must have done a thousand decoy runs and he never passed it to me once. I joked to him once that he would finish me off, taking years off my career by letting me run miles and miles dragging full-backs out of position. But how could I complain when I saw everything that he achieved?

His talent was never in doubt, but it was after the 2006 World Cup and that wink – perhaps even because of the wink – that he really began to play his best. He'd go on to enjoy more prolific campaigns, but I look back on 2006/07 as his most effective. It was when we truly saw the blossoming of his genius.

Maybe what happened at the World Cup focused his mind, although I didn't have a problem with him, and nor did Wayne. After our defeat to Portugal and Wazza's red card, I'd gone into their dressing room to wish Cristiano all the best in the tournament. Why not? What had he done wrong? He'd winked. So what? He was trying to win the World Cup.

There were no problems around the United camp, just media hype and stick from fans around the country, but Ronaldo responded in the best way possible. Before the World Cup he'd had excess in his game: too many touches, too much fannying about on the ball, not enough telling delivery. But then a penny dropped. All of a sudden his selection of pass, his decision-making when it came to beating the man or lay- ing it off, became so much more ruthless and consistent. He was maturing mentally and physically. He'd filled out into a muscular lad, with a prize-fighter's build, and that helped him grow into a roving menace.

He was no longer just a winger but a phenomenal centre- forward who could batter centre-halves in the air. In fact, it is a Ronaldo header which I regard as the greatest goal I've ever seen in a United shirt. You might be surprised at the choice.

It was in a Champions League game in Roma's Olympic Stadium in April 2008. The move was sharp, with some slick passing and a great turn by Rooney, but it was the finish that was just sensational. Scholesy hung a cross in the air and, to be honest, it didn't seem to be aimed at anyone in particular. But then Cristiano came charging into the box like a runaway train. He leapt like Michael Jordan and headed it like Joe Jordan. He was a long way out, near the penalty spot, but it flew in like a bullet. Cristiano had turned himself from a prancing winger into probably the greatest attacking force in world football. Lionel Messi has his incredible gifts, but Cristiano could be devastating on the ground and in the air.

The most significant improvement was that he'd become

more team-orientated – perhaps because he realised how much United wanted him when he was being vilified elsewhere. Just as Old Trafford loved Becks even more after his dismissal at the 1998 World Cup and all the abuse he took around the country, the fans took Ronaldo to heart when they heard him get so much stick. They saw how he responded and they embraced him as United fans only do with very special players.

He deserved to have a team built around him even though he wouldn't set about his defensive duties as diligently as Rooney. He wasn't interested in sprinting back, like Wazza will do, even in the ninetieth minute. At United, attackers have always been expected to put in a shift tracking back. But sometimes, very rarely, you come across a player who deserves to be indulged. Releasing Ronaldo from defensive duties was more than compensated for by the energy he saved for his most effective work at the other end.

Previously we'd get frustrated as a team when he swapped wings without plan or consultation, but we learnt to use his versatility as a strength. He had become the main man.

Winning the league in 2007, after three seasons without the trophy, was massive. As rewarding as any of the championships I won. It was a huge achievement for the club after all the doubts of the previous few years. And, personally, the first six months of that season was probably my best form, aside from the Treble season.

The team was brilliantly balanced. Nemanja Vidic joined us and formed a brilliant partnership with Rio. Patrice Evra came from France – another shrewd move by the boss. We had top new signings, we had experienced players with plenty to prove after three seasons without winning the Premiership, and Rooney and Ronaldo hitting their peak. After all the turmoil of the last few years without a title, after all the questioning of the boss and the players, we were embarking on a fantastic new era – the most successful in the club's history.

We got off to a flyer by thrashing Fulham 5–1 in the opening game, and for the first time in a couple of seasons we immediately put Chelsea under pressure. I'd surprised a few people by saying I was delighted when they signed Michael Ballack and Andrei Shevchenko – the rumblings that those players had been foisted on Mourinho were music to my ears. Anything to disrupt Chelsea's machine.

By the time we hit Christmas we'd lost only two league matches – a big improvement on previous campaigns. Things were on the up, and Chelsea weren't the same team. Our only problem came off the pitch when, in good spirits, we turned up for our annual Christmas piss-up in the Great John Street Hotel. By the end of the night, Jonny Evans, our young Irish defender, had been arrested.

The way it was written up you'd think the whole party was some kind of wild orgy. I can confirm it was one hell of a bash, but Christmas do's always are at United. I pride myself on my professionalism, but I'm also pretty proud of our parties.

Footballers' Christmas parties have become a symbol of all that's wrong in the game – the drink, the lairyness, overpaid players acting like big-time Charlies. But I've always believed they are an important part of the team experience.

In the early days we used to go to the Grapes in Manchester, the pub owned by Vera Duckworth. We'd get my guitar teacher along and have a singsong all afternoon. That was the highlight for me, the afternoon in the pub with a guitar and a pianist singing cover versions, before the drink set in and we started egging each other on with United chants.

All good, harmless fun, even if some of the foreign lads used to think it wasn't quite their cup of tea, or pint of lager. They might go to the casino for the afternoon before meeting us later. But I wouldn't have missed those nights for the world.

In recent years we'd gone a bit more upmarket, to the Great John Street Hotel. I'd organised it, thinking the place would get us further away from the prying lenses of the paparazzi. Yes, there were lots of girls but there were also a lot of single, eligible blokes. It certainly wasn't the sleaze pit some papers made it out to be, and it was a total stitch-up for poor Jonny. We knew right from the start that he'd done nothing wrong. The allegations were unfounded. But by then the story was all over the papers.

In the manager's mind, the damage was done. He called the whole squad in and started screaming and shouting that he was going to fine every single player, first team and reserves, a week's wages. I recognised that the club had been embarrassed by the bad publicity but, being the union rep, I tried in vain to argue that it was unfair to punish everyone. I had organised the party and felt I should take the rap, and I knew Jonny had been stitched up.

I tried to argue my case with the boss on a couple of occasions after this, but he remained firm on this one. As far as he was concerned, there would be no more Christmases.

It wasn't my only bust-up with the boss that season. The first knock-out round in the Champions League took us to Lille, and there was some tension between the manager and his opposite number, Claude Puel. It was an edgy match which boiled over when Giggsy scored with a quick free-kick while Lille were still assembling their wall. It was entirely legal, a sharp piece of thinking, but the French were furious. After protesting in vain to the referee, they started walking off. I couldn't believe it.

'Come on, get on with the fucking game,' I said to their captain, following him towards the side of the pitch.

The next thing I knew the manager was charging down the touchline shouting at me. 'Neville, what are you doing? Get back on!' He had really snapped.

As far as I was concerned I'd been doing the sensible thing, trying to get everyone to get on with a game we were now leading. But he was furious.

So I snapped back – 'Fuck off' – and walked away.

Now, I've said 'fuck off' a million times to a lot of different people, but this was a first. I'd never said it to the manager before. I knew as the game resumed and we played on that I wasn't going to get away with it.

We won the match, and the boss was waiting for me afterwards. He was apoplectic, just as I'd expected.

Back at the club, Giggsy tried to get me to apologise. I hadn't yet had an opportunity when I got a call to go and see the boss in his office. I guessed it was for another bollocking. I wasn't wrong. He blitzed me, fined me a week's wages, then sent me out of his office.

We were playing at Fulham at the weekend and I had to laugh when he took me all the way down to London and didn't play me. He didn't even put me on the bench. I knew exactly why – to teach me a lesson – but the thing about the manager is that he'll always give you an explanation for leaving you out. It's one of his great traits. You hear stories about some clubs where the teamsheet goes up an hour before a game and that's the first a player knows about being dropped. If you started the previous game and he's about to drop you, the boss will always call you into his office and tell you why, without fail. He's a brilliant communicator like that. You might not like the explanation, but at least you've been told, to your face.

'I need some height so I'm going with Wes in the team and O'Shea on the bench,' he said to me that day. 'I need the tall lads against Fulham.'

I just started laughing. 'Boss, you played me at centre-half against Wimbledon's Crazy Gang when I was twenty-one. I've marked Duncan Ferguson in an FA Cup Final.'

'No, Gary. They're dangerous from set-pieces, Fulham.'

Imagine how chuffed I was when we got down there and they had Alexei Smertin on the left flank, all four foot six inches of him, or whatever he is.

'I could have played you after all,' the manager said in the dressing room, looking at their teamsheet. He was laughing.

Three days later he took me down to Reading and left me in the stands again. The seventeenth man. 'What have you brought me for?' I said. 'I could have trained back at the club.'

The trip was a total waste of time, but the boss had asserted his authority. I wouldn't be swearing at him again. He'd slapped me down hard, as he was never slow to do with anyone who stepped out of line, particularly those of us who'd come through the youth ranks.

It always felt like he was harsher with us than with the players he signed because we were the kids he'd brought through. Perhaps he took it more personally if we did something rebellious. I didn't feel that I had done much wrong in Lille but I knew it wasn't worth pursuing with the manager – not unless I wanted to spend even longer out of the team.

Even through my frustration I realised the importance of the win the lads claimed at Fulham in my absence. A 2–1 win at Craven Cottage at the end of February is not the sort of match many people will remember as pivotal. But it was. We were in danger of throwing away a couple of crucial points when Ronaldo popped up with a brilliant solo goal with seconds left on the clock. Great players make decisive interventions at critical times. And this was one of many times that season when Ronaldo made the difference.

The manager recalled me a week later for the trip to Anfield. It was another huge win, one of those matches that clinches titles. We survived endless pressure from Liverpool before John O'Shea popped up with a late winner, not just over our old enemy but right in front of the Kop. As I told him afterwards, 'You just lived my dream.'

We were buoyant, champions-elect, mostly thanks to Ronaldo. I never saw George Best play, but I said at the time I'd be amazed if he was as good as Cristiano. And the way he carried us in 2006/07 marks it out as his best season. I felt I owed him my championship medal in a way that had only really happened before with Schmeichel and Cantona in 1995/96.

It was a great feeling winning the title for the first time since 2002/03, claiming it back after all the doubts. Only eighteen months earlier everyone had been wondering if it was all over in terms of United domination. There had been calls for the manager to quit. There were times when, even inside the dressing room, we wondered whether long-term decline had set in. Chelsea had spent all that money, they'd looked so dominant, so we had a massive celebration now that we were back on top. To win the championship that year was un- believable, up there with my first in 1996 and the Treble in 1999 as the best of my career.

The disappointment was the injury ten games before the end of the season which meant that I had to hobble to collect the trophy with Giggsy. Initially I'd just been gutted to have my season interrupted. I'd been feeling brilliant, enjoying my football and the captaincy. It was a joy to play. It took a while for the seriousness of the injury to hit me.

At the moment it happened, in March at home to Bolton, I couldn't have known how bad it was. I just knew it hurt. Early in the game, Rio played a ball behind me and I dilly- dallied getting it under control and had to take a couple of touches. I could feel Gary Speed coming at me fast so I went to play it down the line. Bang! That's when he nailed me.

It wasn't the best of tackles – more man than ball – but he was only doing what a lot of us try to do: put in a hard tackle early on, particularly away from home. But the full weight of his body landed on my ankle. I knew straight away that my ligaments had been damaged.

It was my wife's birthday that evening and we were due out for a meal, but I couldn't move. I felt terrible. I had ice on to reduce the swelling but the ankle seemed to be getting bigger and more painful. In the end I called the club doctor and asked him to bring some painkillers. 'I think my ankle's going to explode,' I told him through the pain.

I still thought it would be a case of ten to twelve weeks out, not seventeen months before I started to play regularly again. I was even trying to get back for the Cup final, the first game at the new Wembley, when we'd lose to Chelsea. In early May I went out to try and train with one of the physios. I lasted about three minutes.

There was something wrong inside the ankle so I went for an operation to wash it out. They removed some floating junk and shaved two bones. Eager to get back for the 2007/08 season, I worked every day in rehab. Even on holiday I was in the gym.

But when we started pre-season, something still wasn't right. I felt I was running differently and I kept picking up all sorts of problems – in my calves, my groin, my thighs. It was one problem after another. I'd get fit enough to join the reserves but then something else would go.

When I was younger, I used to look at David May or Ronny Johnsen or Louis Saha and think, 'It can't be that bad. Can't they just run it off? They look fit to me.' Now I was the one with the ice pack after training, in an ice bath, or asking the doctor for a trolley load of anti-inflammatories.

I'd never been particularly sympathetic to players who were ruled out but now I began to realise that it's hard work being injured. It's a strain on your time, your confidence. While everyone else is in a good mood going into a new season, an injured player is lonely in the gym. And then there is the constant risk of set-backs.

Just before Christmas I played a few reserve games. I'd been training properly for several weeks. Carlos saw me one morning. 'Great to have you back, Gary.'

We were training one Sunday morning, a practice match. I felt a bit odd for the first twenty minutes. Then I went to do some running and my calf just pinged. A muscle tear. That was another five weeks, but it was the damage to morale that was worse. It was another five weeks on top of eight months.

People would try to cheer me up. It's only a little strain. But I'd just be thinking about how I hadn't recovered from the first injury yet. It was two steps forward, four back.

It reached the point where I actually thought I didn't want to come back in 2007/08, even though I was close by the spring. The lads were enjoying such a great season and I didn't want to be a risk. No manager in his right mind was going to disrupt a team going for a Treble, and that's what we were chasing.

I was thrilled for the club. I don't doubt there are some players who've been dropped or injured and hope the team gets beaten, or the player selected in their position has a bad game. With England I'd be certain that has happened. But I think the manager knows the sort of characters he has at United, and there have been very few bitter, jealous types. Don't be feeling sorry for yourself, we'd been told since we were kids whenever we were dropped or injured. I was chuffed to see the team thriving without me.

I really wasn't sure I was ready to come back when the manager stuck me on the bench. It was April 2008, fully thirteen months after the injury, when I came on in the European Cup quarter-final second leg against AS Roma with the tie well won. 'You're going on in central midfield,' the manager said. I hadn't expected that, or the standing ovation as I ran on to the pitch.

I was embarrassed as much as overwhelmed by the reception. All this fuss for me? I just wanted to get stuck in, to get hold of the ball, to calm my nerves. But it was a lovely thing for the fans to give me such a welcome back. It had been a long slog, but that one moment justified all those long, lonely hours in the gym.

Those nine minutes were all I played in the entire season as, wisely, the manager decided to stick with the players who were carrying us towards a league and European Double. If it hadn't been for a silly home defeat to Portsmouth in the FA Cup I might have been forced to revise my opinion that the Treble would never be repeated.

After beating Roma, we were through to the semi-finals to face Barcelona – and what a test this would be with the talents of Eto'o, Iniesta, Deco and Messi. Credit to Carlos. Beating Barcelona was his finest hour as the manager's assistant. This was when his technical expertise, the way he'd taught us to be a more adaptable European side, paid dividends.

For years, training had always been based around how we'd play, but this time Carlos was obsessive about stopping Barcelona. We'd never seen such attention to detail. He put sit-up mats on the training pitch to mark exactly where he wanted our players to be to the nearest yard. We rehearsed time and again, sometimes walking through the tactics slowly with the ball in our hands.

The instructions were simple enough. Ronaldo up front tying them up, Carlos Tevez dropping on to Yaya Touré every time he got the ball. Let their centre-halves have it. They couldn't hurt us. With Ji-Sung Park and Rooney out wide, the full-backs had two hard-working wingers to help shackle Messi and Iniesta. But the really complex part was for Scholes and Carrick. Carlos had worked out precise positions for each of them, depending on the other's whereabouts. They'd have to pivot in tandem. It would require huge concentration but it was necessary to stop Deco and Xavi feeding the ball through to Eto'o.

Barcelona were such a complex team to counter, and we had to close down all these potential lines of attack. They were a better footballing team than us. Suffocation was a necessary tactic.

The hope for the first leg in the Nou Camp was that Ronaldo could catch them on the break, but it didn't work out that way after he missed an early penalty. Instead it was a defensive masterclass, orchestrated by Carlos.

The second in command can have a great effect on the team. The manager puts a huge amount of trust in his coaches. We learnt from Brian Kidd, from Steve McClaren, and from Carlos Queiroz. We suffered in the periods when we didn't have coaches of that calibre. Carlos could come over a bit dry at times, but we learnt to control games under him.

After a 0–0 draw in the Nou Camp, we came back to Old Trafford in good heart. The return was a nail-biter but then Scholesy hit a wonder goal into the top corner. A great strike from a great player at a vital moment. Sheer class. We'd stopped Barcelona from scoring in 180 minutes which very, very few teams have done over the last five years. And we were back in the European Cup final for the first time in nine years.

The night before we played Chelsea in Moscow I had that feeling of magic in the air. Thinking it might be close, I went through our penalty takers. I fancied our chances; though, with hindsight, I know things might have been very different if John Terry hadn't slipped.

I felt sure we were going to win and I couldn't have hand-picked a more fitting player than Giggsy to score the decisive penalty on the night he made his 759th appearance for the club and surpassed Bobby Charlton's record. Like the 1999 final taking place on Sir Matt Busby's birthday, the wonderful thing about United is that you are always surrounded by this incredible history.

Later that night we presented Giggsy with a watch to mark his appearances record. Part of me wondered whether he should walk away from football there and then. How could you beat the perfection of an occasion like that? He'd become United's most decorated player, the club's greatest servant, and taken the winning kick in a European Cup final. How could you possibly top that?

But the reason he is a legend is that he never thinks of quitting. He was still in love with the game, and why give it up if you are playing brilliantly week after week?

It's been an incredible career, a one-off in English football. Everyone the world over rightly hails Paolo Maldini for his class and his incredible longevity. Well, Giggsy is our Maldini.

The only thing lacking in his CV is an appearance in a World Cup finals, but there's not a lot he could have done about that. Understandably, he used to get very ratty when people came up to him saying, 'Come and play for England.' There was this hope that he might switch because he'd played for England Schools, but Giggsy was born in Wales and is a hundred per cent Welsh.

There have been other long-serving players, but to have done it in his position, with the bravery to take the ball and to keep taking players on, is something extra special. He's been so intelligent, adjusting his game. He's learnt to play central midfield, second striker, even full-back.

You look back on how he began, as this flying winger right out on the touchline, and then think about how he managed to control matches from the heart of the pitch twenty years later. He's managed to remain relevant, and brilliant. Partly that's by being tough. He's got a steely way about him, Giggsy, on and off the pitch. I've hardly ever heard him raise his voice, but he doesn't need to. He's slight, but people know he's not to be messed with.

Anyone who plays until he is thirty-seven needs a bit of luck with injuries, but Giggsy has taken incredible care of his body. Me, Giggsy and Keano took up yoga together but Roy and I managed to fall out very quickly with the teacher. She got tired of me talking all the way through the classes. Giggsy has kept going, and he's looked after himself.

You talk about the great legends of United and Giggsy's up there with the very best. Busby, Ferguson, Charlton, Giggs – that's the quartet who sit at the top of this club. You can separate them from everybody else, with their longevity, their games and their medals, but also the way they embody everything that's great about United.

United is a club that values people and understands the importance of loyalty. Like any player Giggsy had his downturns, his losses of form and confidence, but he always came through. The club always backed him to come good. And he always did.

Our success in the Champions League was a monkey off the manager's back, too. This accusation that we had underachieved in Europe had stalked him all his career, before and after 1999. But in 2008 he joined that very select group of managers who have won the European Cup twice. Only Bob Paisley had beaten that. And while it had taken nine long years, the manager deserved every tribute.

We would go one better by winning the Fifa Club World Cup, too, in Japan, to become the best team in the world. It's a trophy that matters to the players, but I wish there was a format that worked better for the fans. In 1999 we beat Palmeiras, the champions of South America, in a one-off game, the Intercontinental Cup, but it felt strange playing it in Tokyo on neutral soil. It would have been a far better experience to play two legs, one at home and then the great experience of a truly hostile crowd in South America. Football is now a truly global game and I can understand why Fifa want to include teams from Asia and elsewhere, but maybe the tournament has to move around the world so that fans of every continent learn to love it. European supporters don't really get it, partly because it's screened out of their time zone, which is a great shame because to become the best team in the world is the highlight of a club career. For the players it is a massive achievement. You've had to win the Champions League just to qualify.

What made the 2008 triumphs so special was how the boss had moved with the times. If the 1994 team was obviously British and muscular, and the 1999 vintage a little more refined, by 2008 we'd taken on a continental feel. We might still play 4–4–2 at times but there was no comparison with a decade earlier. We had so much more variation. Sometimes our opponents wouldn't know who was centre-forward. Accused in the past of fielding a naive, gung-ho team, the manager had embraced new ideas.

A regular criticism from people who didn't understand how

we'd evolved was that we lacked a warrior, particularly in midfield. I'd hear the question 'Where is our Robson, our Keane, our leader?' But where is Barcelona's warrior? The idea that you need some battle-hardened hero does not stack up. What you need is good footballers. We had plenty of bite in players like Fletcher and Hargreaves and match-winning power in Scholes, Giggs, Rooney, Ronaldo and Tevez.

Of course we'd have loved another Keane, Ince, Robson. But it had become a different game, full of rotation, different strategies, more sophistication. We had a strong squad, good competition so that the players were all on their toes, and the spirit of adventure that runs through all the great United teams. And in Carlos the manager had found a coach whose knowledge (even if at times he bored us with his tactical talks) he could plunder and combine with his own natural aggression and boldness to build another great team.

There was no Treble, but comparisons with 1999 don't show much between the two sides. If I had to choose, I would say that the 1999 squad had a greater ability to pull off results through sheer force of will. But 2008 had more flair and versatility.

We could win playing our way but we could also stop the other team. We could adapt, which is what Arsenal have failed to do. After 2005 we never feared them because we knew exactly what to expect. The manager's approach to them was always the same: stop them, match them, then the football will come, and their heads will go. It was exactly what happened in the European Cup semi-final the following season. We frustrated them and then, bang!, on the counter. They are just too naive. They won't win trophies unless they wise up.

We had learnt, and in 2008 we were European champions again. That night I recalled a text Roy had sent me about six months after he left the club. 'Rooney and Ronaldo will win you the European Cup,' he wrote. Not a lot of people were giving us a prayer at that time. But he knew, as the manager did, that we had a squad full of outstanding players. And one borderline genius in Ronaldo.

22

Steve

I played in five tournaments for England, which is something to be proud of, but there have been times when I reflected on my international career and just thought, 'Well, that was a massive waste of time.'

Sorry for sounding sour, but my best mate got butchered in 1998, then my brother in 2000. The whole lot of us got it in the neck at other times. Sometimes we deserved it, but playing for England was one long rollercoaster: some ups and downs but also quite a few moments when you're not really sure if you are enjoying the ride.

It should be fantastic. Representing your country should be the best moments of your life. But there is no doubt that too many players spend too much time fearing the consequences of failure when they pull on an England shirt. The best managers – Terry, Sven in his early years, Capello in patches – have banished those fears for periods, but it doesn't take much to go wrong before the dread comes flooding back.

I was really struck by one meeting Steve McClaren organised with Bill Beswick, the sports psychologist, and the whole squad. I saw young players really affected, terrified of what was in front of them. A few of them were saying they weren't enjoying England at all. The team wasn't winning and they were getting slaughtered by the fans and the media.

Many supporters will argue that players need to be stronger than that if they want to play for their country. And perhaps they're right. But after my fourth international against Norway, I picked up the *Sun* and saw I'd been given 4/10. 'Nervous wreck,' it said. 'Totally out of his depth.' I actually thought I'd played well! I wouldn't be human if I didn't start doubting myself after that, particularly as a young player. Terry Venables rang me up and said, 'Honestly, Gary, I don't know how they've seen that. Don't worry about it.' But it's not easy to shrug off when you are inexperienced and haven't developed a thick skin.

You can't overestimate the impact the media can have at the national level because you're far more exposed playing for England than for your club. The criticism can eat into your confidence, and then the fans get influenced by the media. I've seen the cycle at work. You are loved at first, a fresh face on the scene. Then they start finding flaws. Then you are OK again, then you're past it, then you're valued for your experience, then you're finished. You should be tested playing for England, but some players struggle to get through that first dip. Have a bad start and they're on to you. And every time we don't win a tournament, it becomes a disastrous failure. We can never just lose. Someone has to be blamed.

This lurching rollercoaster was most violently demostrated with Becks. From one year to the next he could be superhero or arch villain. Boo him, love him, boo him again. Make him captain, strip him of the armband. It was like a soap opera in the national jersey. It was embarrassing. You might get the odd bit of dissent at United but never the crazy hysteria.

A healthy edge of nerves at club level would become fear at national level – a fear that if we lost the world was going to end. Too many players were frightened of what would be said or written about them, of making a mistake. And in my time we never got together a group of players who could quite cast off those inhibitions.

We got closest at Euro 96. We were a whisker away. We played close to our peak and had a squad, and manager, capable of winning a major tournament. Perhaps in 2004, too, but were we ever really a Golden Generation? We had some good players, and a few great ones. Cole, Rio, Becks and Gerrard could have played in any international team.

Steve is undoubtedly a world-class player and I wish he'd played for United. In fact I went on a personal tapping-up mission at Euro 2004 when I knew Chelsea were trying to take advantage of Liverpool being in turmoil.

'Come play for United,' I said one day when we were in the hotel. 'The fans will take to you in no time.'

He just laughed. 'I'll do it if you go to Anfield.'

He's a top, top player, Steve, but he has never quite shown how good when playing for England. Is that down to him, to the managers, to the expectations, or to the fact that we never had a great team around him?

You could write a whole book just trying to answer that question, but I think it involves several factors, on and off the pitch. For example, there's no doubt that the FA mishandled managerial appointments, letting Terry go way too easily and appointing Glenn Hoddle and Steve McClaren before they were ready. But would any manager in the world have turned us into England's first trophy-winners since 1966?

We had good players, a few great ones, but I'm not sure we ever had the depth of talent, or the right sort of players, to be consistently strong at international level. Because we win trophies galore for our clubs, people seem convinced that we should be winning with England. But they overlook how much our clubs have benefited from the foreign stars sprinkled through the Premier League.

I think the situation is changing and improving but we just haven't produced enough players of the right technical and tactical quality. That's easily proved by the very few times we have held our own against top-quality opponents. Holland in 1996 is pretty much the stand-out match, which tells its own story. We stood toe to toe against Argentina in 1998. We beat a couple of poor German teams, at Euro 2000 and in Munich in 2001. At Euro 2004 we didn't play badly against France and Portugal but we didn't exactly put them to the sword either. There were so many games when we were chasing shadows, incapable of controlling possession or tempo. There were so many times when I was playing for England and thought, 'This is what it must be like coming up against United.'

The FA can help far more than they do. I don't want to damn an entire organisation, but take Geoff Thompson, the chairman during most of my England years. He only ever sought out one conversation with me. Did he want to pick my brains on World Cup preparation? Or ask how the FA could help behind the scenes? No, Mr Thompson wanted to know why I didn't sing the national anthem. 'Gary, we'd rather appreciate it if you joined in,' he said. I had to politely explain that no disrespect was intended, I simply preferred to spend those few minutes, as I'd done all my career, focusing on the match. And that was the extent of my dealings with the chairman of the FA.

The FA has a lot of great staff behind the scenes doing their best to make sure the squad gets the best possible preparation. We never had any complaints about facilities. We had top hotels, our own chef. We never wanted for anything.

But when it comes to grand strategy, the FA has not been blessed with dynamic leadership. There's been a lack of real substance at the top addressing the bigger issues of player and coach production.

We've not had a coaching philosophy, and we've needed one to eradicate all the damage done through the eighties by the Charles Hughes approach to football. With the European ban after Heysel, we lost our way altogether. We became obsessed with power and direct football.

Howard Wilkinson is a decent man who had some success as a club manager, but he ended up dictating coaching policy and the youth set-up without any real experience of European methods or philosophy. His way was very much the old English style.

We've got Trevor Brooking, but he's banging his head against a brick wall and has struggled to drag the game forward. It's good to have a true football man involved at the FA but you have to give him more clout. Everything at the FA seems to take a lifetime. They've finally started working on a National Football Centre, but it has taken years.

The FA needs dragging into the twenty-first century. It's been like the House of Lords for too long. When you think of the FA, who do you hear speaking out for the good of the national team? Who do you trust to be making sure we are doing everything we can to win a World Cup?

I scored my only goal in an England shirt in my very last competitive game. Shame it was in the wrong net. It was that crap night in Croatia in October 2006 when the wheels came off the Euro 2008 qualifying wagon. I rolled a backpass to Paul Robinson and then turned to move upfield. The first I knew about the bobble was when the crowd roared. I turned round to see the ball trickling into the net.

It was a bad trip from start to finish. The coaches sprang 3–5–2 on us a couple of days before what was a massive fixture. I know Terry Venables, Steve's right-hand man, had always wanted to be tactically flexible, but I wasn't comfortable. We'd just come off a bad 0–0 draw with Macedonia and we hadn't had enough time to prepare.

As a player, you like to be able to visualise a game, to have an understanding of how you are going to play and what you need to do to counter an opponent. But I just couldn't get a handle on what was expected from me at right wing-back. I hadn't played there for ten years. I told Phil before the game that I was worried about it. And that was no frame of mind for such a crucial game.

I didn't know if I was capable of delivering what the team needed on the night. And it was clear a few of the other players were just as unsure as me. Jamie Carragher had come in as left centre-back, but he never looked comfortable either.

The biggest problem was that we lacked pace and penetration. With me and Ashley Cole as wing-backs, we weren't exactly set up to cut Croatia apart. We had no width high up the field to provide support for Rooney and Crouch. Carrick, Parker and Lampard were tripping over themselves in midfield. We were slow and predictable.

We deserved to lose, and I saw more mistakes in selection watching from home when Croatia came to Wembley for the return. I couldn't understand why Owen Hargreaves wasn't playing. With an opponent like Luka Modric off the front, it was made for him. Steve went with Gareth Barry. It didn't make sense.

I'd play one more game, a friendly defeat by Spain at Old Trafford in February 2007, but that was my lot. Because of my ankle injury I wouldn't have gone to Euro 2008 even if we had qualified.

I felt sorry for Steve. I hoped things would work out for him. I knew he was a good coach and I thought he could thrive in international football. The players respected him and it seemed a very shrewd appointment to have Terry alongside him. But managing England is a monster of a job.

I liken it to being a goalkeeper at Old Trafford. If you have any insecurities, if you aren't confident in your work, it will kill you. I've seen goalkeepers eaten alive in that penalty area because they have too much time to think, to fret over what they should be doing. England managers are the same.

Steve is a really good coach, but sometimes with England managers coaching is the smallest part of the job, and that must have been difficult for someone who loves to be out working with the players.

It would also turn out to be a mistake dropping Becks, Sol Campbell and David James from his first squad. We could all see what he was trying to do. He was trying to start a new regime. But to drop Becks altogether didn't make sense. He was never going to become a bad influence – that's not his character. He's not going to be a cancer in the dressing room. He just wanted to play.

Becks rang me with the news, and I was shocked. Very shocked. They were three big calls, and with hindsight Steve would have been better leaving it for a few months and seeing what he needed. He ended up recalling Becks, but by then he was under big pressure.

Steve was criticised in the media for being too chummy, but I wouldn't say that at all. Yes, he organised the occasional dinner with groups of players, but it was well-intentioned. There was a long time between matches and Steve wanted to go through his thoughts and make us feel like we were all in it together. I thought it was a good idea, but that all becomes irrelevant when you don't win your big matches.

I would have one more call-up under Fabio Capello, in June 2009, for the trip to Kazakhstan. That's a long way to go not to play. I never made it on to the pitch, and a few days later I sat on the bench as we thrashed Andorra 6–0, but I liked what I saw around the camp. Training was sharp and focused. Capello didn't tolerate lateness or slackness in any way. A couple of players were late for a stretch and he pulled them up. Someone had a mobile at lunch and he snapped. On the training pitch, everything was 'quicker, quicker'. He was pushing people even when warming up. There was a real focus in training.

I was impressed with everything he did, which made it even

more bizarre when he became so erratic in the build-up to the 2010 World Cup in South Africa. Even the way he named his squad seemed chaotic.

He brought in Jamie Carragher instead of Wes Brown, who is quicker and more suited to international football. Then he rang up Scholesy the day before he was about to announce his squad having not spoken to him for two years. He left out Walcott who had been an ace in his pack, even if he hadn't had a great six months. Then he called Phil at Everton, totally out of the blue. It looked desperate.

In the World Cup he never recovered from it, and made the biggest mistake of all. I've been advocating 4–3–3 with England for years and I couldn't understand why Capello didn't turn to it. He went with the traditional two banks of four, and it looked predictable and out of date. I'm not saying we'd have won the tournament with better tactics, but we'd have got closer than we did. We might not have been overrun in midfield by the Germans and we'd have kept hold of possession. As soon as Capello switched to 4–3–3 in the Euro 2012 qualifiers the team looked a much better shape. Why didn't he even look at that formation a year earlier?

But for injury I'd have been out there myself and would have won well over a hundred caps. There was a spot at right-back for quite a few years. To be blunt, there's a spot there today. Instead, I fell one short of Kenny Sansom's record of eighty-six for a full-back, though overtaking him wouldn't have meant much to me.

The truth is I was honoured to play for my country and I would have loved to have been part of a successful team. Winning the World Cup with England would have been incredible. The country would have come to a standstill;

there'd have been millions out on the streets. It would have been bedlam.

I regard myself as patriotic but, truth be told, playing for England was a bonus. Winning for my club was always the most important thing, and given a straight choice of a European Cup with United or a European Championship with England, it's United every time. It was United who were my heart and soul as a kid. They are the team I will watch when I am ninety, God willing.

As a kid, England meant very little. England was Bryan Robson. He was the only reason I watched the 1982 World Cup. England had no pull on me whatsoever. Going to Old Trafford on a Saturday was the big deal in my life. Wembley was on a distant planet.

None of this ever stopped me giving my all for my country, or being gutted every time we went out of a tournament. But I almost feel a bit sorry for the England players coming through now because they are caught between these massive expectations and the reality of being good, sometimes very good, but probably not of tournament-winning quality.

Jack Wilshere is a fantastic young talent of true international calibre, but it is going to be a while before we are producing enough players of his class. I think we are heading in the right direction, though. The Premier League years have seen a rise in technique and skills and tactical intelligence. When I started at United we were playing balls into the channels. That's not happening now.

Kids have had role models like Zola, Henry, Bergkamp. There's been change at the top end and I think it's filtering down through most clubs and most academies to the park pitches and the kids.

But it's not a transformation that can happen overnight. It will take time. We have our football culture in this country based on the traditional power player and I don't see us competing seriously for a major tournament for at least ten years. We are heading the right way, but I'm afraid we still have a lot of catching up to do.

23

Money Talks

I've been lucky. I never wanted to play for any club except United. I never lost sleep thinking about a transfer or plotting how to get away. My contract negotiations at Old Trafford would literally take about five minutes, especially because I never had an agent worrying about his cut. I'd walk in with my dad to see Peter Kenyon or David Gill with a number in my head, and, give or take a few quid, they'd have the same figure in mind too. Check the wording, give me a pen, where do I sign.

The only time I had a problem was when Phil was offered less than me when he wasn't in the team every week. I told Kenyon that wasn't fair and the club added some incentives to bring Phil level.

As for my teammates, I never worried for a moment if I was on the same money. I never had a clue what the likes of Scholesy or Giggsy were earning in all my time at Old Trafford. I just hope it was a lot more than me.

My life was simple when it came to money and contracts. I wish it was the same for more footballers but every day we hear about the influence of leeching agents. There are even some so-called super-agents. Super at what? Counting their take?

Everyone in football, apart from agents themselves, agrees that far too much money goes out of the game to middlemen, so why aren't we doing more about it? The Premier League has started publishing what clubs pay to agents to shame them into bringing down the huge sums leaking out of the game – but it is the players who should really take a lead.

Many players have become so reliant on agents it's ridiculous. I'm not going to damn every agent and, certainly for the top players, there is work to be done in terms of commercial contracts and sponsorships. A big-name player at United is a business. And massive moves, especially abroad, need to be handled by someone who can be trusted and who has contacts. There is a place for good representation, but too many footballers end up relying on an agent just to fix a lightbulb. They stop thinking for themselves. They get lazy and they get careless. They turn their whole life over to an agent, and in doing so they lose track of whether advice given is in their best interest.

For years I've been banging on about this. I've been wanting the various football organisations – the PFA, FA, LMA and the clubs – to come together to try and look at ways of weeding out this cancer.

The players themselves can do more. I always tell young players to employ a good accountant or lawyer who can deal with contracts. If you are renegotiating, why do you need an agent taking a slice that you've worked so hard to earn, practising since the age of six? Why should agents ever take a percentage? You can pay an accountant or a lawyer by the hour for the service they provide. That shouldn't cost more than a few thousand quid – much less than the fortunes going to some agents.

I can't understand why clubs and players agree to pay them so much. Just because a deal is worth £30 million it's not necessarily ten times the work of a £3 million move. But clubs and players don't demand value for money.

It's time for players to do their bit, and to make a start I'd take the radical step of publicising every player's wage in this country. We always hear in the media what a player earns so why not be transparent like they are in American sports? Let's take the mystery out of it.

It will cause initial envy – 'Look at what he's earning!' – but everyone will get accustomed to it soon enough. And hopefully it will get players to think, 'I don't need an agent to tell me what I should be on, or what a club's pay-scale is.' It should tell them they don't need to bother with Mr Ten Per Cent.

I signed quite a few long-term contracts – the longer the better as far as I was concerned. My 2004 contract was the biggest because I was captain, at my peak. I found a simple way of working out a fair rate: I would speak to the PFA and they would give me a ballpark figure based on what the going salary was for international defenders.

At that time I was more established than any other right-back in the country. I'm sure there were plenty of other defenders, including Rio at United, earning much more, but I never worried about pushing too hard. Money was never a huge thing for me.

*

Because I've found negotiations so simple, being so committed to United, it has sometimes been hard for me to accept that other players could have their heads turned by rival clubs or want to leave Old Trafford. But 2009 would see Cristiano Ronaldo and Carlos Tevez deciding that they were better off elsewhere.

In the case of Cristiano, a move had become inevitable. We had known that he wanted to leave since the summer of 2008. He would talk openly in the dressing room about Madrid. He wanted to play in the warmth, and the history of Real was always a draw. When someone is set on a dream, it's difficult to stop him. Cristiano dreamt of playing in the white shirt.

'I need to get out of this place and go somewhere hot,' he would say.

I'd have a go back. 'You don't know how good you've got it here. You'll miss us more than you know.'

'Why should I listen to you?' he'd come back. 'You'd never leave Manchester, even on holiday.'

He was totally open about his ambitions and I never had a problem with Cristiano for that. How could you? He stayed totally professional through 2008/09 even though he was counting down the months to his departure. Maybe his form wasn't quite as spectacular as the previous couple of seasons, but we'd had six years out of him – three when the club had given him everything in terms of education, polishing the diamond, and three when he'd sparkled and been truly sensational.

I was sure he would miss us, and I'm sure he has. With all the chopping and changing at the Bernabéu, how can they possibly have the special camaraderie we'd built at Old

Trafford? As for the adulation, Ronaldo couldn't be more popular than he'd been among United supporters. And then there is the small fact that we have carried on winning honours and reaching Champions League finals. Real haven't found that easy, for all their money.

The grass isn't always greener. But Cristiano's heart was set on the move and it was an offer United couldn't turn down. Any club would sell at a world record £80 million.

In the case of Carlos, it was a lot more complicated. The arrival of Dimitar Berbatov in September 2008 had been a challenge he hadn't risen to. He was in and out of the team and he became insecure. After the hunger of the first year, he'd started to toss it off a bit in training. He was constantly saying his back was sore. He'd become very fond of a massage.

Don't get me wrong, I rate him as a player and like him as a person. Forget the handbags between us after he left, he's a brilliant striker, as he proved for City. But I can only judge on what he did in that second season and, to all of us at United, it seemed that his heart wasn't in it.

He'd been upset by the signing of Berba, and Carlos is a player who needs to feel the love. He's not someone who can play one game in three and be happy. Given the strikers we had through 2008/09 there was no way the manager could promise him a starting place, so he became disheartened and then made it worse by trying to get the fans on his side against the manager. That was never going to be a good idea. So it was time for his agent to line up another massive payday.

Carlos was in the unusual position of being 'owned' by a third party, and I can imagine, knowing their principles, that United would have been uncomfortable with the thought of paying a huge transfer fee to agents. This was going to be tens of millions going straight out of the game. Rumour had it that the fee City eventually signed him for was astronomical and, based on his mood in his last year at United, it didn't make sense to compete with that sort of financial deal. United faced a hard decision at the time and there was no great surprise in the dressing room when he left.

He was an impact signing for City and, of course, they made the most of it. They put up the 'Welcome to Manchester' posters, but I never had a problem with that. You give some stick and you take it back. You have to try to beat them on the pitch. That's what United do best. That's what really kills people, winning trophies.

Carlos and I had a little argument after he went. He over-reacted to one innocent comment I made, and when we played City he gave me the big-mouth gesture. I stuck a finger up. It would have made for a quieter life if I hadn't reacted, but sometimes, in the heat of the moment, we can all be daft. I couldn't walk down the streets in Manchester for weeks without either United fans slapping me on the back or City supporters giving me dog's abuse. But that's all noise. It's what matters on the pitch that counts, and if Carlos really thought he'd be happier and more successful at City than United, that was his call, even if I didn't think it made sense.

Within a couple of seasons he was agitating for another transfer. I think he's the type of person who will keep moving on. I suspect he won't stay anywhere for longer than two or three years, and now he's said he wants to leave Manchester. This is the city where he won trophies and became world famous so I was surprised to hear him say he couldn't stand the place. Manchester was the making of him.

*

Ronaldo and Tevez, on top of Wazza and Berba, had given us the sort of attacking depth we hadn't enjoyed since 1999 – though it was still not enough to overcome Barcelona in the Champions League final in 2009 in what would be the last United game for Tevez and Ronaldo. That final in Rome has gone down as one of the great disappointments of the Ferguson era because we never played like a United team can. We didn't go down with all guns blazing.

There has been criticism that we paid for a negative approach, but it was never our intention to see so little of the ball. The manager's last words before the lads went out in Rome's Olympic Stadium were as positive as ever: 'Come on, you are European champions. Show the world what you're made of.'

We had set up to combat Barcelona, in a similar way to how we knocked them out in the semi-final twelve months earlier. That victory provided our tactical blueprint: a five-man midfield closing down the gaps and then Ronaldo causing them problems.

The manager had shown us a video of all the goals Barcelona had conceded that season and we wanted to exploit a weakness. We knew Gerard Pique well from his time at United and were confident you could get at him one-on-one around the penalty area. He's a big, tall lad and not always comfortable facing real pace. That's why we were playing Ronaldo high up the field, in an effort to get him running at Pique. But our old teammate turned out to be brilliant.

I have to say, in the first five minutes Pique showed guts I've rarely seen in a young defender. We were pressing Barcelona like mad but he kept taking the ball off Valdés and playing it out from the back. A couple of times he played unbelievably risky passes, but he trusted in the way he'd been taught. As a team, Barcelona didn't wobble under pressure, they stuck to their passing game. That takes talent and a fantastic temperament. It's what makes this Barcelona team of recent years so special. They'd do exactly the same after we blitzed them early at Wembley in the Champions League final of 2011.

With Pique turning out to be such a fine defender, a world champion, people wondered why United had got rid of him, but it was timing and culture. At that time he didn't fit the English mentality. He had incredible ability, was a great passer of the ball, strong and composed and enthusiastic around the changing room. But he wasn't always at ease in the Premier League. A game at Bolton on a Saturday afternoon with Kevin Davies banging into him came as a shock to him and it affected his confidence. He probably needed to go back to Spain and develop as a player within his own culture. He was a fish out of water in England, and he couldn't get the games to develop because we had Vidic and Ferdinand at their peak. It was just bad timing for him, but we were all very happy at United to see him enjoy success elsewhere – just a shame that he should have been so brilliant against us in two Champions League finals.

Thanks to Pique, Barcelona weathered that early burst in 2009. When Samuel Eto'o scored with their first attack it knocked the stuffing out of us. They settled into their passing rhythm and we couldn't get hold of the ball. We couldn't do much at all. It was so strange for a United team not to have that fightback. Even if we are not playing well we can normally summon something. Get one goal, and then we'll get two. Get two and a third will arrive. That's the mentality.

But the moment never came. They had mastery of the match, and we didn't even begin to rattle them. They scored a second through Messi's free header.

People questioned the team selection, but the system and the approach was good enough to have beaten Barcelona a year earlier. Inevitably the critics pored over Ronaldo's performance, too. He was always going to draw the most scrutiny, but at least he took the game to Barcelona. There were many disappointing individual performances that night. Ronaldo wasn't blameless but I wouldn't begin to put him in the line of fire. There were other players who will know that they did not perform close to what was expected.

I watched all this unfold from the stands. I had to accept that I was now an occasional player, a squad member. I wasn't even on the bench for the final, with John O'Shea in the team and Rafael da Silva as back-up. I couldn't complain, given how I was now battling with a variety of aches, pains and niggles.

I made sixteen league appearances that season and felt I had contributed to another championship. It felt sweet lifting that trophy knowing that we had drawn level with Liverpool on eighteen titles. It had taken a while but, finally, we were alongside them in the history books – an unbelievable achievement given where we'd started from. But no one was going to rest until we'd broken the record.

24

Wazza and the Boss

How many times have we seen the boss doubted? And how many times has he made all those critics look like fools? I'd have thought people would know better, but within a year of us reaching consecutive Champions League finals for the first time in the club's history there was a sense of doom and gloom around Old Trafford.

The loss of Tevez and Ronaldo was, in the fans' eyes, the end of an era. We were champions of England and still among the very best in Europe, but suddenly the terraces were plunged into pessimism. The fans and the media were convinced we were in a period of decline. Failing to win a trophy in 2009/10 was taken as proof of that.

The supporters were twitchy that we'd not lured a marquee signing to replace either of our departing strikers. Antonio Valencia was a very shrewd buy in the summer of 2009, as he has proved, but he wasn't a name. We had a look at Karim

Benzema but he went to Real Madrid for £35 million and the manager complained publicly about the lack of value in the market. The fans decided that he'd had his hands tied by the owners. So suddenly, despite all the success, the Green and Gold campaign started.

It's very difficult for anyone within the club to comment on the Glazers. I grew up as a United fan and the last thing I did as a young kid was look to see who was in the directors' box. My thoughts were with the team, the players, the fans, the atmosphere. I have never allowed that youthful enthusiasm and innocence to turn to cynicism.

In all my time supporting the club I've never known any owners who were popular. Even when the club was a plc there were unhappy fans. But inside the club we have not been affected by changes of ownership; you wouldn't have a clue that anything is different under the Glazer family. David Gill and the manager have been allowed to run the football side without interference. And make no mistake, in the boss and David Gill, United have the best possible people.

When I look at the success of the last five or six years, the stability of the club, and the fan base, I would bet that 99 per cent of clubs wish they were in our place. You hear stories at some big clubs where owner interference and politics are rife, and I think United are in an excellent position.

This has been an historic period for the club, but there is no doubting that the fans saw the glass as half empty in 2009. Rio had started picking up a few injuries, and at the time Vidic hadn't signed a new contract. We'd lost Cristiano, and any team would miss the best player in the world. Chelsea, under Carlo Ancelotti, were making a new assault on the title and we had dropped off the pace.

It wasn't a vintage season for either club. We lost seven league games, they lost six. We put in some poor performances but still only lost the title to Chelsea by a single point. I admire Ancelotti, a good manager with a lot of class who never deserved the sack a year after the Double, but Chelsea weren't particularly convincing.

They had a little helping hand to win that 2009/10 title. Some thought it would be a big test for Chelsea playing at Anfield with a couple of games to go and the title still up for grabs, but at United we knew that Liverpool would ease off if that meant depriving us of the championship – especially a nineteenth championship that would take us past their record. We'd heard rumours during the week that some Liverpool players had turned round to one of their young lads and said, 'There's not a fucking chance that we're going to let United win this league.' I've no idea whether that rumour was true or not, but you could see that the game was a nice end-of-season stroll for Liverpool. You could see half their players on their summer holidays.

We couldn't complain, not publicly. It was up to us to make sure we weren't in a vulnerable position. But it didn't say much for Liverpool, or what they'd been reduced to under Rafa Benitez.

With no trophy to show, surely Manchester United was going through a wobbly patch? But it was yet another example – and I'd seen it on enough occasions – of everyone outside the club leaping to wild conclusions that the rot had set in at Old Trafford. We'd be back in another Champions League final a year later, but you'd never have guessed that from the public mood.

I ask again, how many times, going right back to the

eighties, had the club and the manager been doubted? I couldn't believe people had fallen into the old trap of questioning him. He was soon to prove why he is one of the great managers the game has seen.

In October 2010, Wayne stunned everyone by deciding he wanted out of United.

I say 'stunned', but it wasn't a complete shock. There had been rumblings through pre-season that he was unsettled and it was clear his head was all over the place. England and Wayne had had a poor World Cup in South Africa and he was being attacked professionally and personally. He didn't look happy in himself. Wazza is normally one of the most bubbly, noisy players in the dressing room. But after the World Cup he'd lost all that spark, that energy. We all noticed, though it was still a surprise when it leaked out that he was thinking about leaving.

If a player wants to go elsewhere, that's his concern. I'll never understand someone who wants to leave United, but that's their issue. But with Wayne it wasn't just the decision but the way it was handled that was so bad. He acknowledged that himself when everything calmed down.

With so much turmoil in his head and his form poor, what he needed was good advice. The last thing he needed was disruption and controversy. Going public was crazy. Like the fans, the players were discovering most of the club's news through the papers, which was a massive mistake on Wayne's part. It's simply not the United way to agitate for a move through the media. In the end, the manager didn't have any choice but to go public himself.

The boss's performance at that press conference when he

talked about Wazza was unbelievable. My jaw hit the floor when I switched on the TV. You could see the boss was hurting that a senior player was questioning the club, but you could also see the defiance. He wouldn't stand back and let United be picked apart by any player, however talented. It was like watching one of the manager's team talks played out in public. The rest of the world could see what a great, inspiring leader he is.

From the way the manager spoke, the situation seemed irretrievable. I think that is honestly the way the club felt at that point. And that was before Wayne escalated the situation the next day.

We were just walking into the dressing room an hour or so before our Champions League game against Bursaspor and, as usual, the televisions were on in the corner. That's when we saw on the bottom of the screen 'Breaking News'. Wayne had put out a statement saying that he wanted to leave because the club lacked ambition and the squad wasn't good enough. It would have been a bad thing to say at any time but it was madness to be putting it out an hour before a big game. He knew there was a match on, and so did his representatives. He's a good lad, Wayne, not a troublemaker, so we were dumbfounded.

I stood stunned in the dressing room. 'What idiot has allowed him to put that out?'

I know he must have been stung by the manager's press conference but Wayne just needed to keep his head down. He's a proud lad, a fighter, but his advisers should have been taking a deep breath, not putting out statements to the media.

The manager came into the dressing room. He was pumped up. He'd had his team talk written for him.

It was a testing moment. Our form wasn't good. We were behind in the league and our star player was kicking off. But that's when the manager is at his best. Something is triggered inside him. If he's challenged, he fights back with everything he's got. And that boldness transmitted itself to the team.

It was all the motivation we needed to go out and win the game that night, and you could feel the fans rallying right behind the lads. The manager had taken the bull by the horns with his press conference. He'd shown once again that no player is bigger than the club, and never can be. The fans will have their idols but they know that's the way it has to be.

The next morning, I saw Wayne at the training ground.

'What are you doing?'

'I'm staying.'

'Fuck off! Really? Well, if you are, I think you're going to have to apologise.'

I don't think he needed telling. Already his people were involved in damage limitation as well as sorting out a new contract with David Gill.

Within twenty-four hours Wayne had called the players together at the training ground and said sorry to the lads. Then he'd say it to the supporters.

It was a massive moment for him, and for the club. As usual, the lads started taking the piss. Patrice Evra told Wazza he must have crapped himself when he saw the gang of United fans outside his house. 'So you shit yourself, eh Wayne, when you saw the balaclavas?'

Genuinely I was happy that he'd made the best decision of his life. He'd made a mistake and misread the situation, but you had to wonder about the advice he was getting.

Now that he's committed to staying at United, I believe Wayne can become the new Keane or Robson. He's in a different position but he has the power, the ability and the talismanic qualities. He's still got that temper in him and always will have. But he's approaching his peak years now. We've seen with many top players that you can't take anything for granted once you are over thirty. In Wayne's case, with the way he throws himself into the game, the running he does, the physicality in his football, I can't see him still doing it at thirty-five. He started so young, a regular for club and country at eighteen. The next few years should be his best, and I look forward to watching him from my seat in the stands.

He's great around the changing room. He's funny and good company. And he gives a hundred per cent every single match. You have a lot of time for players who are talented and also give their all like he does. United need special players like Wazza. The fans have embraced him again. They know what a player he is and how important he is to the future of the club. He's always had it within him to be a United legend.

He was bound to feel guilty, and, in one way, that could only help the club. The best way for him to make amends was to play better and to help the team win trophies. The manager could count on a new, improved Rooney now the whole nonsense was behind him.

Only our manager could turn a crisis to the club's advantage. You can imagine other teams being rocked for months. Look at how the sacking of Ray Wilkins unsettled Chelsea. It was still being talked about months later. But the manager has such authority that the Rooney situation was dealt with in a matter of days. Everyone else was going into overdrive but he kept his nerve yet again and played his hand brilliantly.

The manager has seen everything and he knows how to use that experience. He's seen Eric Cantona threaten to quit at his peak and chased him around Paris. He's seen Ronaldo want to leave and talked him into staying for another season.

For twenty-four hours I genuinely did think that the Wazza situation had gone too far, but the manager retrieved it, and a couple of months later we were top of the league, unbeaten. And Wayne was back to his best world-class form as we made a mockery of the talks of a crisis by charging towards another title and another Champions League final.

This was the manager at his very best, proving at sixty-nine why he'll be an impossible man to replace. There'll be other United managers, perhaps very successful ones. But to have stayed on top for as long as he has, inspiring young men to give their very best for United for twenty-five years, steering the club through crisis after crisis, proving the critics wrong time and time again to win trophies – well, the truth is we may never see his like again. When the statue is built for him outside Old Trafford, fans will stop in their droves to marvel at what he did.

I know what loyalty he inspires in people. I'd trust him with my life. Sometimes I wish his detractors could see him around the club, the way he looks after the staff. It's thanks to him that we've had receptionists and lots of backroom staff who've worked at the club for twenty years. He makes every-one feel important.

He treats the club as a family he has to protect, and that's why he defends it so ferociously.

Plenty on the outside have criticised him for being blindly loyal to his club, to his players. But look at it from his perspective. United has been central to his life. He's been devoted to the club every hour of every day. And how do you, how does anyone react when their family is attacked? They defend it with their lives.

It's why he reacts to media intrusion like it's a personal insult. To come into his club and unsettle his players is like criticising his family. He might slaughter a player in private but like any good mother or father he will never, ever allow those private rows to be played out in public.

It will be a very sad day when he finally bows out. It may be a while yet judging from his enthusiasm, so who can guess who the candidates to replace him will be? The obvious names people come up with are José Mourinho and Pep Guardiola. They've both enjoyed incredible success in very different ways. I do think style of football has to figure in the deliberations. United, deservedly, have a reputation for playing good, attacking football. The boss has kept the philosophy passed down by Sir Matt Busby that the team has a duty to entertain. The next manager of Manchester United will have to be true to that spirit. He'll have to be bold and he'll have to have balls. It's the way United was under Busby: he told the football authorities that he was taking his team into the European Cup whether they liked it or not. Our boss has also been a pioneer.

I'll be as interested to see how the club handles the transition, because perhaps the boss's greatest achievement has been in proving that no one is irreplaceable. We cannot possibly allow the club to falter as it did after Sir Matt left. Hard as it is, the club will have to move on even without the boss, which is what he'd expect.

In words and deeds he has made it clear to us that United

is a conveyor belt. You fall off at the end and someone else gets on at the start. That's a culture encouraged by the manager, and rightly so. You've never cracked it. There's never a time to put your feet up. Celebrate your successes, but be ready to report for work first thing the next day.

Perhaps that's what the club got wrong at the end of the great Best–Law–Charlton era, and when Sir Matt Busby moved on. Too much looking back. The challenge for the club will be to prove that we aren't harking back to the Ferguson era.

United are in safe hands for a while yet. I can see the emergence of another brilliant team. There's great youthful talent in Rafael and Fabio da Silva, Chris Smalling and Chicharito. The signing of Phil Jones is another statement of intent – he's already got the look of a future United and England captain. Watching him play for England Under 21s in the summer, he looked an absolute steal for £16.5 million.

I can feel the manager making the bold changes necessary to take us on again. There's a good blend of experience and youth, and new talent coming in with Jones, Ashley Young and David de Gea. It's not as if we are far off.

I know we lost the 2011 Champions League final at Wembley, and it looked to the world as if we'd been out-classed, but I think then you were seeing Barcelona at the absolute peak of their powers. This was a great team, one of the very best, at the pinnacle. But I've been around football long enough to know that you cannot possibly sustain that level of excellence. Xavi, Messi and Iniesta were all on top form, but they can't go on for ever. Something has to give. A major player starts to get older, the manager might leave, and then the wheel of fortune turns again.

I'm not taking anything away from Barcelona. They gave us a lesson at Wembley. If I hadn't felt so bad for our lads, I'd have enjoyed watching their skills. But I am a hundred per cent confident that the gap will get smaller. I can see the evolution of another top United team and I don't believe that Barcelona will retain their Champions League title. You heard it here first: Real Madrid or United will be champions in 2012. Our boss is ready to go again.

25

Definitely the End

The end came for me on New Year's Day, 2011 – and it came on a toilet at the Hawthorns. It wasn't the way I'd have chosen to finish, but I knew for certain that this was my last game.

After eighteen years at Manchester United, after 602 first-team appearances, I was in the middle of playing for my team for the last time. And I couldn't wait for it to be over.

In the dressing room, the manager was barking instructions about how we were going to improve on a dire first-half performance against West Brom. But I just wanted to get home, to disappear. In the sanctuary of the toilet, my mind was elsewhere.

I'd been really poor in the first half but that hadn't stopped the fans singing my name. 'Gary Neville is a Red, is a Red . . .' For the first time in my life I'd been embarrassed to hear it.

Don't sing that. I don't deserve it. Maybe in the past, but not today.

I was beating myself up even as the game was going on around me.

What am I doing out here? How soon will this be over?

My mind was racing at a thousand miles an hour, full of doubts and vulnerabilities.

This wasn't like me at all. I was normally full of drive and commitment and focus. Normally I'd be the one barking instructions, telling others to concentrate. I'd prepared for every game in my life knowing that however much my opponent wanted it, I wanted it more. But now all I could think was 'please get me out of here without making a terrible mistake'.

I'd known I wasn't right from the moment the manager pulled me on the Thursday after training to tell me I was playing. He wanted my experience, he said. We'd been panicking a bit at the back, let in a sloppy late goal at Birmingham City a few days earlier. But this would be my first start for more than two months. I'd not played since the trip to Stoke City the previous October when I'd not exactly covered myself in glory. We'd won, but I should have been sent off for a scything tackle that was several minutes late.

I'd made four appearances in four months and never felt properly fit. It had been a hard struggle with injury ever since my ankle went in 2007. I'd been ready to bow out in the spring of 2010 so it caught me by surprise when the boss asked me to stay on for another year. I had my doubts, but I couldn't turn down the invitation. Who wants to walk away from the job of your dreams?

I signed on happily for another season, but the first day back in pre-season I pulled my calf. Then I pulled my groin, and then my ankle went again in the game at Stoke. I was caught in a nasty Catch-22: I needed matches to regain my sharpness, but with Rafael starting to blossom as my long-term successor I knew the manager couldn't give me a run of games.

With my obsessive attention to detailed preparation – the right number of leg weights, sprints, stretches – I knew I wasn't ready. Others might get away with cutting corners but, right through my career, if I wasn't in the right condition, I was half the player.

When I saw Scholesy in the canteen after I'd spoken to the manager, I told him my fears. 'This is going to be messy,' I said.

He laughed. 'You don't mean Lionel.'

Typical Scholesy, ready to take the mickey.

So now, at half-time against West Brom, I was staring at the toilet door and all my worst fears were coming true. I was making Jerome Thomas look like Ronaldo. It would have been even worse if the referee had spotted my trip on Graham Dorrans in the box. I deserved a red card; if justice had been done, my career would have finished there and then with a lonely, embarrassed walk to the dressing room. I'd got off lightly, but I wasn't going to avoid the wrath of the manager at half-time. I walked into a predictable, and deserved, blast for poor positioning.

Perhaps sensing my troubles, Rio stuck up for me, offering to take the blame for one of West Brom's chances. It was good of him to put his hand up because I didn't have the stomach to argue back at the manager. All I wanted to do was get through the second half and get home.

Out of the toilet I came and, bizarrely, I enjoyed my twenty-five minutes after half-time. I felt a renewed sense of calm, probably from knowing it would soon be over. My mind was back on the job though my legs were still pleading for a rest.

I went for an attacking run, and it seemed to take all day to get back in position. There was no chance of me lasting until the final whistle, and when the ball ran out of play near the bench I saw Mick Phelan wander over for a word.

'You're fucked, aren't you?'

'Yes.'

Now the end was only seconds away.

I saw Rafael warming up, and soon the board was out – a big number two, up in lights. Off I went for the last time. I knew it was over.

Gary Neville, the former Manchester United defender.

I don't know if anyone else on the bench knew this was the end for me. If they did, they weren't saying. There were no reassuring pats on the back or words of comfort, and I wasn't expecting any. There was a match still to be won, so I grabbed my coat, pulled the hood over my head for a moment of quiet reflection, and then watched to see if we could turn a scrappy draw into a victory.

We were playing really poorly, but I knew we were going to win. I'd have bet my life on it. This team has the spirit – the Manchester United spirit – I'd first detected as a teenage apprentice. It is the need to win, the hunger for it, and the ability to find a way.

This is the DNA of the club established by the boss: play great football if you can, and if not, dig deep within yourself and win with guts and heart and determination. And that's exactly what the lads did at West Brom, Chicharito popping up with the winner from a corner. It was a horrible performance. But we found a way.

'Only Manchester United could have won playing that badly,' I said to the manager the next day when I went into his office to tell him I was retiring. That unquenchable fire is the greatest quality at United, but, as I explained to the boss, you also have to know when to quit.

I knew this was my time to go. I'd had a sleepless night fretting over it. I woke up Emma in the middle of the night with my tossing and turning.

'What do you think I should do?'

'Why are you asking me?' she laughed. 'You'll do what you want anyway.'

I lay in bed going over and over it, asking myself again and again if that was it. What if I went away on a training camp? What if I got fit? What if the manager suddenly needed me for the run-in? My brain was still racing when I went in at 7.30 that Sunday morning to see the manager and tell him I was bowing out. I sat in my car for an hour in the car park, not realising the manager was already in his office – first in, as ever.

It wasn't an easy decision to make but, deep down, I knew one hundred per cent it was the right one.

The boss tried to talk me round – 'Typical Neville, over-reacting, getting emotional.' He told me to go for a break, which I did, to Dubai with my family. It must have been the only week in history when it rained there every day.

I had plenty of time to sit and ponder my options, but I knew I was finished. I didn't want to be a liability to my team. I felt like I could cost us points, maybe even the title, if I carried on playing.

Briefly I thought of whether I could hang on for ten appearances. Then I might finish with another championship medal, and what a sweet one it would be given that we'd be passing Liverpool's tally of eighteen titles. But it was a fleeting thought. My time had been and gone. United could win the championship without me. I was ready to accept it gracefully and count my blessings.

I'm the type who makes a decision and wants to get everything sorted immediately. I hate things dragging on for weeks. So although we'd talked about waiting until the end of the season to make a decision, I wanted it out. I didn't want to live a lie. So on 2 February, the club announced that I was retiring with immediate effect.

You read about some sportsmen really struggling to face up to the end of their playing careers. Sport is all they've known and they can't face life without it. But there hasn't been a moment of panic for me.

The thought of never playing for United again was bound to feel like a massive wrench but I'd had plenty of time to prepare for it with the injuries I'd had. And it was made easier by knowing I had plenty to get on with. I knew I wouldn't be rattling around the house with nothing to do, getting depressed.

So, what next? It won't be management, not any time soon. I need plenty of convincing that my future lies in the dug-out. I've done my badges up to Uefa 'A' level and some coaching with junior United teams but I face the same dilemma that confronts all of us who have played at the top level for many years: can I find the motivation to work obsessively which is necessary to be a good manager?

First I need a break. I've been on the same ship with the same routine for a quarter of a century and I need time off. I've been controlled. I've been told where to be, what to do, when to do it. I've known what I was going to eat, when I was going to train, how far I was going to run. I need a breather.

It's a complete guess, but I imagine that assistant manager of United would be a dream job. That way you spend time on the practice ground and you work with the players without all the other hassles of management, and you learn your trade. But that's easy to say. How do you prove you are worthy of it?

You can't stage-manage a career in management. If you are serious about management you have to be willing to learn the trade. The most successful managers have done that: Mourinho, Wenger, Ferguson, Redknapp. They've worked their way up.

It's a job that takes suffering, mistakes, the sack. To be good, you've got to give it everything. I see old teammates like Keano, Brucey and Incey and the traumas they put themselves through, jumping up and down on the sidelines like they are going to have a heart attack. I wonder if I have the stomach to put myself through all that tension again.

What also puts you off is the knowledge that, in this country, you get written off so quickly and brutally. Steve McClaren's reputation was so battered after the England job that he had to go abroad. Glenn Hoddle still has something to contribute, but you get a reputation in this country, especially when you have failed at England level. Robbo, Keano – they've all been judged in five minutes.

We write managers off when they have endured a bad run. We personalise it. I look at Spain and see managers rotating. Real Madrid will sack somebody and then five years later they'll make him manager again. In England we have a mentality that you're either a success or a failure and there's no in-between. It's the same with the English national team – always on the brink of total calamity.

Even some very good managers have bad seasons. Look at Carlo Ancelotti, sacked despite winning trophies at Chelsea. Clubs so rarely show patience and it makes a hard job even more stressful and unsettling. Is that really what I need?

I do think we fail to harness the knowledge and experience of ex-players in this country, though. The PFA membership contains some of the most high-profile people in England. With fame comes a certain amount of power, but we don't use it as well as we could.

Players should have a voice in the big decisions being made by the Premier League and the FA. There are some big issues that need to be addressed – too many matches, the winter break, better coaching courses – so why aren't we consulted? We keep bemoaning the fact that we don't have a Platini, a Beckenbauer. Well, let's encourage the players to take on that responsibility.

By the way, this is not a personal pitch for leadership. I don't fancy Gordon Taylor's post whenever he steps down at the PFA. After the magnificent job he has done he will be very difficult to replace. I've plenty else to occupy me for the next few years. I've signed up to work for Sky and I believe I've something to contribute on TV having played at the top level for almost twenty years. Of course United is in my blood but I'll strive to be as open, honest and impartial as I can be.

I'm involved with a few business projects as well, notably property and a sustainability company. Those two interests have combined with the supporters' club I'm helping to build using proceeds from my testimonial. United fans have never had somewhere around Old Trafford to gather and I'm hoping it will become a focal point before games.

I look forward to going in there myself. I've become an ambassador for the club, but above all I'm a fan. I always said that when I retired I looked forward to sitting in the stands with my mates, having a drink and cheering my team.

That's why I went on the terraces at Stamford Bridge in March. I got three tickets for me and a couple of mates and we sat in the away end, just like I'd wanted to do for years. I had a great night, but I've been advised that it might not be the safest thing in future.

It's sad that it's come to that, but as the fame and the money has grown in football, so has the hostility. There are massive rewards for players today but there's also more intrusion, more hassle, more aggression. There's a frightening amount of scrutiny, which I won't miss.

The most common question you get asked as you approach the end of your career is how you want to be remembered. For me, it's simple really: I want to be remembered for giving everything to United. That's what my dad told me when I started as a kid: don't look back wishing you could have done more.

I wasn't the most skilful player around. I've always joked that I'll have six out of ten on my gravestone because that's the perception of me – a steady Eddie in a team of stars like Cantona, Robson, Beckham, Ronaldo, Scholes, Giggs. Never bad but never great either.

But that's OK. All that matters is that you make the most of yourself. I've never been a pin-up but I'm not a bad example for anyone out there who wonders if they've quite got the skill to make it to the top. I'm proof of what can be achieved if you keep working.

I think that's the greatest quality that can be said of all of us who came through from the class of '92. You see how Giggsy is still going strong; Becks is still playing out in the States; Phil has just signed a new contract at Everton; and Scholesy kept going for as long as possible. We've all tried to squeeze every drop out of our careers. That's the best that any footballer can do, whatever their talent level.

I couldn't have given more, but now my time is up. I went out with the lads to celebrate our historic nineteenth title. I felt total joy to have finally moved ahead of Liverpool. It's a phenomenal achievement. I was thrilled for the whole club and for the lads as they sang their songs and drank their pints. But as the party moved on into the night, I was also a little bit detached from it, if I'm honest.

I'd had my time. I was already retired, starting out on my new life, and the club had moved on too, winning trophies without me. What an amazing time I'd had, but as the players continued to celebrate their championship, I slipped away into the night. I wouldn't be missed, which is just how it should be.

Epilogue

Best United XI

I've been lucky to play with some of the true greats of the game – so many fantastic players that I've always been reluctant to choose the very best. But I've been asked so many times to select my Manchester United XI that I've had to give in.

It was an agonising process, and I've changed my mind about twenty times. There are world-class players, United legends, who have been left out. No room for Eric? That's how hard it is to get in this team.

Goalkeeper

How do you separate two of the greatest ever goalkeepers? Peter Schmeichel and Edwin van der Sar would grace any team. Edwin was the first goalkeeper since Peter left who mastered the position. He is a sweeper-keeper with great shot-saving ability and fantastic distribution. But, best of all, he exuded calm confidence. It's a very hard job being a United goalkeeper but Edwin was never flustered, however big the occasion.

Edwin is a class act, but in the end I had to go with the longevity of Peter who was not just a great goalkeeper but a massive presence when I was coming into the side. He was one of those ferociously driven players who made all the young lads realise what it took to reach the top. He would slaughter me in training. He could be brutal. But that was just his raging desire to win. Peter was unarguably the best in the world for quite a few years and has to go down as one of the manager's greatest signings.

Defence

Denis Irwin was so good you could put him at left- or right-back and he would be brilliant in either position. It's hard to remember a mistake he made, and, on top of his reliability, he could attack and take penalties and free-kicks.

He played more as a left-back for United but he'll have to go on the right in this team because I'm going for Patrice Evra at left-back. Patrice was not an instant hit at United, taking a little time to adjust to the physicality of the Premier League, but he proved a very quick learner and has been throwing himself into challenges ever since. And attacking-wise, there are few better full-backs in the world.

Centre-half was a massive dilemma. Steve Bruce, Gary Pallister, Jaap Stam, Nemanja Vidic, Rio Ferdinand – you could take any two of them and have a top-quality pairing. I knew I'd never get into the team at centre-half when I saw Brucey and Pallister. They were great players and fantastic people to be around when we were coming into the team.

But I'm going for the modern-day pairing of Vidic and Rio as my choice, though how I am leaving out Jaap I'll never know. Jaap was brilliant, colossal. In his first season we won the Treble and he should have been at United for longer, as the manager has admitted.

But Vidic has to be in the team. That's non-negotiable. How he didn't win Player of the Year in 2010/11 is beyond me. He was easily the most consistent, influential player in the league. There's an argument that Rio and Vidic need each other to be at their best, and that's why, in the end, I am going for the two of them together. They are a fantastic combination, a great blend, with Rio's wonderful all-round ability to see the game, to make interceptions and to play the ball in the tightest of spaces alongside Vidic getting in the way of everything. The bottom line is they have played in three Champions League finals together during the club's golden period.

Midfield

The Treble-winning midfield quartet of David Beckham, Roy Keane, Paul Scholes and Ryan Giggs walk into the team. They are inseparable. That four had everything.

There was Giggsy's dribbling on one side and Becks' delivery on the other, allied to Keano's incredible drive and tenacity and Scholesy's laser-passing and goalscoring ability. Tenacity, passing, penetration, energy, technical quality, tackling – all of it in spades. What more could you want from a midfield?

It has become harder to play a flat four in modern football. The game has moved on. Teams work on outnumbering you in that area of the field. But I've not seen a four that has complemented one another so well, and I wouldn't put it past them to have flourished today even with the tactical changes in the game.

They were all very intelligent players, had bags of skill, and they all worked like dogs. They had it all. It was a privilege to be in the same team.

Attack

Cristiano Ronaldo is a cert up front. The goals he scored for United, added to the fact that he had so much ability to frighten players, mean he is a must. For three years from around 2006 to 2009 Cristiano was the best player in the world, and that is why he has to be in.

Rooney or Cantona as his partner? This one took a lot of consideration, and I was tempted to go for Eric. He is a Messiah at this club, an all-time icon. I think back to that 1995/96 season and I know we couldn't have won the league without him. It's sad that he didn't stay around to win the Champions League.

But Wayne has helped us to reach three European finals in four years and that's why he just gets the nod. These should be his peak years now and everything's set up for him to become an Old Trafford legend. The stage is set for him.

That leaves out Ruud van Nistelrooy, who was the greatest goalscorer I ever played with; Dwight Yorke, who set us alight in that Treble season; Mark Hughes, who was just an incredible warrior for United as well as a great striker; and Andy Cole, who overcame a difficult start at Old Trafford to become a goalscoring machine.

But if the team is weighted more to the present day, that's because it's hard to ignore the phenomenal success that's been enjoyed in reaching all those Champions League finals. This has been a special time in United's history.

So there you have it: Schmeichel – Irwin, Ferdinand, Vidic, Evra – Beckham, Keane, Scholes, Giggs – Rooney, Ronaldo.

As for me, I'll be lucky if I make it on to the bench.

Acknowledgements

My thanks to Matt Dickinson for helping to put this book together.

Picture Acknowledgements

Unless otherwise stated, all pictures are personally provided courtesy of the author, with thanks to Manchester United FC, the *Bury Times*, the *Manchester Evening News* and the photographers who have followed his life and career over the years. Every effort has been made to obtain the necessary permissions with reference to illustrative copyright material. We apologise for any omissions in this respect and will be pleased to make the appropriate acknowledgements in any future edition.

Second section, p. 2: Gascoigne and Beckham goal celebrations; p. 5: Turin celebrations; p. 7: Rooney in Moscow all © Press Association Images.

Second section, p. 5: Neville brothers in Barcelona; p. 6: Carling Cup and Premier League celebrations; p. 7: lifting Champions League trophy in Moscow and celebrating with Ronaldo; p. 8: testimonial photographs all © Getty Images.

Index

ABOUT THE AUTHOR

Gary Neville was born on 18 February 1975 and became one of the most decorated footballers in the history of the game with Manchester United. He was captain of the United team that won the FA Youth Cup in 1992, and after making his first-team debut that autumn he went on to make 602 appearances for the club.

He won the Premier League eight times (skippering the Red Devils to their victories in 2007, 2008 and 2009), the FA Cup three times, the League Cup twice and the Champions League in 1999 to complete a remarkable set of medals. He also won 85 caps for England – a record for a right-back – and appeared in two World Cups and three European Championships for his country.